MOVIES
AND THE
MODERN PSYCHE

MOVIES
AND THE
MODERN PSYCHE

Sharon Packer

PRAEGER

Westport, Connecticut
London

Library of Congress Cataloging-in-Publication Data

Packer, Sharon.
   Movies and the modern psyche / Sharon Packer.
      p. cm.
   Includes bibliographical references and index.
   ISBN-13: 978–0–275–99359–7 (alk. paper)
   1.   Motion pictures—Psychological aspects.   I. Title.
   PN1995.P215 2007
   791.4301'9—dc22   2007027874

British Library Cataloguing in Publication Data is available.

Library of Congress Catalog Card Number: 2007027874
ISBN-13: 978–0–275–99359–7

First published in 2007

Praeger Publishers, 88 Post Road West, Westport, CT 06881
An imprint of Greenwood Publishing Group, Inc.
www.praeger.com

Printed in the United States of America

The paper used in this book complies with the
Permanent Paper Standard issued by the National
Information Standards Organization (Z39.48–1984).

10   9   8   7   6   5   4   3   2   1

$50. 05

In Memory of

Professor and Chair Emeritus, Jack Peter Green, PhD, M.D.
Department of Pharmacology, Mt. Sinai School of Medicine

CONTENTS

PREFACE

Flash back to college years in the sixties. If anyone had said that I would someday write a book on film, and not just one book, but two (so far), I would surely have thought them insane. For film studies were not a serious subject of study in the sixties, and pre-meds like me had to be serious about our studies if we wanted to make it to med school. So I balanced my science and psych courses with art history (and classical Greek), and I continued advanced Judaica classes, for I had been brought up to believe that proven cultural products of the past were superior to pop culture of the present. It was difficult to imagine that anything as new as film could compete with centuries of artistic achievement.

Back then, I was unaware of how much early cinematic art intertwined with fine art. One had to appreciate German Expressionism and the so-called decadent art of the Weimar years to make that connection. But the sixties were still too close to the Holocaust to think clearly about that emotionally laden era. I also admit that I developed telescopic vision from peering into too many microscopes in biology labs. For I lost sight of the fact that cinema was also a science. It took the dawning of the computer era to make me think about the scientific significance of cinema.

Most importantly, I was completely unaware of how much movies had molded my personal plans to become a psychiatrist. It was only after researching my last book, *Dreams in Myth, Medicine, & Movies*, and teaching college courses on Movies and Madness and on Film and Dream, that I realized how much *Psycho, Three Faces of Eve*, and *Spellbound* had increased my intrigue with psychoanalysis (which was essentially synonymous with psychiatry at the time). Until that relatively late point in life, I truly believed that it was the books I read at the age of ten, such as Lucy Freeman's *Story of Psychoanalysis* and *The 50 Minute Hour*, that had set me on this path.

Unfortunately, my film-fed infatuation with psychoanalysis started to fade after medical school introduced me to neuroscience and biochemistry and more modern approaches to the machinations of the mind. My very early training in psychoanalytically oriented psychiatry proved to be disappointing and more fanciful than some of the "couch cures" seen on the screen.

What did not disappoint me in the least were cinematic couch cures. I had the good fortune to complete my psychiatry residency in Greenwich Village, not far from Film Forum, where film festivals occurred monthly, and where film afficionados stood in line, discussing films with the same seriousness that psychiatrists-in-training applied to their patients' psychopathology. What began as an evening's escape from the intensity of working on psych wards by day turned into something much more enduring over the years.

In those days, art houses and revival houses dotted the blocks of downtown Manhattan. Reading broadsides provided by Film Forum motivated me to read more works in film studies, once my schedule permitted. I was intrigued to see how film scholars recycled psychoanalytic theories at the same time that most of those theories were being abandoned by neuroscientists. At last, I could find a good use for the psychoanalytic lectures I attended in my first year of psychiatry training! Even if couch cures could not cure real patients, the theory behind them could be applied to the movies, to characters' motivations, and to understanding the plot.

Two books by psychiatrists proved equally compelling and equally inspiring: the Gabbards' *Psychiatry and the Cinema* and Greenberg's *Screen Memories*. But it was Kracauer's *From Caligari to Hitler* (1947) that really set the wheels whirling. That book made me revisit an ugly period from the past, the Holocaust, to see how it intertwined with film and art, as well as with psychiatry and psychology. I talk a lot about Kracauer's study in this book, perhaps too much, because it was impossible to push its thesis out of my mind after reading it.

Kracauer's subject is a sad one, to say the least, but the topic of movies and the modern mind is a delightful one, at least in *my* mind, and hopefully in your mind also. The idea that film both forms and reflects our understanding of a subject as serious as the psyche is both awesome and annoying. Surely, the idea that movies mold our mindset about the mind as much as modern science does annoys the scientifically minded. But at least those movies are fun to watch, and they turn into an art form that is often more enduring than the treatments they depict.

I suspect that it is my appreciation of both art and antiquity that makes me like those movies so much, and that compelled me to write an entire book on this topic and to share those ideas with you. For, even as psychoanalysis fades into the shadows, and even as the latest scientific advance makes the last "advance" look silly, we can still appreciate film for what it is: a cultural document and a commentary on the struggles of the society that conceived it. Even though the technology of earlier cinema is inevitably supplanted by later technology, we can still turn back to those films and appreciate them as art products.

Unfortunately, I cannot say the same for psychiatry. For outdated psychiatry does not turn into an "art product" or a "scientific artifact." Mostly, it turns into superstition. Luckily, psychiatric superstitions can be recycled as cinema! Any disappointment provoked by the inflated promises of psychoanalysis becomes diluted, once we see how much those couch cures contributed to mid-twentieth-century cinema and produced an impressive tapestry of film and Freud.

Besides, times changed, both for cinematic subjects and for psychiatric treatment. Today, we live in an action-adventure age. In the past, people were content when a psychiatrist showed them how their past affected their present. Today they do not want to simply understand their situations; they want to CHANGE those situations, like actors in action-adventure films. Quick cures are better suited for a faster-paced society that also appreciates faster-paced films.

The chapters to come represent just a smattering of everything that can be said on this vast and expanding subject. Please forgive my omissions of important films for the sake of brevity. I hope that discussing my omissions can stimulate your own conversations, and your own studies, and that some of you may chose to share those ideas with me at sharonpacker@msn.com.

ACKNOWLEDGMENTS

This book would not have been possible without the efforts of two people: Dan Harmon and George Higham. Dan Harmon is an editor whose endless enthusiasm and encouragement are matched only by his vast knowledge of media and movies and his ability to turn a "lump of clay" into a (nearly) living book form. George's nonstop personal support, as well as his lifelong film work and his uncanny ability to unearth the obscure films and out-of-print books needed for this study, were essential to shaping this book. I thank Susie Yates for her patient and punctilious project management, Tom Graney of *Hollywood Outsider,* Jim Carlson for tireless tech support, journalists John Strausbaugh and Jim Knipfel, Dr. Fuat Ulas's listserv on psychiatry and cinema, Dr. Don Mender of the Association for the Advancement of Psychiatry and Philosophy for his books on the Holocaust, Dr. Richard Cumberlin for alerting me to the philosophical value of sci-fi, Dr. Phil Miller for hosting Hebrew Union College's unforgettable Yiddish film festival, Association for the Advancement of Technology and Psychiatry members, Dr. George Makari's History of Psychiatry seminars, New York Academy of Medicine's library staff and History of Medicine lectures, Anthology Film Archives' curators and librarians, and old friends from medical school and residency Stephen A. Berman, M.D., PhD; Joel L. Steinberg, M.D.; Terry Sukenik, M.D.; Merle Robinson, M.D.; and Stephanie Spanos, M.D. I appreciate Prof. Susan Ko's and the late Steve Rossen's last-minute alerts about *Lilith.* Finally, I thank the anonymous people who let me eavesdrop on their erudite conversations as they stood in ticket lines at East Village art houses, such as Anthology Film Archives, Film Forum, Cinema Classics, Bleecker Street and Van Dam cinemas, and other art houses of blessed memory. I hope that this book helps keep such revival houses as Anthology and Film Forum alive.

Chapter 1

Introduction

Film, as a medium, is inherently psychological in nature. The fact that cinema and psychoanalysis grew up together at the turn of the twentieth century only strengthens this association. Freud coined the term "psychoanalysis" at the same time that the first films screened. We can only wonder if Freud's seminal book *The Interpretation of Dreams* would have gained as much fame as it did, and wielded the wide influence that it did, had the book not appeared at the same time that cinema was in its infancy. For cinema also screened dreamlike scenes in the dark, just as sleep does. Moreover, cinema was a scientific invention, and Freud also touted his innovative dream interpretations as "scientific."

These coincidences alone would have been enough to cement the connection between psychology and cinema forever. Yet another "coincidence" had already occurred slightly earlier in the nineteenth century. Science was pushing forward when a photographer named Muybridge succeeded in producing motion photography. That year was 1878, the very same year that the first experimental psychology laboratory opened in Germany. This German lab bore no direct connection to Muybridge's photographic experiments in America. But those photographic experiments (performed by the photographer and not by the psychologist) paved a direct path to the cinema and also led to pivotal discoveries in perceptual psychology some thirty years later.

These chronological convergences were striking, even if they were simply coincidences. These convergences encouraged cinema to showcase shifts in psychological theories and treatments as they occurred, and to record both public and professional reactions to different treatments and theories. Cinema could excavate the past, comment on the present, and predict the future of psychiatry. And it did just that, as different genres developed over the course of the century. But cinema's purpose was not to record the history of psychiatry or psychology per se (even though some mental-health lobbying groups act as though this *should* be the purpose).

Cinema's purposes were to tell a good story, showcase special effects, add interesting settings, develop a character, or intensify dramatic conflict. Psychiatric conditions, psychiatric institutions, and psychiatric practitioners—and their sideshow or super-natural predecessors, such as hypnotists or exorcists—were perfectly suited for the same purposes. Although some films and filmmakers were motivated by political pur-poses when they conceived stories about psychiatry, most filmmakers were motivated by their desire to engage their audiences. They were willing to exploit people or places or professions to reach this goal.

It has been said that film influences popular opinion about the causes and cures of mental illness as much as scientific studies do. Many scientific studies support such allegations. In addition, scientific studies—conducted by health professionals—show that film also influences professional opinion. For instance, medical students' attitudes toward electroconvulsive therapy shifted after "seeing" Jack Nicholson sub-jected to such therapy in *One Flew over the Cuckoo's Nest* (1975). Films also provoke professional outrage and public outcries when professionals feel that they—or their patients—are not represented respectfully on screen, as happens more often than not.

To add insult to injury, of the four films that have swept all major Academy Awards since the awards began in 1927, two revolved around psychiatry and psychiatrists—but they depicted bad psychiatrists and worse psychiatric institutions! *One Flew Over the Cuckoo's Nest* (1975) and *The Silence of the Lambs* (1991), the two award-winning films, showed the darkest shadows of psychiatry. One wonders if *The Cabinet of Dr. Caligari* (1919) would have made the short list of great films on bad psychiatrists had the awards started in 1917 instead of 1927.

Ironically, early in the twentieth century Freud dismissed film's significance. Yet film therapy gained ground as a treatment technique in the late twentieth century. Ever since the memorably titled book *Rent Two Films and Let's Talk in the Morning* appeared in 1998,[1] more and more self-help books about film therapy have surfaced. More and more treatment programs (and especially substance abuse treatment pro-grams) mesh film therapy with traditional group therapy. Programs that are con-cerned with capping the high cost of health care and with servicing broader patient populations seem especially eager to substitute low-cost DVDs for pricey talk therapy.

It's not just that there is an obvious economic advantage to film therapy. It is equally important that these DVD-driven programs are well-accepted, and some-times preferred, by patients. Many people have difficulties putting their thoughts into words, as traditional talk therapy requires. They feel pressured when asked to "think of something to say," so they say nothing. Yet many can comment on cinema and thereby enter into a psychological dialogue about their thoughts and feelings. People who are new to the therapeutic setting, or people who are not schooled in expressing themselves, or visual artists who think in images rather than words, often like film therapy, as do many educated people who are familiar with film. When cultural chasms distance patients and professionals, film therapy bridges that gap. For mass media create a common culture and make patients feel that they share the same ground as their therapists.

The use of film to treat psychological problems might seem far-fetched, or strictly motivated by profit-driven maneuvers that try to treat the largest number of patients with the least amount of staff so as to make the most money. Perhaps that is true, to a degree. But film therapy is a natural idea, for film, as a medium, is so psychological in nature. Even Parker Tyler, the late and great film critic, referred to film as the "poor man's psychoanalyst."[2] (Tyler made that comment at a time when costly psychoanalysis was the gold standard, reserved for the wealthy.)

Films encourage viewers to free-associate, just as analysands do in psychoanalytic sessions. Virtually no one can watch a film without being reminded of a similar (or completely dissimilar) situation in one's own life or one's own past. Even people who recognize that their own lives are completely opposite of the screen (or off-screen) life of their favorite actor or director or singer can step into the actor's shoes for a moment and envision themselves living a different life. They might look to film to learn the steps that they need to take should they choose to step up to new and unfamiliar social roles. Alternatively, films that show bad behavior are blamed for corrupting morals of minors (or adults), because viewers model their own actions on the actions of actors.

Films also substitute for the drug experience (which may be another reason why film therapy is particularly popular in drug treatment programs). The spectator dissociates from everyday reality and retreats into unreality for an hour or two. Viewers shift into cinema's (non-chemically) altered state of consciousness and enjoy these so-called Hollywood hallucinations, without the aid of dangerous or addicting drugs. They learn new ways to live drug-free lives.

With their sound, light, color, and drama, films contain a myriad of different stimuli. Because they play on almost all senses, they become even more engrossing. Olfactory, taste, and tactile perceptions, which are absent from the celluloid itself, are still invoked in movie houses. The soothing smell of freshly buttered popcorn or the slimy feel of gum stuck on fabric-covered theater seats brings back memories, just as the taste of a lemon-flavored madeleine reminded Proust to write a thousand-plus pages' worth of *Remembrances of Things Past*. For many people, tasting the same "movie candies" that were eaten during childhood movie-going rituals with favored relatives brings back fond remembrances and makes later movie-going more fun.

It is natural for each individual to respond to any of the many stimuli in film and to use those stimuli as stepping stones to personal psychological insights. Interestingly, people who suffer from schizophrenia often avoid films, precisely because their brains cannot process so many stimuli simultaneously. For them, the viewing experience is overwhelming and unpleasant.

But for most of us (since schizophrenia mercifully strikes only 1 percent of the population), films offer many other psychological functions. First and foremost, film functions as a fantasy escape because it removes viewers from everyday reality and transports them to unreal realms that are otherwise available only through dreams or drugs. But films are even more useful than dreams or drugs, because films produce fantasies on demand, whereas dreams demand that the dreamer make do with whatever the unconscious cooks up that evening. The spectator chooses the unreal adventures of the evening. Luckily, films do not destroy the liver, or permanently raise blood pressure, or transmit infection, as drugs do.

Films can assuage anxiety because they allow the audience to "do-undo" events that were experienced vicariously while viewing the film. To use Freudian terminology, viewers practice "repetition-compulsion" as they view experiences that troubled them in the past. Spectators identify with a character. They emote with that character.

They imagine that they are experiencing the same events that the actor experiences. Or they try to understand how opposing characters thought or felt or functioned and why they did what they did (or did not do what they should have done).

At the end, when the credits roll and the lights go on, audiences are usually relieved to learn that it was only the actor—rather than they themselves—who was shot on the range, or who died on the battlefield, or who rolled off a cliff in a car. (Occasionally, viewers suffer disappointment when they realize that they must return to their own unmade bed, and walk over the crumpled potato chip bags left from the night before, rather than returning to the sparkling penthouse or sprawling mansion or teeming jungle that they have made-believe they lived in for the last two hours.)

Films can also induce anxiety, because they tap into realistic or unrealistic fears about the past, present, or future. It is not uncommon for patients to call a psychiatrist, claiming that their sleep problems or panic attacks began after seeing a specific film. In the author's experience, *Donnie Darko* (2001) holds the record for inducing male anxiety. This cult film about a young man who relives the last twenty-eight days, six hours, forty-two minutes, and twelve seconds of his life—until the audience learns that he died in a plane crash as the film starts—was uncannily similar to the airplane attack on the World Trade Center, so much so that it was pulled from theaters soon after its initial release in 2001. Alternatively, Hitchcock's *Psycho* (1960) and its immortalized shower slasher scene was known for panicking young women. Steven Spielberg's *Jaws* (1975) was an equal opportunity phobia-producer. *Jaws* became the first "summer blockbuster" film, and it proved that anxiety-inducing films raise box office revenue as well as heart rate!

Although it sounds paradoxical, anxiety-inducing films also function as anxiety-relieving films. Under the best of circumstances, films relieve anxiety because they convince viewers that their own anxieties are not unique. The filmmaker or screen writer already endured similar fears, for how else could he or she have conceived of the subject matter in the first place? Seeing other people sitting in the audience alongside them, or standing in the same video rental line, reassures the spectator that other people share their concerns. Why else would others pay the price of the movie ticket or the rental fee for the DVD?

There is another important connection between cinema and psychology, and that has to do with film's inherent similarity to dream. Seeing images projected on screen, and strung together in ways that defy retelling with words, occurs in both dream and film. Even the very experience of movie-going is deliberately dreamlike. Sitting in a dark setting, while immobilized in an enclosed space, seeing flashing images and experiencing highly emotional content, is similar to experiencing events that transpire in sleep laboratories. Those who believe that dreams are the "royal road to the unconscious" (as Freud put it) will be beckoned into the movie house's "dream chamber," and will want to dissect films (and their associations to those films) as if those films were personal dreams. Discussing films with friends turns the film-going experience into a quick, cheap, and often effective form of group therapy. In both places, personal insights are shared with others, who respond with their own comments and conjectures.

Because films are dreamlike, by their very nature they evoke associations with Freudian psychoanalysis, which penetrated the public's consciousness through Freud's century-changing book *The Interpretation of Dreams* (1900). Because dream interpretation is associated with Freudian (and with Jungian) analysis, dream scenes, and dream interpretation scenes, often find their way into film. That is one reason why we see so many dream scenes on screen, but there are artistic reasons as well, for dream scenes showcase special effects and computer-generated imagery (CGI). Dream scenes show off the cinematographer's special talents and premiere cinema's latest innovations, at the same time that they add intriguing dimensions to the art direction or reveal the characters' hidden motivations, fantasy lives, or repressed recollections. Dream scenes can be more memorable than the story itself. For instance, many people remember Salvador Dali's dream sequences in *Spellbound* (1945) better than they remember Bergman's or Peck's or Carroll's faces.

The mere fact that psychoanalytic dream scenes are so perfectly suited to cinema was reason enough for filmmakers to focus on psychoanalysis. For psychoanalysis emphasizes dreams. But there were even better reasons to showcase talk therapy so much (unwittingly making the public believe that psychoanalysis is the premiere psychiatric treatment). Because psychoanalysis provided the best dramatic driving devices for film, the couch cure received special attention on screen. Psychoanalysis serves as a story-telling device that uncovers hidden secrets and deep-seated motives. The analyst performs the same plot-driving function as the detective in police procedural films. The psychiatrist substitutes for a letter or a telegram or an eavesdropping device, revealing information to audiences and providing viewers with privileged communication.

For these reasons, and for many more reasons that will be discussed in chapters to come, it is no wonder that the subject of psychology—or psychiatry—in the cinema has long attracted the attention of psychiatrists, therapists, film critics, and movie directors—not to mention audiences and prospective psychiatric patients. Many spectators look to the movies to understand their personal problems, to find a quick and current diagnosis, and to decide who (or what) can best address their issues. Such similarities have contributed to a continual, strong, and mutually beneficial relationship between these seemingly divergent disciplines.

Even though psychiatrists are quick to condemn unflattering portrayals of psychiatrists and psychiatric patients on film, they are just as eager to exploit cinema for the lessons it can teach psychiatrists-in-training. Each year, at its annual conference, the American Psychiatric Association (and Dr. Steven Hyler) offer a for-credit, extra-cost course on "Teaching Psychiatry? Let Hollywood Help!" Each year, that course sells out. It is so popular that the catalogue carries a special warning, reminding attendees to register well in advance. Dozens of other courses are offered simultaneously, yet, to my knowledge, no other course carries this warning, and certainly not for so many consecutive years. Apparently its appeal endures.

Psychiatrists show interest in cinema more than just once a year. Columns about psychiatry and cinema are popular year round. All psychiatric tabloids (which summarize complicated studies from academic journals) include regular columns on film. Entire journals are devoted to psychoanalysis and cinema or to media and psychology.

Some tabloids featured educational articles about film therapy and encouraged practitioners to add this treatment technique to their armamentarium.

Aside from film therapy, film has a long legacy of clinical use in psychiatry and psychotherapy. Family therapists recognized that film captures real-life interactions that can be replayed and compared to personal recollections. Showing videos of family sessions allows family members to see their relationships with their relatives as others see them and to alter their behavior accordingly.

Therapists-in-training are typically videotaped as they interview patients (with the patient's permission). Watching those videos, in the company of their supervisors, helps them hone their interview skills and see nuances of their interactions with patients and identify subtle psychopathology that eluded them during stressful face-to-face interviews. Video viewing (with subsequent diagnostic discussion) is an essential element of the psychiatry board examination.

Telepsychiatry is about to provide another twist to video viewings. Forensic interviews can be conducted in prisons to offer opportunities to determine competency to stand trial or even to provide treatment. Although this approach is in its infancy, it still promises to increase access to psychiatric assessment and treatment, especially in underserved rural regions. One wonders if telepsychiatry, once fully developed, will become the preferred treatment vehicle for people with limited travel time, or with demanding family or work obligations. Maybe it will make treatment more accessible, especially for those who fear stigma if seen entering a psychiatrist's office.

Like most people, psychiatrists and psychotherapists are eager to observe their own images in cinema. They are quick to comment (or complain) about their reflections (or their distortions) in the movie mirror. Since the start of the century, there was never a time when psychiatrists or psychoanalysts did not appear in cinema. From the mind-controlling villains of early horror films (such as *Caligari* or the *Mabuse* movies) to Cold War thrillers (such as *The Ipcress File*), to the asylums that house political allegories along with personal dramas (such as *Shock Corridor*, *Spellbound*, *One Flew over the Cuckoo's Nest*, and *Girl, Interrupted*), to the drugs, phobias, and other disorders that pervade so many of our favorite films (including, as a small sample, *Vertigo*, *Night of the Hunter*, *Psycho*, *Rainman*, *Fight Club*, and *Requiem for a Dream*), there is no escaping either psychology in the movies, or the movies in psychology.

By looking at the interactions between cinema and psychology, this book offers readers clear and basic insights into the many reasons why film is such an important influence in our lives today.

In the next chapter on "A Century of Psychology and Cinema," we look at how advances in perceptual psychology, psychoanalysis, and behavioral conditioning corresponded with advances in cinematography. In "Freud and Film," we see how Freud's development of psychoanalysis and his abandonment of hypnotic treatments coincided with the birth of film. We see how "repressed memories" excavated by psychoanalysts turn into film flashbacks that serve as dramatic plot devices and add depth to characters. Chapter 4, "The Dream," highlights film's inherent similarity to dream and suggests that Freud's *Interpretation of Dreams* (1900) increased interest in film's "dream screen" and vice versa. We also examine Freudian-influenced dream themes in cinema, from Cocteau's creations to Dali's dream sequences in *Spellbound*.

The chapter on "Hypnosis" unveils the "evil twin" of psychoanalytic free associations: hypnosis and Pavlovian conditioning. We show how these authoritarian techniques penetrated German expressionism of the twenties, resurfaced in horror films of the thirties, infiltrated films noir of the forties, and contributed to Cold War paranoia of the fifties. We discuss *Caligari*, *Mabuse*, *Nightmare Alley*, *Manchurian Candidate*, and horror films great and horrid.

We move to "Madhouses, Haunted Houses, and Political Polemics" to show how pre-sound asylum thrillers (*Caligari, Mabuse*) morphed into a horror subgenre and evolved into psychological-supernatural works such as *House on Haunted Hill*. We trace the continuum between double-dealing doctors (*Spellbound*) to sadistic shock or straightjacket scenes (*Snakepit, Shock Corridor, The Jacket*) to political polemics (*Cuckoo's Nest, King of Hearts*) and compare those insufferable asylums to the romanticized rest homes and sorority house settings of *Now, Voyager*; *David and Lisa*; and *Girl, Interrupted*, and to the more realistic institutions in *Rainman* and *Spider*.

The chapter on "Psychological Thrillers and Serial Killers and the Motif of Madness" explores the meaning behind this once common category and shows how its popularity peaked after psychology permeated mainstream movies in the fifties. It shows how Hitchcock's "faux psychology" convinced audiences that "repressed memories" cause mental illness and that couch cures relieve them. Favorites of the 1940s and 1950s are discussed, such as *Cat People, Psycho, Three Faces of Eve, Spellbound*, and *Rope*, as well as forensic psychiatry–influenced films about serial killers, such as Hannibal Lecter. We see why films that indirectly imply the presence of psychosis (*Night of the Hunter, Cape Fear*) are more disturbing and more "psychologically thrilling" than more straightforward films.

The chapter on "Freudian Westerns and Films Noir" shows how movies such as *Johnny Guitar*, *Red River*, and *Gun Crazy* foreshadowed such contemporary gay-themed films as *Brokeback Mountain*. We find Freudian themes (such as Oedipal issues, sex role conflicts, preoccupation with past), as well as film noir influences, adding psychological dimensions in post-1950s cowboy films. We then deal with sexual transgression and sexual fetishism when we turn to film noir, with its femme fatales, dream themes, flashbacks, and psychoanalytic-style voice-overs. We mention academic texts on feminist film criticism that were inspired by film noir femme fatales and allude to their relationship to Freudianism and to film studies in general.

"Cold War Paranoia and Postwar PTSD" traces the influence of McCarthyism, the Cold War, and Korean War captives on paranoia-tinged films of the fifties, such as *Dr. Strangelove, Seconds, The Ipcress File*, and *The Manchurian Candidate*. We see how the fear of being watched (paranoia) transforms into a fascination with watching others (voyeurism) in *Rear Window* and *Peeping Tom*.

In "Drugs and Other Demons" we compare the drug culture's fascination with viewing films "under the influence" (*Wizard of Oz, Willy Wonka, Yellow Submarine, 2001, Fantasia*) with earlier and later films about dangers of drink/drug abuse (*Dr. Jekyll and Mr. Hyde, Lost Weekend, Altered States, Jacob's Ladder, Requiem for a Dream, Valley of the Dolls*). We contrast early opium-dream films with latter-day psychedelic-themed films (*The Game, American Beauty, Matrix*). A look at Charlie Chaplin's *Tramp* and *The Cure* adds perspective to cinema's portrayal of alcoholism.

A chapter on "Doubles and Doppelgängers" explains why the early intrigue with doubles (*Student of Prague, The Picture of Dorian Gray, Dr. Jekyll and Mr. Hyde*) occurred when photo and film discoveries compounded Freudian concepts about the "double consciousness." We see how "double identities" of the computer era ushered in a new era of "doubles" in *Fight Club, The Jacket,* and *Jacob's Ladder,* and why World War II experiences increased interest in films about twisted twins and secret selves.

"Woody Allen's Worries" shows how psychoanalysis fell from grace (and was replaced by the post-Prozac era) just as Woody fell from grace (and abandoned his analysis in favor of a union with a forbidden woman). We muse about how much Woody's about-face paved the path to public acceptance of psychopharmacology, especially since it was Allen who had personally promoted the couch cure for the thirty years that preceded psychiatry's striking paradigm shift.

Finally, "The Psyche Assumes Physical Form" shows that brain exchanges between humans and apes appeared in early film, when Darwinian debates were prominent. We see how the "race to space" produced sci-fi films about alien brain exchanges (*Brain from Planet Arous, Body Snatchers, Donovan's Brain*) that foreshadowed latter-day neuropsychiatric themes in *Total Recall, Scanners, eXistenZ, Flatliners, Minority Report,* and *Memento.* We conclude by musing about the ways that twenty-first-century technological advances, such as virtual reality and computer gaming, might impact future film-going and movie making. But before we talk about the future and our ending, let's turn back in time, to see how psychology and cinema played off one another from the start.

CHAPTER 2

A CENTURY OF PSYCHOLOGY AND CINEMA

SCIENCE, PSYCHOLOGY, AND PSYCHOANALYSIS

To appreciate the connections between cinema and scientific psychology (or experimental psychology, as the field came to be called), we must start by discussing science's contribution to cinema. For cinema is the only art form that fully depends upon scientific invention: cinema could not have come into being had it not been for science. It was a convenient coincidence that cinema and psychoanalysis grew up together, and that the two fields cross-pollinated each other, making each better than it would have on its own. The combination of cinema and psychoanalysis was an optional addition and a convenient quirk of history. However, the combination of science and cinema was not optional. It was essential.

Science and technological advances *had to* be in place before cinema, the seventh art, could emerge. Let me say it again: cinema could not exist without the technological innovations that preceded it. Curiously, cinema was developed as a scientific aid, not as a venue for entertainment or artistic expression.

Proto-cinema began with magic lantern shows in the 1660s (although some say that the Chinese used these techniques in the second century). Magic lantern shows progressed into optical toys and shadow shows. Those toys turned into *zoogyroscopes*, which morphed into cinematographs, and so on and so forth. A long list of inventions, innovations, and improvements preceded cinema. Many of their names are too difficult to pronounce, and even more difficult to remember. Some of those inventions were fascinating, some were fiascos, and some were half-failures, but all encouraged the great leap forward that followed.

Once cinema appeared, improvements increased progressively, since scientific progress often snowballs once it starts. "Movies" became "talkies," and turn-of-the-century magic tricks turned into computer-generated imagery, and on and on. True, there were times when two steps forward were followed by the proverbial one step back, but overall cinema advanced.

But what of psychology? How does that field fit into the picture? That is the question we will answer in chapters to follow.

Psychology is now one of the behavioral sciences, but it started as philosophy. Philosophy is speculation. Aristotle speculated about psychology some 2,500 years earlier and started a long tradition. Psychology as we know it today did not come into being until the last quarter of the nineteenth century. At that point, psychology turned into a science that tested its theories in the laboratory, rather than in the library or the living room. Soon psychology became a subject of university study. Until then, psychology had been a topic of conversation for *philosophes* and other intellectuals who sat in the proverbial armchairs and thought and talked.

Freud, the founder of psychoanalysis, was called the "last of the philosophes" because he preferred to speculate about psychoanalysis without testing his theories scientifically—even though he trained as a physician, practiced neurology, published scientific papers, and was educated in an era that embraced scientific positivism. But Freud forsook the laboratory studies of his early career when he took up the cause of psychoanalysis. He put his research on the intersexuality of eels behind him, pushed aside his neurological experiments on aphasia (the inability to express oneself in words), and pursued philosophically inclined psychoanalytic studies at the very time that mainstream psychology was becoming scientific.

Freud changed the way the world thought—even though he himself is not thought of nearly so well by the world today as he once was. Freud indirectly changed the way cinema developed, because his psychoanalytic ideas infiltrated cinema as cinema was evolving. Freud founded psychoanalysis, an entirely new field that originally attracted other neurologists like him, but eventually included psychiatrists, psychologists (after 1980), and, in Europe only, lay practitioners who were not formally schooled in either medicine or psychology.

In addition to an understanding of how experimental psychology evolved from speculative philosophy, and of Freud's beginnings as a neurologist and neurology researcher, something else is equally important to our discussion of the *psyche* and how it was represented (or misrepresented) in twentieth-century cinema: psychology and psychiatry are *not* one and the same, and psychologists and psychiatrists are *not* interchangeable, and psychoanalysis is an entity unto itself. True, these words all begin with the Greek root *psyche*, and all these fields concern themselves with the "mind" (also known as the psyche). But there are reasons why these different professions exist. Filmmakers sometimes confuse the fields, but at other times they send out significant though subtle messages when they represent one type of treatment on film rather than another.

Many viewers wonder why psychologists were rare in early film, and why they were typically depicted as test givers rather than talk therapists. The answer to the question is easy: clinical psychology did not exist until 1962. In that year, psychologists were given the right to determine competency to stand trial and could testify about sanity and insanity and participate in courtroom scenes that are staples of police procedural films. Until 1962, psychologists invented tests, conducted tests, or ran experiments.

Because psychologists were lower on the power totem pole, and because they were not medically trained as physicians, they could not administer such medical-type treatments as shock therapy. They could not order restraints. They could not inject tranquilizers or truth serum (as Nurse Ratched did in *One Flew over the Cuckoo's Nest*). So they tend to appear in more compassionate roles than psychiatrists, who often act as "the agents of the state" in cinema. There are exceptions to this rule, as dramatized by the carnivorous "consulting psychologist" in *Nightmare Alley* (1947).

This positive stereotyping of cinematic psychologists forgives the fact that psychologists Watson and Skinner "invented" behavioral conditioning in 1919 and 1953, respectively. Behavioral conditioning is a potent form of mind control. It is comparable to hypnosis, but falls short of lobotomy or high doses of Thorazine or shock therapy. Watson's early experiments on little Albert are frankly frightening. He trained Albert to fear white mice and to develop a full-blown phobia. This achievement found its way into *1984*, the dystopian book and film about a totalitarian state that controlled citizens like Winston, known to have a rat phobia, by forcing his face into a rat-filled cage.

A relatively recent development in mental health care delivery is the psychiatric or clinical social worker (CSW) who has one or two years of post-college training. CSWs were initially intended to provide lower-cost treatment in community health centers that serve all economic strata (unlike psychoanalysis, which was elitist, expensive, time-consuming, and reserved for the rich).

When CSWs received the right to bill insurance companies, times changed. Many left the community mental health centers and hospital-based programs where they started, and started private practice as "psychotherapists." Eventually, they outnumbered PhD-level talk therapists. Since the time that psychiatric social workers entered private practice, remarkable changes have occurred in mental health care. For one thing, "managed mental health care" emerged reining in reimbursement for talk therapy. By then, psychopharmacology had advanced enough to make the long-term talk therapy that we see in movies fade into gray. The 1990s were dubbed "the decade of the brain"—but not until the psychiatrist who once headed the American Psychoanalytic Association conceded that psychoanalysis is an art rather than a science.

Once compensation for psychotherapy had dropped dramatically, most psychiatrists moved to psychopharmacology. Lower-paid and lesser-trained psychiatric social workers provided "talk therapy." Many psychologists veered toward more structured and experimentally studied "cognitive-behavioral therapy." Because psychoanalysis was no longer as prestigious, provable, or profitable as it was in its heyday, fewer and fewer psychiatrists entered psychoanalytic training programs. Fewer and fewer psychiatrists practiced the "cinema psychiatry" portrayed in film's golden age of psychiatry (1947–53). To stay open, psychoanalytic institutions trained more and more social workers in psychoanalysis, which is now considered defunct as a science.

Cinema captured these changes. *The Cell* (2000), starring the pop icon Jennifer Lopez, tells how J-Lo's character started her career as a social worker before becoming a psychotherapist. Only now, in this futuristic sci-fi film, she works in a sleep lab of sorts and functions as a technician who manipulates hi-tech machinery that lets her "get into the head" of her psychotic patient. This sci-film introduces the social worker as a true mental health technician. It also prepares us for upcoming technological breakthroughs in psychiatric treatments. Some of those changes are happening already, as vagal nerve stimulation (VNS) and brain pacers and implants move from experimental stages to controlled clinical trials with human subjects. Perhaps *The Cell* is telling us that technicians—rather than therapists—will soon be curing psychosis. This far-fetched suggestion may not be so inconceivable in the future, especially now that lab tests for defects in neurotransmitter synthesis are becoming available.

Prime (2005), a very different film about a psychiatric social worker/psychotherapist, stars Meryl Streep. *Prime* is not futuristic like *The Cell*. Rather, it is regressive. It parodies psychoanalysts and uses humor to poke fun at a dying tradition. We see Streep listening to clients' stories about sex, as if she were part Jewish mother (which Streep is not), part bearded Viennese analyst (which she also is not) and part yenta (from *Fiddler on the Roof*), who meddles with relationships and arranges marriages. Again, this film prepares us for shifts in society and science, this time through parody (the end stage of comedy) rather than sci-fi.

Unlike psychology, psychiatry always existed, in one form or another. Psychiatry is all about praxis, or practice, even if it was practiced by people known as alienists or soul doctors rather than psychiatrists. Psychiatry was the first recognized American medical specialty, and it came into being in 1844, before the Civil War started in 1861. Our current American Psychiatric Association was called the Association of Medical Superintendents of American Institutions for the Insane. The organization was convened by thirteen "asylum doctors" who worked in asylums that housed the insane, indigents, and petty criminals.

Most asylums were little more than warehouses for these unfortunates, although important research was being conducted at the Salpêtrière in Paris and the Burgholzi in Switzerland. Some asylums encouraged visitors, who paid a few pence to watch madmen and madwomen assume strange postures and behave bizarrely. Some asylums hosted Lunatics' Balls for both lunatics and "admiring audiences," who "appreciated" the antics of psychotics decades before exploitative "madhouse movies" appeared in grind houses or drive-ins.

For film makers, it was fortuitous that so many aspects of psychiatry have been and still are controversial, or conflict-ridden—for drama revolves around conflict. Conflict drives the plot. Comedy parodies conflict. How boring it would be if there were nothing to debate, and if we were stuck watching films about *Fred Ott's Sneeze* (an early short that literally shows an Edison employee sneezing, and nothing more).

One of the hottest areas of debate revolves around the relationship between psychiatry and the state. This subject was perfectly suited to cinema, as the far-reaching influence of *One Flew Over the Cuckoo's Nest* proved. Psychiatrists know that psychiatry was (and sometimes still is) used as a political ploy or as a means of social control. Historically, psychiatry was used to save society from harm or inconvenience as much as (or even more than) it was used to save psychiatric patients from personal harm. Often, psychiatric treatment was a means of containing (but not necessarily curing or caring for) people whose aberrant behavior disrupted the social order. This is also a worthy subject for cinema, as shown by such thrillers as *House on Haunted Hill* (remake, 1999) and *Spellbound*.

Yet psychiatrists did not always wield such control. Until the late eighteenth century, psychiatry was the province of church doctors rather than medical doctors. Many aspects of psychiatry were barely distinguishable from superstition and occultism. Men such as Franz Anton Mesmer (1734–1815) deliberately blurred the boundaries between medicine and magic. Mesmer was a medical doctor when he invented "animal magnetism," also known as mesmerism. Although medical overseers ran Mesmer out of his native Austria, the charismatic Mesmer was welcomed in Paris. His mesmerism (and his charming personality) proved to be popular with Parisian ladies. Mesmerism, along with its distant relative, hypnosis, would be revived and resuscitated many times over on the silver screen, which itself is said to be mesmerizing and mind-controlling.

These historical associations between psychiatry and superstition, and between psychiatric asylums and prisons, may have been embarrassing for psychiatry, but they worked very well for film. Freud's invention of psychoanalysis, and his abandonment of hypnosis, called more attention to these old techniques. Science may have wanted to forget its origins, but filmmakers mined the past for good plots and refused to let such an entertaining legacy die a natural death.

For filmmakers eagerly exploit any good dramatic device, as *The Exorcist* and its sequels demonstrated in the 1970s, and as *Jacob's Ladder* (1999) and *The Sixth Sense* proved in the 1990s. Boundary blurring between neuropsychiatry and the supernatural persisted throughout the decade of the brain, as the 1990s was known. In 2006 *Silent Hill*, a film based on a video game, attributed a child's sleepwalking and psychotic episodes to atavistic memory traces from the haunted village she inhabited in her former life. One wonders if contemporary psychiatry's demand for evidence-based medicine will cast even more attention on these arcane concepts. It is curious that *Silent Hill*'s subject matter is so similar to the *Dybbuk* story and films.

PERCEPTUAL PSYCHOLOGY, SCIENCE, AND CINEMA

Let us turn to perceptual psychology, which began as a science and which remains a science, and which is also intimately intertwined with cinema. As mentioned earlier, there is cause for concern about the connections between science and cinema. Scientific innovation was essential to cinema. Were it not for fast film, motion picture projectors, and photographic inventions, cinema could not exist. Likewise, were it not for fine points of perceptual psychology, we would not be able to perceive "moving pictures." However, one does not need to understand the perceptual psychology that underlies the perception of motion in order to develop cinema or to appreciate cinema. In fact, cinema was based on *false* premises about the perception of motion and *false* premises about perceptual psychology. The invention of cinema *preceded* important discoveries in perceptual psychology, and *inspired* discoveries in perceptual psychology, rather than the other way around.

Impressionism also deserves credit for changing assumptions about the psychology of perception. The first Impressionist paintings were exhibited in Paris in 1874, just one year before Exner conducted critical experiments concerning the perception of light and motion. In 1875 Exner proved that people cannot identify lights that flash more frequently than 45 milliseconds as distinct objects. They "see" a single object in motion instead of seeing separate lights. But the Impressionist painters made it possible to appreciate these scientific discoveries about perception.

Between 1912 and 1916, psychologist Max Wertheimer and physician-turned-psychologist Hugo Munsterberg developed their theories about perception. Their discoveries earned extra attention because the public wanted to understand the psychology and the science behind movies, motion picture cameras, and projectors. When Exner conducted his original studies on the perception of motion in 1875, his research did not attract much attention, largely because cinema had not yet appeared and because the influence of the Impressionists had not yet spread. In contrast, Wertheimer worked in 1912, after cinema had become an art form, and after Freud had lectured in America and made people wonder about the machinations of the mind.

Until Wertheimer and Munsterberg proved otherwise, it was believed that the "persistence of vision" made motion pictures possible. The ancient Egyptians discussed persistence of vision, as did Aristotle, Newton, and others. The "persistence of vision" premise rested upon the belief that the eye deceives the mind. Then Wertheimer analyzed the stroboscopic effect and showed that it was the other way around: the mind deceives the eye. The brain provides a mental bridge between movie frames, so that a series of static images appears to be a single continuous movement. Wertheimer named his discovery *gestalt psychology*. *Gestalt psychology* inspired Fritz Perls's *gestalt therapy*, which was popular in the 1960s. Apart from its name and its inspiration, however, *gestalt therapy* bears no connection to experimental *gestalt psychology*.

As the story goes, Wertheimer became intrigued with this "flicker phenomenon" as he watched light bulbs "move" on a Broadway theater marquee. Electric lights had recently been invented and had turned Broadway into the Great White Way. Lights lured theater-goers each evening. One evening, Wertheimer realized that one bulb burned out and changed the look of the whole (*gestalt*) marquee and made the marquee appear to be moving.

Wertheimer's studies in the psychology of perception persisted through his student Rudolf Arnheim, whose book on *Film as Art* (1932) remains a must-read for cinema studies. Like Wertheimer (and psychiatrist Fritz Perls), Arnheim was one of many, mostly Jewish, intellectuals who fled Europe in the 1930s as Hitler came to power. In 1954, the prolific Arnheim published his most important work, *Art and Visual Perception: A Psychology of the Creative Eye* (1954). Arnheim died in June 2007, at the age of 102, and was profusely eulogized by the *New York Times*.

In 1924 Peter Mark Roget proved that the retina retains images of an object for half a second. This discovery confirmed that the retina was *not* responsible for the illusion of movement. Later, it was learned that the brain cannot process images that move too quickly, and that "the mind's eye" sees rapidly moving objects as a single continuous image rather than as a discrete object. Because film moves at a speed of twenty-four frames/second, it bypasses the brain's threshold of perception, and so we see separate film frames as one continuous course of action.

The study of perception, and the interplay between mind and eye (or other sensory organs), falls under the rubric of perceptual psychology. Perception takes place without our conscious awareness and without our volition or our intent. From that angle, perceptual psychology is similar to psychoanalysis, which also claims that the mind operates without our conscious awareness, and makes us remember people or places differently from the way they appeared in real life.

The psychoanalyst posits that personal memories and unconscious associations and forgotten family drama alter perception and lead to misperceptions. Perceptual psychologists concern themselves with universal principles, whereas psychoanalysts focus on individual experiences. Perceptual psychologists conduct experiments confirming that people do not perceive reality as it really is. Cinema is the ultimate confirmation of these principles from perceptual psychology, for cinema makes us believe (temporarily) that events taking place on screen are real.

As for our topic of movies and the modern psyche, we can see how these two twentieth-century innovations—psychoanalysis and perceptual psychology—both called attention to the fact that the mind (psyche) processes information and reinterprets information, in spite of our intent. The mind, or psyche, overrides our will, which was once thought to be inviolable. The conjoint inventions of cinema and psychoanalysis made people perceive the world differently. The modern era arrived, not just because of a time change, but because of these—and other—inventions and ideas. The world would not be the same, were it not for cinema, and were it not for psychoanalysis. Discoveries in the field of perceptual psychology did not change the way the world thought, but simply fortified the claims of the psychoanalysts (or depth psychologists) who said that "something beneath the surface" affected perception.

Cinema provided the ultimate proof that people must learn how to perceive. When the Lumière brothers' *The Arrival of a Train at the Station* first screened in 1895 France, spectators ran from the theater in fear. They saw the smoke-blowing train rush forward, moving toward them. Because they were unfamiliar with film, audience members believed that the train could leave the screen and run them over, like a real locomotive. By the time that Edwin A. Porter's *Great Train Robbery* screened in 1903, showing a man aiming his pistol at the audience, they were surely startled, as action-adventure audiences should be, but they were not deceived by this illusion. Close to a century later, Woody Allen referenced these early reactions to cinema in *Purple Rose of Cairo* (1985). There, a character steps out of the screen, moves into the audience, and speaks to Mia Farrow as she sits in the theater. She embraces the possibility that "reel life" can penetrate "real life" and leave the screen, and she starts a futile love affair with the actor.

Perceptual psychology is always at work as we view film. Perceptual psychology is like the stagehand who labors backstage, moving props and dimming lighting and making sounds with such finesse that the theatrical audience forgets that the stagehand exists. On the surface, the psychology of perception seems to be the least dramatic form of psychology, especially when compared to psychoanalysis, which evolved around the same time.

Yet, as already hinted, perceptual psychology was not invented by psychologists, even though psychologist Wertheimer and physician-turned-psychologist and later film scholar Munsterberg got credit for developing the field. Perceptual psychology owes it origins to someone who was entangled in a triangle so dramatic, and so deadly, that even a psychoanalyst would be shocked. That person's name is Edward Muybridge. Muybridge was a photographer, already acclaimed for his photographs of Yosemite National Park when he was offered the opportunity to participate in an unusual photographic experiment. Before he achieved photographic fame, Muybridge was also known for his eccentricities, which were attributed to a head injury suffered during a stagecoach accident in 1860. While recovering from his injury, he learned photography and grew skilled enough to win a job on an expedition to Alaska. His discoveries in photography and perceptual psychology were delayed because of an unplanned foray into the field of forensic psychiatry.

In 1874 Muybridge murdered his younger wife's lover after he learned that the boy whom he believed to be his own son had instead been fathered by the lover. Muybridge was nearly lynched, but he entered a plea of insanity just before the trial. Oddly enough, the judge rejected his plea and acquitted him, implying that a reasonable man would have reacted the way Muybridge did. One need not be insane to do what Muybridge had done.

After the trial, Muybridge returned to his photographic career. In 1878 he made good on a bet placed by racehorse breeder and former Senator Leland Stanford. Stanford hired Muybridge to photograph a galloping horse to see if all four legs left the ground at one time as the horse galloped. Muybridge proved Stanford's theory by placing cameras and trip lines at predetermined points along the race track. The newly developed fast film captured successive images of the horse in motion as the horse tripped lines that connected to the cameras and set off their shutters.

By 1880 Muybridge had developed a device that projected successive photographs of this galloping horse and thereby simulated the horse's motion. He called these devices zoogyroscopes. Zoogyroscopes became popular immediately. They recollected the "magic lantern" shows developed by a monk named Athanasius Kirschner in the mid-1600s.

It is interesting to note that 1878—the year Muybridge began his photographic experiments—was the same year that physician-turned-psychologist Wilhelm Wundt founded the first laboratory for experimental psychology in Germany. Even though Muybridge's photographic study had no direct connection to Wendt's laboratory, it seems that photographic invention and scientific discovery were in the air in the 1880s. One discovery played off another. One innovation drew on the last innovation. Scientific advances stimulated more studies.

For sure, technology and perceptual psychology were snowballing. In 1876 Bell invented the telephone. Edison's phonograph arrived a year later. As we have seen, 1878 was a historic year, thanks to Muybridge's photographic experiments (in the United States) and Wundt's experimental psychology laboratory (in Germany).

By 1879 Edison (or one of his employees) had invented the electric carbon-filament light. This electric light would be essential to film projectors. The following year, 1880, brought Muybridge's zoogyroscope, which was arguably the most important proto-cinema innovation since the monk's magic lantern shows. It was now just a matter of time before cinema appeared. Science was snowballing, and society was receptive.

PSYCHOANALYSIS AND CINEMA: CURIOUS COINCIDENCES

As we have seen, some very curious coincidences occurred as the nineteenth century ended. Some of these were not coincidental at all, since they involved scientific discovery. It is well known that one discovery begets another discovery, and that science snowballs at certain times and in certain places. Because cinema is the first and only art form that is fully dependent upon scientific discoveries, it makes sense that scientific progress pushed cinema forward. Because cinema also depends upon perceptual psychology, it makes sense these fields advanced one another.

However, there was another coincidence—the coincidental convergence between the discovery of cinema and the discovery of psychoanalysis—that has little or no connection to science as we know it. Psychoanalysis was not essential to the discovery of cinema, and cinema would have emerged whether or not psychoanalysis existed. But psychoanalysis made movies that were made in its wake more interesting and more modern. One could say that cinema and perceptual psychology provided the skeleton, but psychoanalysis added flesh to the bone, giving movies more dimensions. Because these curious chronological coincidences are directly relevant to the interplay between movies and the modern mind, they deserve to be described in detail below.

In 1894 an Edison employee named Dickson filmed another employee who engaged in a rather ordinary act. The employee was named Fred Ott, an ordinary engineer whose name would have faded from history, had it not been for the fact that he sneezed at the right time, and that his sneeze was captured in an extraordinary way. For Dickson recorded *Fred Ott's Sneeze* on a newly invented kinetograph. *Fred Ott's Sneeze* (1894) entered history, as did Ott.

That same year the name *kinetograph* was changed to *kinetoscope*. After a few improvements were made, the first kinetoscope parlor opened in New York City, also in 1894. This kinetoscope was the forerunner of the motion picture projector.

One year later, in 1895, the Lumière brothers screened the first film in France, using their *cinematograph*. Our word *cinema* comes from cinematograph. Among the audience at that first screening was Georges Méliès, a French magician and illusionist who owned his own theater. Méliès was an entertainer by nature. He earned his living by sleight-of-hand, and he appreciated the entertainment potential of the celluloid illusions. Méliès's more scientifically minded predecessors focused only on the scientific aspects of cinema. Even the enterprising Edison viewed cinema as a scientific device that could scientifically document events.

Méliès, on the other hand, realized that cinema could construct stories and fabricate fiction. Méliès became the "father of narrative film" and changed the course of cinema. He produced his first film, *Une Partie de Cartes*, in 1896.

Now that we have fast-forwarded to 1896, let us magically move east to Vienna, where we find a brash young neurologist named Sigmund Freud. Some years previous, while still a medical student, Freud had published an academic paper on the intersexuality of eels. This otherwise arcane topic foreshadowed the flamboyant psychosexual theories that Freud would be remembered for. But that would come later. In 1896 Freud focused on hysteria, and on differentiating the loss of words that follows a brain injury from the loss of words produced by psychological trauma alone.

Freud had previously published scientific papers on aphasia (the loss of ability to express oneself with words). He was already experimenting with hypnosis as a cure for hysteria. Then, in 1896, Freud claimed that he could cure hysteria through a never-before-discovered technique: psychoanalysis. Freud's experimental psychoanalytic treatment technique would become known as the talking cure. Colloquially, it was called the couch cure because it took place on a couch, which was common in Victorian-era parlors. The important point is that both psychoanalysis and cinema came into being nearly simultaneously, in the short span of two years.

In 1898, two years after he coined the concept of psychoanalysis, and recanted earlier ideas about using hypnosis to cure hysteria, Freud published a ground-breaking paper called *Sexuality in the Aetiology of Neuroses*. The following year, in 1899, this self-styled connoisseur of the unconscious wrote an equally important essay called *Screen Memories*. The term *screen memories* refers to the snapshot memories that we carry with us from childhood. In the name of that essay, Freud made an unconscious (and almost unconscionable) association: he referenced this new invention of film, the importance of which he would soon dismiss. Curiously, photography was also pushing forward in those same years, thanks to the inventions of George Eastman. But by using the term *screen* memories, Freud saluted cinema as the supreme signature of the unconscious.

Freud never gave cinema much credit, neither in this book nor in his other writings or his meticulously recorded conversations and correspondence. In fact, when given the chance to comment on movies, he denigrated them and dismissed their importance. (Freud also thought that religion was an illusion that would disappear in due time, and that America was unimportant, and we know what became of those prophecies!) Freud's opinion about film is, for now, irrelevant.

The important issue is that psychoanalysis and cinema were invented at the same time, albeit independently of one another. Both psychoanalysis and cinema were children of the turn-of-the-twentieth century. They basked in the same cultural climate, and breathed the same social concerns of the day. They reflected the same intellectual arguments and the same scientific accomplishments, and they commented on the same political conflicts that colored their era. They influenced one another, and they interacted with one another, from the start, as I shall explain in the chapters ahead. Each reconfigured the human mind and reworked the powers of perception. Each operated independently, in its own way, but both were more forceful when acting together.

The story does not end there: rather, the story is just starting. For now, let us inch forward to the turn of the century, to November 1899, when Freud's century-changing book about dreams arrived. Freud's expressed goal was to "shake the sleep of mankind." He succeeded. Cinema succeeded, also, even though its early promoters never aspired as high as Freud did. Cinema's creators never fathomed that their invention would mold the modern mind, much less that it would prime that modern mind to accept century-changing psychoanalytic theories about the unconscious control of dreams and ordinary human interactions and emotions.

It was fortunate for Freud that movies were viewed in a dark chamber that mimicked a bedchamber and that reminded spectators of dreams. Now that cinema had been invented, and was appreciated by far more people than appreciated Freudian theories, nighttime dreams could be seen as mind movies that flashed across the consciousness of the sleeper. This curious coincidence—the simultaneous "discovery" of "scientific" approaches to dreams in both films and in psychoanalysis—helped

Freudian theory gain ground in serious circles at the same time that less serious people patronized peep shows and peaked at dreamlike scenes projected on screen.

By 1899 movies were popular attractions in amusement arcades, music halls, traveling fairs, wax museums, and vaudeville houses. Movies made their way to many countries. They were a slightly more high-brow attraction in Europe than in America. In America, movies were especially popular with southern and eastern European immigrants who flooded Ellis Island at the turn of the century, buoyed by dreams about opportunities in America but knowing no English. These immigrants appreciated cheap silent cinema that did not require an understanding of English.

Movies were gaining ground in France at the same time that Ellis Island was welcoming immigrants. In 1899 Méliès produced *Cendrillon* [Cinderella], a fantasy if there ever was one. The story of Cinderella endures to this day. Disney catapulted Cinderella to fame through his animated cartoons. But fact is sometimes stranger than fiction, and the fact is that this fantasy film *Cendrillon* was the first film to use prearranged scenes. Thus Méliès's *Cendrillon* ushered in the era of the narrative (story-telling) film and changed the course of cinema. This narrative technique would remain with us for decades, and would dominate cinematic exposition until post-modernism—and disrupted narrative—appeared at the twilight of the twentieth century and interjected itself into such films as *Pulp Fiction* (1994) and *Memento* (2000).

This narrative technique complemented changes that were taking place in novels and in the roman à clef in particular. Movies motivated psychoanalytic patients to retell their life tales as though their lives were driven by the same kind of MacGuffin that drives movie plots. (*MacGuffin* is the term that Hitchcock used to describe the element that pushes the plot and recurs throughout the film.) Movies made people believe that their lives can be transformed as easily as movie scenes. That belief proved to be a selling point for psychoanalysis and for the "human potential movement" that appeared much later in the twentieth century. Near the end of the twentieth century, Neal Gabler wrote a book called *Life the Movie* (1998). He observed that media-driven Americans expected their lives to unfold like film, and that they had little ability—and little inclination—to distinguish between "real life" and "reel life." The *inner identity* that was transmitted through their elders intermixed with the *outer identity* that was appropriated from the media.

But we are getting ahead of ourselves. Let us return to the beginning of the twentieth century, to see how we wound up where we are. In 1901, just a year after Freud had published his landmark *Interpretation of Dreams* and just a year after Méliès the magician had worked his movie magic with *Cendrillon,* Freud published another world-changing work: *The Psychopathology of Everyday Life*. (It doesn't matter whether you agree with Freud or his ideas; what matters is that his ideas influenced others and changed the way the world thought, at least for a while.)

The Psychopathology of Everyday Life was remarkable for many reasons. For one thing, this book showed that strange psychological events happen to everyone, and not just to madmen. Ordinary people have slips of the tongue (which became known as Freudian slips). They have conflicts with their families and they experience strange sexual sensations. They enter into a state of psychosis, each night, as they dream. Psychopathology was not exclusive to asylum inmates who danced at lunatics' balls.

Psychopathology occurred in everyone, and was on a continuum with psychosis, or so Freud said. This theory was a sea change at the time: it destigmatized psychosis.

Even though Freud's ideas about childhood sexuality were not well-accepted by the medical community, the theories he presented in *The Psychopathology of Everyday Life* resonated with the public. Over time, this book became a best seller. Convinced that everyone suffered from some sort of conflict, the public was primed to see their conflicts—or anyone else's conflicts—displayed on screen. This book set the stage for the psychologically minded cinema that followed.

In 1902 Georges Méliès introduced innovative special effects in the first real science fiction film, *Le voyage dans la lune* [*A Trip to the Moon*]. This film consisted of a series of long shots that were strung together, punctuated with disappearances, double exposures, other trick photography, and elaborate sets.

The magician-turned-movie-maestro projected dream scenes onto film screens, while Freud deciphered dream scenes in psychoanalytic settings. Each toiled in his own setting, at the very same time, even though Freud insisted that he was a scientist (a claim that has been hotly contested), whereas Méliès acknowledged that he used something that was intended to be a scientific tool—cinema—and turned it into entertainment and into a new form of movie magic.

The year 1902 was memorable for other reasons as well. William James's *The Varieties of Religious Experience* was published, to the shock and dismay of James's academic colleagues at Harvard. James, a physician by education but a psychologist by inclination, had published his ground-breaking *Lectures on Psychology* in 1890. He opened America's first psychology laboratory and started Harvard's first psychology department. He showed promise as a serious researcher, one who could push the study of psychology out of the world of superstition and into the realm of science. And now, here he was, returning to his roots, to his Swedenborgian religious roots specifically. He had returned to magic and mysticism, which he apparently preferred to serious psychology. As destiny would have it, James would be remembered for his writings on religion, even though the history of psychology and philosophy recorded his other achievements.

Apparently, the door was swinging both ways as the twentieth century entered the arena. Regardless of how one chooses to remember William James, few forget that James brought Freud to America. He invited Freud to lecture at Clark University and thereby introduced Freud's iconoclastic ideas to American academics. Fortunately for Freud, Americans were far more receptive to his unsettling ideas than were his Austrian compatriots.

Change was on fast forward in the early twentieth century. If we stay in America for a moment, and stay in the year 1903, we find the first stirrings of the history-making American director Edwin S. Porter. Porter was chief of film production at the Edison studio when he shifted to narrative storytelling with *The Life of an American Fireman* (1902). *Fireman* was the first realistic film to use the narrative techniques that Méliès introduced for fantasy subjects.

In 1903 Porter produced another first. *The Great Train Robbery* (1903) was a Western, a quintessentially American genre. More importantly, Porter's twelve-minute *Train Robbery* was the first film to use modern film techniques, such as multiple camera positions, filming out of sequence, and editing the scenes into their proper order afterwards. The art and science of film editing was born! We have to make do with our dreams, but we can edit our films (or the film directors and editors can edit them for us), to produce even more interesting dreams on screen.

The year 1903 was a landmark year for yet another reason: Hollywood was incorporated as a municipality. Hollywood would change the world, and world cinema as well, although not for a while. It took two world wars to establish Hollywood as the undisputed film capital of the world.

In the meantime, Porter's film, with its parallel cross-cutting between scenes, approximated the working of the human mind (or at least it made us believe that the human mind functions as such, manipulating several ideas and images simultaneously). Over the course of the century, psychologists studied human subjects to prove that people experience many thoughts simultaneously, just as the movies suggested. Filmmaking would soar to new heights as a result.

By century's end, television commercials about ADHD had convinced many Americans that they experience too many thoughts simultaneously, and that their confusion could be cured with stimulants and other prescription pills. By then, both film and literature were transformed by the nonchronological narrative of postmodernism. Sequential narratives—the norm since 1904—faded into the background, but did not entirely disappear.

Something else happened in 1904, something that was totally unrelated to film, or to psychoanalysis, or to psychology of perception. Just the same, that "something" proved to be fortuitous for film. In 1904 the Russian physiologist Ivan Pavlov won the Nobel Prize in physiology and medicine. Even though Pavlov's name is synonymous with Pavlovian conditioning, he earned his award for discoveries on digestion and not for advances in psychology. Pavlov's experiments showed that dogs (and people) can be trained to salivate in response to an unrelated stimulus, provided that the stimulus (a bell) is repeatedly paired with food, which automatically evokes a response.

Pavlov did not elaborate on behavioral conditioning for another decade or two; his book on this subject had to wait until 1923. It would be psychologists, rather than physiologists, who carried Pavlov's early experiments to new heights (or deeper depths). In 1919 psychologist John Watson published his findings about behavioral conditioning. From the 1920s onward, debates between behaviorists and psychoanalysts escalated. The behaviorists eventually won in the scientific arena, but the philosophical implications of their work was unpalatable to many Americans.

The idea that behavior could be controlled so completely, and that human beings could be conditioned as easily as animals, and even made to act like animals, was perfect fodder for film. Early in film's history, when Darwinian thought was still fresh, and when the idea that humans had descended from apes was still shocking, several short, silent films showed scientists exchanging human brains with ape brains. The idea that humans did not control their own destinies was less acceptable to democratically minded Americans than it was to Russians, who were accustomed to the czar and who were attempting to overthrow Russian royalty and to install "the reign of the people" at the very same time that the film industry was coming into being.

For Americans, Freud's idea of free associations was preferred to the Russian model of control. Just the same, a wonderful array of films played upon ideas presented by Pavlov (and Watson and fellow behaviorist B. F. Skinner). *One Flew over the Cuckoo's Nest* is the best known of this genre. The zombie movies of the fifties, as well as sci-fi classics such as *Invasion of the Body Snatchers*, also captured the spirit of behavioral conditioning, and added a little biology and astronomy and anthropology to the mix. *The Manchurian Candidate* (1962) contrasted Korean communist brainwashing (which ingrained lies) to American-style "free dreams" and "free associations" (which told truths) and became the best comparative cinematic study of these themes.

By 1905 the groundwork for the major directions in movies and the modern psyche was in place. Experiments in perceptual psychology were underway. Freudian dream theories were working their way around the world, even though Freud's *Interpretation of Dreams* would not be translated into English until the next decade. In 1905 Binet invented the first intelligence test. Other psychological tests followed. Many such tests were showcased in cinema, particularly tests that were visually intriguing, like the Rorschach inkblot test. Hypnosis had been known since the days of surgeon James Braid but would receive renewed attention once Freud's newly fashioned psychoanalysis replaced it. Jung's conflation of psychiatry and the supernatural was cemented when he completed his dissertation on mediums and the occult in 1905.

Pavlov laid the groundwork for mind-control techniques that proved popular in Weimar Germany and in Cold War America. Drugs such as opium, cocaine, alcohol, and even hallucinogens were already well known to doctors and to filmmakers. The visual hallucinosis of alcohol withdrawal (DTs) and opium dreams were ideal for silent cinema. Psychosurgery (such as lobotomies and leukotomies) had not yet been invented, but that did not stop filmmakers from exercising their imaginations and depicting brain exchanges. Shock therapy was three decades away, but mental patients were subjected to other horrific treatments, such as chains and racks that were reminiscent of the witch burnings and water dunkings of the Middle Ages. These treatments were exploited early on, as *Witchcraft through the Ages* (1922) proves.

Fortunately for filmmakers, but unfortunately for the poor people who experienced these cruelties, cruel cures for mental illness had existed for centuries and could be compared to the more compassionate and more modern couch cure. The couch cure could also be exploited endlessly, especially since psychoanalysts emphasized sexual origins of civilized behavior. Besides, the connection between *couch* and *bed* was obvious even to someone who had never seen an erotic and exotic nineteenth century *Odalisque* reclining on a divan and posing for a painting.

Some compassionate cures, such as the nature cure that was inspired by the poet Wordsworth, or the moral treatment that was coined by Quakers, were in place in the late nineteenth century. Filmmakers could choose peaceful mountain retreats, a la *Now, Voyager* (1942) or *A Razor's Edge* (1946/1984). Or they could showcase scary asylums that were dingier than Count Dracula's castle. Mental illness, mental health practitioners, and mental asylums provided a wide array of dramatic backdrops, settings, characters, moods, and plots. There was no end to mental illness's inspiration.

The year 1919 proved to be especially productive for film, for behavioral conditioning, and for cementing the association between psychiatry and cinema. World War I had just ended, having been fought between 1914 and 1918. The influenza epidemic raged even after the war. That epidemic claimed more lives than any other epidemic in history. Soldiers were returning, shell-shocked, having seen battle scenes more intense than any seen before.

In 1919 Dr. Watson, the behaviorist, had just succeeded in conditioning poor Little Albert to fear white mice. Pavlov had already won his Nobel Prize. Freud's name was known far and wide, and his writings were available in English.

While Pavlov's book on *Behavioral Conditioning* had to wait until 1923, the world was in for a very different kind of treat in 1919. For it was then that Robert Weine's *The Cabinet of Dr. Caligari* was released. *Caligari* proved to be the prototype of anti-psychiatry and anti–mind control movies (even though evil hypnotists had appeared on the silent screen almost from the start of cinema). *Caligari* was considered to be the forerunner, if not also the foremost example, of German Expressionism, an art and film form that surfaced in the 1920s and faded away some five years later. Some latter-day critics suspected that Dr. Caligari really represented Dr. Freud, given the publicity that Freud was attracting for his newfound mind cures. Others said just the opposite, claiming that *Caligari* represented the old school of psychiatry that Freud had replaced with his emphasis on free associations. *Caligari* spawned many progeny over the century. Horror films in particular owed their inspiration to *Caligari*, according to Prawer's influential book *Caligari's Children*. Other authors, such as Siegfried Kracauer, contended that *Caligari* conjured up far worse connotations, and said that *Caligari* foreshadowed the arrival of Hitler.

German Expressionism in film led to film noir in America some twenty years later, and to many other permutations, including Tim Burton's *Beetlejuice* (1988) and Dr. Seuss's *5,000 Fingers of Dr. T* (1953). More immediately, *Caligari* led to Fritz Lang's long-running *Dr. Mabuse* series about evil psychiatrists. One can draw a dotted line between Dr. Caligari and Hannibal the Cannibal, who debuted in *Manhunter* (1986) before appearing in sequels and prequels about *Silence of the Lambs*.

Caligari was not a German film per se but was actually the brainchild of two Czech writers. As a silent film, its subtitles translated easily into any language. Yet *Caligari* is intimately connected to German history because German Expressionism as an art movement carried potent political implications and because *Caligari*'s name appears in the title of Kracauer's unforgettable book, *From Caligari to Hitler*. German Expressionism carries bittersweet memories. It flourished when the German economy plummeted and when politics started to go awry and when creative energies poured into the arts. Hitler suppressed this genre when he took power: the Third Reich condemned all Expressionist art as decadent and burned paintings of expressionist artists.

In the 1930s the Nazis passed more and more restrictive Nuremberg Laws and purged the German film industry (and other industries and other professions) of Jews. Film professionals, along with artists, actors, and writers left the country en masse, as did the psychoanalysts. Altogether, some 60,000 artists fled. Most set sail for the Americas, and many resettled in Hollywood.

Fritz Lang's legendary (and perhaps fictionalized) escape from Europe and his subsequent flight to America was prompted by the Nazi take-over of Europe. Lang's dramatic departure reads like a screenplay of his *Cloak and Dagger* or other noir films, which became popular in America in the 1940s and 1950s. Those noirs transmitted the artistic and thematic and psychological legacy of German Expressionism, largely because they were made by émigrés who were versed in Expressionism.

These dark and dismal and disturbing films noir of the 1940s and 1950s were psychoanalytically-informed. They featured flashbacks and voice-overs and other Freudian-like narrative devices. Many focused on the criminal underworld or on dark deeds of the night. Many included dream scenes that reminded viewers of Freudian ideas about dreams. These films took on a life of their own in the United States. Over the decades, film noir turned into a favorite of film scholars. Film noir festivals appeared i n art houses in the 1970s, 1980s, and 1990s. Film noir femme fatales set off a wave of Freudian-informed feminist film scholarship, which condemned directors for depicting evil, ensnaring women and claimed that such films encouraged misogyny (hatred of women) and reflected fears of women's rising power. By the twenty-first century, the film noir genre carried so much cachet that virtually any black-and-white film of that era was promoted as a film noir, even if it was only tangentially connected to "true" film noir (if indeed there is such a genre as film noir).

As we look back in time, and revisit the time when Robert Weine conceived of *Dr. Caligari*, and when Dr. Watson perfected his phobia-producing experiments on Little Albert, we are tempted to say that these two events were unrelated, save for a chronological convergence that is evident only in retrospect. However, I doubt that these "coincidences" were merely coincidental. I suspect that there is a tangential connection, even though there is no direct connection. For film (like all other art forms) reflects ideas that are in the air. It presents those ideas to the public, in veiled form, even before those ideas are verified by scientific studies and disseminated through scientific circles. Artists veer toward the vanguard, expressing unconventional ideas and attitudes that are still simmering among scientists and serious scholars. Such was the case with the Surrealists, who promulgated Freudian dream theories through poems and paintings long before psychiatrists and other therapists adopted Freudian techniques.

Biographers confirm that *Caligari's* screen writers were inspired by personal or family forays with psychiatry and insanity and suicide. It was no accident that they focused their film on an evil psychiatrist who turned out to be a sideshow charlatan and an asylum inmate. But the film version of *Caligari* bears yet another connection to the fascinating interface between psychiatry and cinema. *The Cabinet of Dr. Caligari* inspired one of the most controversial, but one of the most thought-provoking, books ever written on this topic: *From Caligari to Hitler.*

Published in 1947 and written by Sigmund Kracauer, *From Caligari to Hitler* called attention to the topic of movies and the modern mind. This book also called attention to the *Caligari* film itself, and cemented its place in film history and in the popular imagination. Kracauer contended that Caligari and other mind-controlling psychiatric villains of early German cinema foreshadowed the coming of the despotic Hitler, as well as the German people's willingness to accept the Reich's authoritarianism and mind control. Kracauer's book appeared shortly after World War II ended in 1945, and shortly after he had settled on American shores. Over the years, Kracauer's political theories were hotly contested, and his film history was questioned and corrected. Yet this book was reprinted many times over, and it remains in print sixty years after it first appeared.

There is no debate about one thing: *From Caligari to Hitler* made readers reflect on the relationship of cinema, psychology, and society. It made them rethink theories about movies and the modern mind. The author of this book is one of countless people who have read, and reread, *From Caligari to Hitler*. Had it not been for Kracauer, my book about *Movies and the Modern Psyche* might never have been born.

CHAPTER 3

FREUD AND FILM

THE SIGNIFICANCE OF ST. SIGMUND

Freud's name is invoked so often (in my own writings and in the writings of so many others) that one starts to wonder when historians will start to demarcate time as either BF or AF (Before Freud or After Freud). For St. Sigmund (as he is sometimes known, facetiously rather than affectionately) cast a spell on the twentieth century. Some seventy years after his death in 1939, he functions as a near-religious icon for his faithful followers. His memory has been resurrected and his story told many times over, even though most of his "scientific" theories have been laid to rest by social scientists and neuroscientists. Devotees defend his doctrines reflexively and passionately. The opposite reaction occurs among apostates. Opponents are called to arms, like crusaders, whenever Freud receives more reverence than he deserves. Sometimes, the mere mention of his name causes psychic convulsions, if not also political protests. Yet his name appears in many places, including this chapter's title.

Sigmund Freud's theories about the way we think changed the very way we think, at least temporarily. His ideas dominated the twentieth century. They inspired debate among social scientists, political scientists, psychiatrists, neuroscientists, and anthropologists. His ideas infiltrated art, literature, cinema, philosophy, and even theology. Had it not been for St. Sigmund's inspiration, we might not be so concerned with consciousness or motivation or deep-seated meanings or family dramas or sexual symbolism. Freud made us think about the role of the unconscious in everyday life, even though Freud himself was *not* the first to "discover" the "unconscious." (That was the brainchild of Romantic philosopher C. G. Carus.) Still, it was Freud who made us *self-conscious* about the differences between conscious acts and unconscious thoughts.

As influential as Freud was to twentieth century arts and letters, his psychoanalytic studies did not weather well among scientists. The heyday of Freudian psychology was the mid-twentieth century. Freud's influence lasted a little longer in psychiatry departments of medical schools. By the 1980s, serious scientists were more likely to lambast than to laud Freud's totalizing theories. When the Smithsonian announced plans for a Freud exhibition in the 1990s, public protests began before the doors opened, and nearly stopped the show. This time, it was not the clergy or the Catholic Church or the creationists who opposed Freud's emphasis on sex or evolution or atheism. Rather, it was the scientifically minded public and many offended feminists who objected.

Regardless of one's stance on Freud, we must acknowledge that Freud's writings introduced us to concepts such as the ego and the id and the superego. Freud alerted us to the Oedipus complex and the Electra complex. He told us that emotional catharsis occurs when viewers watch a play, identify with the characters, experience their emotions and conflicts, and then purge (or de-cathect) themselves of those emotions after the drama ends.

It was beside the point that Greek dramaturgists described the concept of catharsis 2,500 years before Freud's birth. The point is that Freud reintroduced those ideas to the Western world, and to the American public in particular. Because Freud was educated in the classics as well as in the sciences, like all well-educated persons of his era, he was familiar with ancient ideas about drama and was able to appropriate those ideas and parlay them into his new (pseudo)science of psychoanalysis. He made classical concepts appealing to twentieth-century citizens.

By the end of the twentieth century, that psychoanalytic lingo had turned into psychobabble and entered everyone's vocabulary. Freud repackaged classical myths and theatrical themes so well that most Americans were not aware of their ancient origins, or so said conservative political philosopher and University of Chicago professor, Alan Bloom, in his best-selling book *The Closing of the American Mind* (1987).

Ironically, Freud himself had little time to attend theater. Yet he was familiar enough with the plays of Aeschylus, Euripides, and Sophocles to incorporate their insights into his theories. He acknowledged Shakespeare and Goethe, and he noted that poets were the first psychologists. In his 1919 essay *The Uncanny*, he wrote about marionettes (and perhaps even alluded to the Salzburg Marionettes that premiered near his native Vienna in 1913). Freud's appreciation of literature and drama (as well as his own fine writing style and storytelling techniques) were rewarded when he received the Goethe Prize for Literature in 1930.

Once we see how much Freud owed his ideas—or at least his terminology—to myth and drama, we are no longer surprised to see how easily Freud's theories were adapted to artistic theories of the twentieth century. Freud's near-successor and one-time heir apparent, Carl Jung, turned to myth and drama even more than his mentor. Jung used theatrical terms such as "persona" to describe the public personality that conceals the private self that is rarely revealed to outsiders. In Greek theater, the term *persona* referred to the mask worn on stage by actors, to make their characters easily recognizable by audiences. Jung's writings about myths and archetypes penetrated the arts and the dance world easily, especially because he emphasized the visual much more than Freud did.

Before Jung's influence spread to the arts, Freud's writings had already inspired filmmakers, novelists, poets, and painters to depict Freudian ideas artistically or dramatically. Twentieth-century literary luminaries such as Thomas Mann and D. H. Lawrence deliberately worked Freudian theories into their plots. Mann and Lawrence and other writers convinced many otherwise educated people (who were unaware of this fact) that literature and arts and cinema validated Freud's psychological theories about family romances and Oedipal dramas and castrating women and latent homosexuality. If such great writers wrote about being torn between "scorching sense and icy intellect," as Thomas Mann did in *Death in Venice*, then surely Freud was right! This solipsism worked, to a point.

By the 1920s, such playwrights as Eugene O'Neill incorporated Freudian ideas and terminology into their titles and their texts. O'Neill's *Mourning Becomes Electra* is just one example. Tennessee Williams was also Freudian-influenced, as demonstrated by the movie version of *Night of the Iguana* (1962).

When we learn that Freud's writings arrived first, and that these great fictional writings came second, and that these acclaimed writers intentionally incorporated Freudian ideas into their dramas, we are no longer so convinced that Freud identified universal truths that are reified by myth and literature. We will soon see how and why cinema compounded the effect of Freudianism in literature, and how Freudian influences in film further cemented the stranglehold of Freudian theories on the modern American mind. For filmmakers were equally eager to add Freudian ideas to their movies, because those theories produced convoluted plots and amplified characters' personalities and elucidated their motivation.

In addition, Freud's theories were modern and were meant to replace (presumably) outmoded ideas about the biological basis of behavior or about the inheritability of degeneration. Movies were also modern, so it was only appropriate that they broached modern themes such as psychoanalysis. It was not long before filmmakers and movie moguls sprinkled their films with Freudian theories and treatments, just as their literary and dramatic counterparts had done earlier in the twentieth century. Because film reached wider audiences than the written word, it introduced far more people to Freudianism than serious literature did.

The twentieth century would not have been the same, had it not been for the inventions of Sigmund Freud and the Freudians who carried his message from Austria and to America, where Freudianism found more fertile soil and grew deeper roots than it did in its native Europe. That is not to say that everything would be better . . . or that everything would be worse. It simply means that things would be different. We would think differently. We would approach concepts such as sex and aggression and family romances differently than we do, had we grown up with, say, Marxist dogma rather than Freudian psychoanalytic theory, or if the biologically based neuropsychiatry of the late nineteenth century had continued, unchecked.

Cinema would not be the same had it not surfaced at the same time as Freudian psychoanalysis. For cinema absorbed Freudian influences like a sponge. Still, cinema did not showcase psychoanalytic approaches to treatment immediately, for several reasons. For one thing, cinema's earliest influence derived from magic, and from the magic of Méliès in particular. Méliès was a magician before he was a filmmaker. Magic was a throwback to supernaturalism and superstition, so it made sense that these magical movies showed magical themes at the start.

In addition, as discussed in the previous chapter, early moving pictures, or moving photography, were especially equipped to improve upon the "waking dream" and to showcase the world of sleep and dreams, which was both magical and modern, and the subject of Freudian studies and superstition.

Equally important, film technology could not do justice to Freudian-style talk therapy immediately, for talkies did not arrive until 1927. Subtitles were poor substitutes. Yet cinema was superbly suited to depict dreams, and did just that, even before Freud published *The Interpretation of Dreams* in 1900. Last, but equally important, it takes time to absorb new ideas, digest them, and rework those ideas for any medium. It would take a little longer to work those themes into a still embryonic medium such as cinema.

And so early cinema showered attention on hypnosis, which was well-known at the turn of the century. It was a favorite of psychiatrists and charlatans and showmen, and was a perfect subject for a magical medium like movies. This crossover between magic and medicine was a throwback to the supernaturalism and spiritualism of the nineteenth-century Romantic era. Hypnosis was a throwback to Freud's early experiments from his pre-psychoanalytic years.

Hypnosis would come to represent the old school of psychiatry as opposed to Freud's more modern, turn-of-the-twentieth-century psychoanalytic talking approach. For Freud had studied hypnosis at the Salpêtrière, in Paris, where "hysterics" performed on stage, swooning and seizing, gyrating and gesticulating, as physicians and artists joined the audience to observe the psychiatric theatrics. Hypnosis was not just for showmen. It inspired serious scientific debate even before Freud published an important paper about using hypnosis as a cure for hysteria.

WHO WAS FREUD?

Now that we know chronological correlations between Freud's invention of psychoanalysis and the invention of modern cinema, we can take a closer look at Freud the person, Freud the scientist, Freud the psychoanalyst, and even Freud the Jew. We know that other important events (filmic and otherwise) occurred during the course of Freud's long life. In fact, films produced in Freud's final years of life were critical to transmitting his message after his death in 1939. It was no accident that historian Peter Gay, who wrote prolifically about Freud and about modern European history, subtitled his biography of Freud as *A Life for Our Times*. For Freud's life crossed two centuries and two continents, and ushered us into modernity, the same modernity that brought movies and mass media.

Who was this man of near mythic proportions, and why did his ideas infiltrate film to the extent that they did? Before he became a physician and a neurologist and the founder of the psychoanalytic movement, Freud was a self-described "Godless Jew" born in Moravia, which is now part of Czech Republic. His birthplace was much more rural than Vienna, where Freud's parents moved when he was three. It was in Vienna that Freud studied medicine and practiced psychoanalysis, at 18 Bergasse Street.

Young Freud returned to Moravia during the summers to visit Chasidic relatives in those rural enclaves. Moravia's residents were far more religious and far less sophisticated than the Viennese. Throughout his life, Freud remained self-conscious of his Jewish connections, and expressed fears that his fledgling psychoanalytic science would be dismissed because its early followers were Jewish.

In 1933 his fears proved founded. His books were among the first to be burned by the Nazis. Psychoanalysis was condemned as "the Jewish science." Jewish doctors and analysts were forced to resign from the German Committee for Medical Psychotherapy. Carl Jung took over for the ousted Jewish chair. Freud, who was occasionally dismissed as a Kabbalist (a Jewish mystic), now found that his Jewish origins put his life—as well as his life's work—in danger. Already ill with advanced cancer, Freud fled Austria in 1938 and relocated to North London, where the Freud Museum still stands. Freud, the Godless Jew, died in 1939, on Yom Kippur, the Jewish day of atonement. That year, Hitler annexed Poland and Czechoslovakia and World War II began. In 1939, some of the greatest American films were made.

Freud did not live long enough to witness the death camps, which began in 1941, and which claimed the lives of his sisters. Yet Freud's memory is forever connected to the Holocaust, partly because he left his Viennese headquarters when the Nazis annexed Austria, and partly because the Nazis' Nuremberg Laws sent psychoanalysts sailing for America, where this so-called Jewish science found a warmer welcome than it received in its native Austria. Psychoanalysts were prohibited from practicing, and so were the first professionals to exit Europe. Many settled in Hollywood (and in New York, Chicago, and Buenos Aires). The film industry acquired these psychoanalytic influences along with the abundant film talent of the refugees.

While still a medical student, Freud conducted scientific research into the intersexuality of eels. These studies of sexual dimorphism anticipated his later psychoanalytic theories about the sexual sources of behavior. After graduating from medical school in 1881, Freud experimented with cocaine and wrote his *Cocaine Papers*. These *Cocaine Papers* were purged from Freud's collected works, but they were spoofed by drug culture filmmakers in *The Seven Percent Solution* (1976). When he opened his private neurology practice, he continued to treat hysterics, first with the hypnosis that he had studied in Paris, and then with the talking cure that turned into his revolutionary new idea of psychoanalysis. He also published neurologically oriented papers.

In 1896 Freud had coined the concept of psychoanalysis. In 1897 he borrowed from Greek drama when he identified the Oedipus complex, a concept that would be recycled in film and literature innumerable times. The end of 1899 brought his century-changing book *The Interpretation of Dreams.* He is remembered for this book more than for any other, and he himself favored this book more than all his other works. Because he designated dreams as "the royal road to the unconscious," and because this book was a blueprint for deciphering dreams, it firmly cemented psychoanalysis and cinema.

About a year later, in 1901, Freud published *The Psychopathology of Everyday Life.* This book proved to be popular with the public, even though his scientific ideas had not yet gained wide acceptance. *The Psychopathology of Everyday Life* introduced the concept of the Freudian slip, which became a lively and entertaining topic of conversation. A year later, the Wednesday Psychological Society started, and Freud's psychoanalytic circle congealed. In 1906 Carl Jung, the Swiss-born son of a Protestant pastor, began correspondence with Freud. Jung would become Freud's heir apparent, but would depart bitterly a few years later. Jung turned into Freud's nemesis during the Nazi era, when he agreed to chair the anti-Semitic German Committee for Medical Psychotherapy.

In the meantime, short silent films were being screened in Europe and in America. Hypnosis was by far the favored theme in early film, and evil hypnotists were particularly popular subjects, but asylum doctors soon appeared on screen. (*Asylum doctors* were distinct from psychoanalysts.) *Dr. Dippy's Sanitarium* (1906) was the first American film to feature a psychiatrist, and an incompetent one at that. Hydrotherapy appeared in an early Méliès film, *Hydrotherapie Fantastique* [*The Doctor's Secret*] (1910).

By 1909 a filmmaker by the name of D. W. Griffith had produced *The Criminal Hypnotist*. Several years later, Griffith created the hallucinatory, psychoanalytically informed *The Avenging Conscience* (1914). This same Griffith entered the annals of film history by virtue of two later films: *The Birth of a Nation* (1915) and *Intolerance* (1916). Although he was repudiated as a racist during the decades that followed, Griffith's skills as a filmmaker were unimpeachable. The fact that a filmmaker of such stature showed interest in Freudian-influenced themes highlighted the growing importance of Freudian themes in cinema, and foreshadowed the interest that American movie moguls would show in Freud and Freudianism. In 1921, when Freudian dream themes were the rage on the Broadway stage, Griffith returned to his early interest, and directed *Dream Street* (1921).

THE GREAT WAR AND THE BATTLES FOR THE MIND

By the time World War I erupted, Freud's works had been translated into English. Freud had already lectured in America, and the New York Psychoanalytic Society was established. Oddly enough, it was the Great War that cemented Freud's reputation and paved the path to Freudianism and to modernism in general. After witnessing the horrors of the Great War first hand, the world was ready to put its past behind, to embrace new art forms, and to entertain new ideas about the way the mind worked.

Shortly before World War I ended, Julius Wagner-Jauregg discovered that he could cure "general paresis of the insane" (tertiary neurosyphilis) by injecting patients with malaria-tainted blood, to induce "quotidian fevers" that sent their temperature skyrocketing to 105. This was a remarkable feat, considering that most inmates in asylums suffered from neurosyphilis. Wagner-Jauregg won a Nobel Prize for this pioneering work in biological psychiatry. By the end of the twentieth century, biological psychiatry had won the "war of the mind." But much transpired during that time.

Before that sea change in the late twentieth century, and before the American Psychiatric Association declared the 1990s to be "the decade of the brain," it was Freud who won the "battle of the mind." It was Freud (and Freudians who followed him) who became the torchbearers of psychological treatments. The decisive moment came just after World War I ended in 1918, when Freud published *Introduction to Psychoanalysis and the War Neuroses.* The year was 1919.

The war had already drawn attention to psychiatrists and psychologists, as soldiers were tested for fitness for duty before the war, and were assessed for disability after the war. Freud's talk therapy was kinder and gentler than Wagner-Jauregg's malaria-induced treatment, and it was less authoritarian than Watson's mean-spirited studies on behavioral conditioning. For Watson's *Psychology from the Standpoint of a Behaviorist* (1919) told how he induced a phobia in a five-year-old boy. Besides, this time around, Freud had a few facts in his favor: his talk therapy had relieved some suffering soldiers. Moreover, soldiers who developed shell shock were not necessarily the same soldiers who came into contact with the atropine-based nerve gas.

When *The Cabinet of Dr. Caligari* appeared in 1919, many assumed that the film's mastermind doctor-imposter was modeled after Dr. Freud. In retrospect, Dr. Caligari seems much closer in spirit to the experimental psychologist Dr. Watson than to Dr. Freud. If anything, the seemingly benign Freudian couch cure made Watson's mind-control techniques seem more evil. It was later learned that both *Caligari* screen writers had other reasons to depict evil mind doctors. One, Alfred Janowitz, hated the psychiatrist who alleged that he faked battle fatigue during the war. The other, Carl Meyer, was embittered because he had lost a brother in the war, and had lost his gambler-father to suicide while still a youth. These details are irrelevant for now. What is relevant is that Freud's fame was so widespread by 1919 that the world wondered if Freud's techniques influenced this masterpiece of German Expressionism.

The following year, 1920, brought the first public radio broadcast. People could hear voices that sounded like their own inner dialogue, or the voice of their own unconscious. People who hallucinated (because they suffered from schizophrenia or neurosyphilis or alcohol withdrawal) could hear public hallucinations over the airwaves. In fact, a typical schizophrenic delusion called thought projection revolves around radio (and later TV): schizophrenics hear voices discussing their private thoughts or their personal acts over the radio.

Two decades later, film noir took this one step further, using voice-overs, as well as visual flashbacks, to mirror the voice of the unconscious, and to evoke Freudian theories in doing so.

These disembodied radio voices were uncanny. When Freud wrote his essay about *The Uncanny*, his words resonated. Freud explained how the familiar becomes unfamiliar, through marionettes, automatons, moving dolls, and mirrors, and thereby creates a sense of the uncanny, or the *unheimlich*, as he called it in German. He did not mention cinema as an example, possibly because moving pictures were so familiar by 1919 that they did not feel as uncanny as early photographs did in the 1830s and 1840s. Had Freud written this essay a few years later, when the German Expressionist genre was better developed, and when Expressionist giants such as F. W. Murnau worked their movie magic, Freud might have had something to say about uncanny film imagery discussed in Lotte Eisner's book *The Haunted Screen*. But that presumes that Freud would have seen those films in the first place. We know that he had not. And that he would not, even if given the opportunity. For Freud dismissed the significance of film.

To this day, Freud's essay on *The Uncanny* is required reading for film majors. It is deemed to be Freud's finest literary work, which is no small accolade, considering that Freud won the Goethe Prize in Literature in 1930 (even though he never won a scientific award). Freud was and is incredibly important to film scholars, who routinely read his essay on the uncanny, and who fossilized Freudian ideas through feminist film scholarship and who filtered Freudian theories through the lens of the French psychoanalyst Jacques Lacan.

Yet Freud himself was no fan of film. He saw only one movie in his lifetime, and that occurred during his tour of America, in 1909. That one film was a Western, no less, a quintessentially American genre. He saw this film more out of curiosity about America than out of curiosity about film. Ironically, by World War II's end, Westerns had evolved into a separate subgenre known as Freudian Westerns. Freudian Westerns started with Howard Hawks's *Red River* (1948), which starred John Wayne (the most popular film star ever) and Montgomery Clift. These Freudian Westerns appeared at the peak of psychoanalysis's influence in film (and in American culture), and made psychoanalytic-style reflectiveness and pensiveness appear more appealing to macho soldiers who were returning home from the war.

Freud's 1919 essay on *The Uncanny* had barely left the press when Fritz Lang's first film about Dr. Mabuse appeared in Europe. Lang's 1922 version of *Dr. Mabuse, der Spieler* [*Dr. Mabuse, the Gambler*] was more offensive to analysts than *Caligari*, perhaps because Dr. Mabuse was a real doctor who ran a sanitarium, rather than an imposter like Caligari. Also, the few years that passed between the 1919 *Caligari* and the 1922 *Mabuse* were enough time for the fledgling psychoanalysts to gain steam and acquire distinctive identities and protest against misrepresentations of their profession. Yet, apparently, not enough time had passed, and not enough steam had been summoned, for the Vienna Psychoanalytic Society did not agree with analyst Paul Federn's request that they formally condemn *Mabuse*'s misrepresentations of analysis.

Lang went on to produce several other versions of *Dr. Mabuse* over the decades. Each film painted a dark portrait of psychoanalysts. The prolific and talented Lang also produced *M* in 1931, just two years before Hitler became chancellor of Germany. This psychological thriller about a psychotic child killer starred Peter Lorre in his breakout role. *M* arguably started the ever-popular (but ever-ambiguous) genre of psychological thrillers. Lorre, in turn, began a long and prestigious film career that began in Europe and ended in America. A decade after *M*, Lorre starred in what was (arguably, as usual) the first film noir, *Stranger on the Third Floor* (1940). The bug-eyed, thickly accented Lorre played another schizotypal murderer whose identity is unveiled through psychoanalytically informed dream themes.

The year after Lang's first 1922 *Dr. Mabuse* film proved to be a better year for Freud, at least in America. By this time, Freudian-influenced, dream-themed plays were appearing on Broadway. Freud was becoming a household name that was synonymous with modernism, the avant-garde, and sexuality. America women had just won the right to vote in 1920. Flappers, with their bobbed hair and short skirts, were asserting themselves, both at the polls and in the playhouses.

Playwrights searched for new themes that reflected the new sensibilities. In 1923 *Flaming Youth* was released. According to Zaretsky's *Secrets of the Soul* (2004), it was called "the film that packaged the 'flapper' for the mass audience." *Flaming Youth* starred Colleen Moore, whose character was shown reading a book by Freud. Moore's publicity agents stressed that she actually read Freud, thereby implying that she was as conversant with Freudian theories about sexual drives as was her filmic character. When Freud's book about *The Ego and the Id* appeared in 1923, Colleen Moore's performance in *Flaming Youth* had already primed the public for a study of sexual desires.

By 1924 Freud's American reputation was strong enough to send movie mogul Sam Goldwyn sailing for Europe, with plans to offer Freud $100,000 for assistance in devising "a really great love story." Sailing for Europe was not easy in 1924, and $100,000 was a vast sum. But Freud was deemed to be the world's expert on love, sex, and romance. Hollywood's star was also rising. America was becoming the movie capital of the world, especially after the German depression of 1923 diverted funds from the UFA (the German national film company) and thereby shifted leverage to the American film industry.

Freud declined the offer, insisting that "plastic representation" of psychoanalytic theory would not do his ideas justice. Although he did not say so, Freud was undoubtedly aware that early Hollywood did not have the social cachet it enjoys today. American films were a lower-class phenomenon that attracted unwashed and unschooled immigrants. A prudent person who sought scientific approval for sexually explicit theories was wise to avoid such shady associations.

Even though Freud refused to collaborate on the making of a psychoanalytic film, his disciples Karl Abraham, Hans Sachs, and Siegfried Bernfeld accepted Goldwyn's offer to act as "scientific consultants" on a film about psychoanalysis. In 1926 G. W. Pabst produced *Secrets of the Soul.* Many consider Pabst to be Germany's finest filmmaker of his era. Yet no one considered *Secrets of the Soul* to be Pabst's finest film. Pabst is better remembered for *Pandora's Box* (1929).

Freud's reluctance to get involved with American film turned out to have some merit, for other reasons. For the couch cure that cinema showcased did not mirror real clinical practice. Cinema psychiatry (as it came to be known) sensationalized the sexual aspects of psychoanalytic theory; it focused on repressed memories that could be represented visually, through dream scenes that showcased specific photographic effects or through dramatic dialogue that held the audience's attention. Cinema psychiatry had to occur quickly, and cures needed to be completed as the reels rolled. Miraculous transformations were one specialty of cinema psychiatrists. Other cinema psychiatrists were simply sinister psychiatrists who increased anxiety, added dramatic tension, and pandered to audiences' worst nightmares.

CINEMA PSYCHIATRY AND THE COUCH CURE

Cinema psychiatry evolved out of a need to depict psychiatric events dramatically, rather than accurately. Cinema psychiatry catered to the commercial concerns of film studios, which banked on entertaining, rather than edifying, their audiences. Because a film's financial success depends in large part upon the film's ability to tap into the hopes and fears of the viewers, film has an uncanny way of excavating unconscious attitudes of the audience, and playing upon unspoken feelings and ideas. Those movies that romanticized and sensationalized the couch cure turned out to be psychoanalysis's most effective spokesperson and PR agent.

As an added bonus, the couch cure had sexual connotations because the couch is so similar to the bed and because Freudian theory centers around sexual conflicts and childhood sexuality. As we all know, and as the censors above all knew, sex, as well as violence, holds special appeal for audiences. The couch cure could quickly convert into a segue for sex. The couch cure could be used as code for sexual innuendo, particularly when the Hays Code was in effect, and when censors forbade too much skin or sex or profanity on screen.[1] And then there were those dream scenes, those wonderful psychoanalytic dream scenes, that were often a treat in themselves, and just one more reason to add a sprinkle of screen psychoanalysis.

When talkies came into being in 1927, and replaced the overly emotive acting of silent cinema, the world was primed for talk therapy. In fact, watching the histrionics of the silent screen and witnessing its "psychic acoustics" may have convinced the public that putting feelings into words could achieve the much-needed catharsis! One wonders how much this transition from movies to talkies promoted public acceptance of talk therapy in the decades that followed.

Because psychoanalytic therapy appeared so often in film, the public came to believe that psychoanalysis was the gold standard of psychiatric treatment. It seemed as though psychoanalytic explorations of the unconscious were the only way to explore the unconscious, or, worse yet, that explorations of the unconscious are essential to cure any psychiatric condition. In spite of Freud's opposition to film, it is hard to believe that psychoanalysis would have achieved such cachet for as long as it did—or that this experimental treatment technique would have enjoyed such long-lived status—had it not been for film, and for the fact that psychoanalysis and cinema grew up together and drew attention to one another.

Cinema would become the "poor man's psychoanalysis," to use the words of the late, great film critic Parker Tyler.[2] Cinema frequently depicted psychiatrists and psychiatric themes, which were evolving at the same time that cinema evolved, and which not only called attention to the latest and greatest treatment techniques of the day, but also reminded everyone of outdated and outmoded mind cures. Not everyone could afford to see a psychoanalyst, and not everyone wanted to, but almost everyone could pay to see psychoanalysts ply their trade on the screen. It was interesting to watch psychoanalysts excavate repressed memories in their patients, and it was entertaining to listen to patients' free associations and slips of the tongue. The instantaneous couch cure seen on screen was inspiring as much as it was entertaining, because it induced the (false) belief that instantaneous cures for long-standing psychological problems were possible.

Thanks to film, psychoanalysis was kept alive far longer than it deserved to be on sheer scientific merit. The couch cure is still recycled as comedy. *Analyze This*, with Billy Crystal starring as a fast-talking Jewish-American psychiatrist and Robert De Niro as a tough-talking Italian-American mobster whose henchmen abduct Crystal, became an unexpected box office hit in 1999. It spawned an equally popular sequel,

Analyze That (2002). In fact, psychoanalysis typically appears as parody in the twenty-first century. Parody signals the last stage of a dying idea.[3]

To this day, Freudian and occasionally Jungian and especially Lacanian theories are fossilized in film theory, and in feminist film theory in particular. Freud's much-criticized concepts about castration anxiety live on through Laura Mulvey's "Visual Pleasure and Narrative Cinema" (1975). In this must-read work, Mulvey posits that men watch films because they are intrigued by the image of "l'homme manquee" (literally, the "lacking man," or the castrated man), and they seek to assuage their own castration anxiety by fixating on screen images of (castrated) women, reassuring themselves that they are indeed different.

Mulvey's position paper about castration anxiety and film spectatorship is controversial, to say the least, even though it remains required reading in film classes because it spearheaded feminist film studies of the seventies and spectator studies that focus on the audiences as much as on the actors or auteurs. But the events during the last years of Freud's life are not subject to debate, and are as intertwined with the fate of film as the very earliest years of psychoanalysis.

Freud died of jaw cancer in 1939, in the same year that Germany annexed Poland and Czechoslovakia, and when World War II began in Europe. *Kristallnacht* had already occurred and the Holocaust started. Nineteen thirty-nine was the year television debuted at the World's Fair, and, by implication, marked the beginning of the decline of (but not the death of) the film industry. Ironically, 1939 was the best year ever for film. More great films were made in 1939 than ever before (or ever after). *The Wizard of Oz* was just one of those films, but it is a film that is especially important to our study of movies and the modern psyche because Dorothy's adventures in Oz and her encounter with the Wizard parallels the promises of psychoanalysis, and it explains why psychoanalysis held such appeal for the American mind.

The Wizard of Oz was the brainchild of Frank Baum. Baum wrote his stories at the turn of the century. Although *Oz* books had existed for decades before the film was made, the film form of *The Wizard of Oz* took on a life of its own and turned into American myth. It is for good reason that this movie has become a Thanksgiving Day television staple. This story of a family lost and found is typically viewed with family, on a uniquely American holiday. There are many ways to interpret *The Wizard of Oz*. The political implications are many-layered. Its Kansas setting spoke loudly and clearly to Depression-era farmers who faced foreclosures. The drug culture of the sixties and seventies found messages in Emerald City that previous generations had not.

Without denying the importance of those political interpretations, we also find important messages about psychoanalysis that partly explains why psychoanalysis rose to such prominence in America, and why Freud took such a fall when some theories were debunked at later dates.

In *The Wizard of Oz* film version, Dorothy suffers from a concussion during a tornado and enters a dream state that leads her down the Yellow Brick Road in search of the Wizard (read analyst) who lives in the mythical Oz. When Dorothy and friends finally meet with this mysterious "wizard," they learn that they themselves already possess the personal strengths they expect the Wizard to confer on them. They simply need someone of the Wizard's stature to excavate their unconscious, refresh their memories, and convince them that they have already demonstrated the same abilities they believe themselves to be deficient in.

Analysis, at least the American version of analysis, offers the same promise: seek out the wizard, confront your worst nightmares (or your dreams), and that wizard/analyst will help you uncover the answer that already lies within yourself (or within your own unconscious). The fact that this film made use of a dream theme, and a Technicolor dream at that, further fortified the significance of Freud's formulations. The film also set the stage for Freud's undoing, for it showed that the Wizard was a fraud who hid behind a screen (read couch).

By the end of the century, American society had concluded that many Freudian ideas were also fraudulent . . . but that did not stop them from loving *The Wizard of Oz*. In fact, *Wizard of Oz* permutated into several new forms. *The Wiz* (1978) was an African American variant, and Walter Murch's *Return to Oz* (1985) was the nightmarish version that made the flying monkeys and the Wicked Witch seem safe and secure. Freud may be dead, but film's Dorothy lives forever!

CHAPTER 4

THE DREAM

Cinematographers and cinemaphiles saw the similarity between dream and film from the start. Early movie moguls referred to movie theaters as dream palaces. Later in the century, Steven Spielberg named his movie company Dreamworks SKG, implying that moviemaking involves the same process that the mind employs to manufacture dreams: Freud had dubbed that process "dream works." Spielberg admitted that many of his movie ideas stemmed from dreams.

When Hortense Powdermaker's book *Hollywood, the Dream Factory* appeared in 1950,[1] it needed no subtitle. It was understood that Hollywood and dreams (both real and metaphorical) were synonymous. Although the book went out of print long ago, the term itself entered our everyday vocabulary, before inspiring a TV documentary of the same name.

Interestingly, India's Bollywood (which is named for Bombay, now Mumbai, and Hollywood) surpasses Hollywood in sheer numbers of films produced. Thus, it is a bigger dream factory than its American namesake. So when a musical about a starry-eyed slum boy who skyrocketed to Bollywood stardom appeared on Broadway, with the title *Bombay Dreams*, the production conjured instant associations between Hollywood and dreams, and between Hollywood and Bollywood.

But Broadway is Broadway, and cinema is cinema (and Bollywood is Bollywood). Movies may have begun as photoplays, but it was not long before they took off in different directions and bore little similarity to staged productions. Likewise, the theater of the 1920s attempted to appear as modern as movies. Theater tried to produce "dream plays" that took Strindberg's *Dream Play* one step further, alluding to Freud's avant-garde ideas about dreams. Try as it might, though, the theater could not compete with cinema when it came to depicting dreams.

Film was by far the closest medium to dream. With its fluid photography, its dissolve shots, and its ever-inventive editing techniques, moving pictures mirrored the changing nature of dream. Film could exploit dream themes and dream techniques to the fullest. Besides being suited to showcase advances in special effects, trick photography, and cinematography, dreams are also convenient framing devices for either theater or film. Dreams can set the stage for the start of a story or add a metanarrative, and tell a story within a story. Embedding a story within a dream emphasizes the fantastic nature of the story. Dreams soften messages by making them seem slightly unreal. Dreams tell us more about the character's motivation and thus push the plot. They are useful as inspiration and as iconography, for film or for other art forms.

Dramatists have known these secrets for centuries. Yet there are reasons why film is so perfectly suited to dream themes, and why dream themes fit so snugly into cinema. In both film and dream, moving images are projected onto a screen. In one case, it is the silver screen. In the other, it is the sleep screen. In both films and dreams, irrational images and memory traces are strung together in sequences that defy logic or reason. These sequences change swiftly, and they disappear within seconds. Images mutate and morph in ways that cannot be described in verbal language. No matter how hard poets try to capture the fleeting imagery of dreams, and the disconnected and disjointed meanings that underlie dream symbols, their efforts pale compared to film's inherent similarity to dream.

The fact that films are viewed in a dark chamber, as spectators sit motionless, evokes even deeper comparisons to sleep. During sleep, mind movies flash in the darkness of night, concealed behind closed eyes that substitute for stage curtains. Voluntary muscles, which ordinarily allow us to move our limbs at will, are paralyzed when the brain enters the rapid eye movement (REM) stage of sleep, when the best dreams appear. Even though the heart beats and the lungs contract during sleep, the body is otherwise immobile. The sleeper, like the cinema spectator, is a captive audience of sleep visions, or mind movies, as dreams are known in film circles.

Fairly early on, filmmakers saluted the similarity between film and dream through special effects that simulated the eye opening and closing. Many films began and ended with animated renditions of "iris openings" and "iris closings" (also called iris-ins and iris-outs). D. W. Griffith used iris-in and iris-out shots as early as 1916, when he made *Intolerance*. By the 1920s, when Freud's ideas about dreams had spread beyond his psychoanalytic circle and spilled into artistic circles, iris-ins and -outs had become a common convention in cinema. Murnau's *Nosferatu* (1922), Eric von Stroheim's *Greed* (1924), and Bunuel's *Un Chien Andalou* (1929) are a few of the many films that begin and end with this literal allusion to sleeping, dreaming, and awakening.

Orson Welles retained this tradition as late as 1941. Welles's *Citizen Kane* (1941) used iris-ins and iris-outs to open and close scenes of Freudian-style flashbacks. This technique suggested that dissociation is similar to dream, and that flashbacks are like waking dreams, because both dreams and flashbacks mine unconscious memories and bring buried associations to the surface. Welles's choice of this metaphor was consistent with the film's theme, for *Citizen Kane* revolved around a Freudian-style motif.

Unearthing Charles Foster Kane's childhood memories was the MacGuffin of the movie. When the movie's media mogul dies, while holding a snow globe in his hands, he utters one last word: "Rosebud." Reporters are told to discover the meaning behind "Rosebud." This quest fleshes out the plot. Reporters comb the globe in search of clues. In true Freudian fashion, "Rosebud" turns out to be the name inscribed on the sled that young Kane rode on the snowy day that news of his inheritance arrived. He was whisked away from his parents, and transplanted into a life of money and power—and lack of love and parental affection. The snow globe apparently reminded him of that snowy day. The closing scene shows the Rosebud sled tossed into the fire, its name unrecognized and its significance to Kane literally going up in smoke.

By the time that *Citizen Kane* appeared, audiences knew enough about Freudian psychoanalysis to understand such concepts as family romances, early childhood memories, and free associations. There was no need to sandwich such ideas in dreams. Yet other films of *Kane*'s era turned into brilliant blackboards for dream themes. For film noir, with its dream themes and psychopathic criminals, began in 1940 with *Stranger on the Third Floor*. Film noir persisted as a cinematic style and as a frame of mind for the next two decades, and produced some of the greatest dream scenes of all times, even though the connection between film and dream was made much, much earlier on.

It was easy for filmmakers to recognize the commonality between dreams and films, especially since cinema had evolved from photography. Movies could augment dreamlike photographic techniques through jump-cuts, zooms, layers, dissolves, double-exposures, and pans. These cinematic techniques were far more advanced than staid and static photographic approaches. Movies also let editors improve upon camera tricks, via cutting and pasting and making montages, much as our minds do to manufacture dreams. A century after its invention in the 1830s, surrealist artist Salvador Dali rekindled the link between photography and dream when he compared his surrealist dreamscapes to "hand-painted dream photographs."[2]

Long before film noir surfaced in 1940, film and Freudian dream theory had crossed paths. The coincidental convergence between Freud's discovery of psychoanalysis and the invention of film was fortuitous for Freud. I doubt that his "revolutionary" new theories about dreams would have had such an impact, had it not been for the fact that his *supposedly* scientific approach to dreams appeared so soon after this *decidedly* scientific depiction of dreams had appeared on cinema screens. (However, I cannot prove this theory, since we cannot put history on rewind like a DVD.) Yet the fact remains that film "spoke to" a far wider audience than his esoteric and select circle of psychoanalysts did.

In fact, he had not yet convened his psychoanalytic circle by the time *Interpretation of Dreams* hit the press in November 1899. For a full five years before, film had set the stage for anticipation of a new approach to dream, an approach that was different from anything that was already available. Ever since the first films screened in 1895, spectators could see dreamlike imagery reproduced before their own eyes, prancing past them, and affirming the importance of this inner imagery. The century brought a new medium, and an appreciation of a new "scientific" study of a subject that had been the domain of supernaturalists and spiritualists.

Cinema turned dream scenes into a shared, group experience, just as religion had done in the past. It released dreams from the confines of private and personal experience, and catapulted dreams into the public imagination. Even though myth and religion also delved into dreams, there was a vast difference between the dream themes of film and the dream depictions of faith. For one thing, cinematography was a state-of-the-art scientific advance, and science was all-important to turn-of-the-century society, which valued scientific positivism above all else.

True, late nineteenth-century society did indulge itself in spiritualism and seances and occasionally confused the unconscious with the uncanny. Claims of "spirit photography" (which turned out to be trick photography) were convincing enough to the masses and to Sir Arthur Conan Doyle (physician and literary father of Sherlock Holmes). But, in general, science was worlds away from faith. Freud's generation had, after all, borne witness to Darwin's heresies about evolution and the *Descent of Man*, and now was willing to tackle even newer scientific advances, such as Freud's self-described "scientific psychology."

Today, we take cinema for granted and rarely think of cinema and science in the same sentence, except perhaps when we contemplate advances with computers and cinema, or marvel at the latest technology in cameras and camcorders or computer-based home editing devices. Most contemporary film fans consider cinema as an art form, rather than a manifestation of applied technology. Yet the basic scientific discovery of cinema was necessary before film could become a blackboard for artists, actors, auteurs, and authors. The nineteenth-century man or woman who witnessed the birth of film was acutely aware of the technological feat that film represented. For such a person, cinema carried the authority of science as much as art.

Freud also invoked the authority of science. He began his book on *The Interpretation of Dreams* with a chapter called "The Scientific Literature Dealing with the Problems of Dreams." This chapter title was intended to distance the work from occult connections. It was essential that Freud include such a caveat, for several reasons. For one, a Jewish mystical work on the interpretation of dreams already existed. This book was popular with Freud's more rural and more pious co-religionists who lived to the east (the *Ostjuden*, or Eastern Jews). Also, an occultist book about the interpretation of dreams and magic was still in print when Freud's *Interpretation of Dreams* appeared. The two books could have been confused, in the absence of a disclaimer.

The fact that cinema was simultaneously scientific and artistic aided Freud's efforts, for he, too, joined scientific investigations with literary presentations. Freud's writings are infused with literary references and function as literature in their own right. Even admirers admit that he was more successful at writing literature than at studying science. The one-time head of the New York Psychoanalytic Association publicly acknowledged that psychoanalysis should be included among the arts rather than the sciences. Cinema's success in bridging art and science may have been one more factor that helped legitimatize Freud's syncretic approach to dreams.

True believers like to say that Freudian dream theories came first, and that dream scenes in film reflected Freud's influence. But history shows us that the reverse was true. For dream scenes in early (primitive) film predated Freudian psychoanalysis. Early dream themes were linked to magic and illusion and were used to showcase filmmakers' fledgling special effects skills. However, it is only fair to say that, once Freudian-style dream themes (as well as Freudian-style family romances) evolved, they took on a life of their own and a look of their own. Freudian-style dream themes, for example, made films noir of the 1940s and 1950s memorable.

MÉLIÈS AND MOVIE MAGIC

Until the 1940s, movie magic and dream themes owed more to Georges Méliès than anyone else. Méliès, the magician who would become the "father of narrative film" produced his first film, *Une Partie de Cartes*, in 1896. That was the same year that Freud conceived of the concept of psychoanalysis. A year before, in 1895, the Lumière brothers screened the first film ever. Méliès was a master of illusion. He basked in the same cultural climate that nurtured the French Symbolist painters who combined occult symbols with sleepy-eyed somnambulists.

The titles of Méliès's early films echo his enchantment with dreams. *The Drunkard's Dream* (1897), *The Artist's Dream* (1898), *The Beggar's Dream* (1898), *The Astronomer's Dream (The Man in the Moon)* (1898), *The Christmas Dream* (1900), *The Rajah's Dream* (1900), *Dream of a Hindu Beggar* (1902), *Dream of the Ballet Master* (1903), *The Clockmaker's Dream* (1904), *The Dream of the Poor Fisherman* (1904), and *Dream of an Opium Fiend* (1908) appear among his credits. Most of these films lasted five minutes or less, as was typical for early film.

In spite of his many dream-themed films, Méliès was better known for his sci-fi-forerunner film, *A Trip to the Moon* (1902). *A Trip to the Moon* was his most "mature" work in that it used editing, cutting, and splicing as well as special effects to make "movie magic."

A Trip to the Moon was fourteen minutes long, yet it used thirty separate tableaus (scenes) with superimposed images, dissolves, and jump cuts. In switching from magic tricks to trick photography, Méliès created a modern-looking, capsulized rocket ship shot into space from a cannon, only to crash into the eye of the man in the moon. Upon arrival at the moon, the voyagers dismount and encounter dream-like moon dwellers at the Moon King's court.

Méliès's foray into special effects occurred by accident rather than by intent. One day, while filming a street scene, his camera jammed. He had pointed his camera at a trolley, but a hearse drove by before the film rolled out. When the film was developed, the trolley magically morphed into the hearse, in much the same way that one image morphs into another in dreams. There is no indication that Méliès ever sought to emulate the "dream works" described by Freud, as Steven Spielberg did seventy years later. Yet he captured the same fleeting, liquid, fantastic feeling that Spielberg alluded to later when he named his production company Dreamworks.

Sadly, Méliès's films fell into oblivion after the initial enthusiasm for his simplistic special effects died down. More advanced techniques appeared and overshadowed his early efforts. The man who was once heir to a shoe factory (but sold his share to his brother so that he could dabble in magic) was left impoverished, having to sell toys on the street in order to survive. In the later years of his life, he was rediscovered on the streets of France and was honored by the government and awarded a government pension. His works have been revived in recent years and play to appreciative audiences at art houses such as Anthology Film Archives.

Méliès died in 1938, one year before Freud succumbed to jaw cancer, and in the same year that Freud abandoned his Viennese headquarters to seek a safer space in North London. Méliès is now revered by filmmakers and film viewers alike, even if his early special effects and dream scenes seem slightly silly. His contribution to film is undisputed. Alternatively, Freud's reputation has suffered. Starting in the late 1930s, sleep science disproved some of Freud's early ideas about dreams. In the twenty-first century, sleep centers have sprung up, promising patients deeper sleep instead of the meaningful dreams that were popular with psychoanalysts.

Although Méliès is now the best-remembered of these early fantasy filmmakers, he was not the only one to depict dream themes and dream scenes. Edwin S. Porter's *The Cavalier's Dream* appeared in 1898, five years before he earned a permanent place in film history for his realistic renditions of *The Life of an American Fireman* (1903) and *The Great Train Robbery* (1906). *Dream of a Rarebit Fiend* (1909), which attributed bad dreams to aged cheese, was one more of some 200 short silent films on the theme of dreams.

Other luminaries of early film started their careers with dream themes. D. W. Griffith created *The Criminal Hypnotist* (1909) early in his career. Then came Griffith's hallucinatory film, *The Avenging Conscience* (1914). On the surface, *The Avenging Conscience* seemed to be informed by Freud or, at the very least, by Dostoevsky's *Crime and Punishment*. Yet the film was based on Poe's pre-psychoanalytic, pre–Civil War tale of *The Tell-Tale Heart*.

In 1921, a year after the first public radio broadcast, Griffith released *Dream Street*, using his Photokinema. Griffith's interest in Freudian-style dream themes foreshadowed the interest that American movie moguls would soon shower on Freud and Freudians. In 1926 G. W. Pabst produced *Secrets of a Soul*, specifically to drama-tize Freud's dream theories. Pabst gained far greater fame for *Pandora's Box*, but *Secrets of a Soul* won him an extra place in history because it was woven into psycho-analytic history.

SECRETS OF A SOUL AND SURREALISM

Freud's services were sought for Pabst's film, but Freud refused. Freud resented the cross-over between film and dream and avoided situations that pinpointed parallels between psychoanalytic dream interpretation and cinema's dream screen. When Freud's disciples, Hans Sachs and Karl Abraham, agreed to be "scientific consultants" for Pabst's *Secrets of a Soul* after Freud refused, Freud saw this collaboration as an ominous sign.

For Freud objected to "visual representation of the unconscious" (even though he later liked Dali). To Freud, this approach was regressive. Furthermore, he was not flat-tered to learn that Hollywood producers wanted to turn his psychoanalytic dream treatments into a feature-length film. He worked hard to build a power base for psy-choanalysis, yet he declined the film industry's offer to spread word about "psychoan-alytic science." He couched his arguments against film in academic terms, but left one wondering if the class-conscious and socially striving Freud consciously (or subcon-sciously) resented the possibility that his "scientific" psychoanalysis could be promul-gated through a lower-class medium that attracted immigrants and illiterates.

Let us also recall that Freud would soon write *Civilization and Its Discontents* (1930). There, he claimed that some sexual drives must be sublimated for civilization to thrive. Perhaps he (correctly) intuited that cinema could cheapen his couch cure by highlighting its sexual connotations. Or that the entertainment industry would sensationalize his theories about sex and pander to the masses. If these hypothetical concerns existed, they were not expressed directly.

Instead, Freud focused on the fact that film, like dream, was governed by "considerations of representation" rather than by "real meaning." Both dream and film use a visual vocabulary instead of a verbal vocabulary. This visual vocabulary is chosen because its symbols make visual sense, and *not* because the symbols best express underlying thoughts or feelings. The images need not be critical to the story, but simply need to be memorable, or meaningful, to the viewer.

It is the *picture* that is primary, in both film and dream. Both film and dream need visual appeal so that they can be recognized by the dreamer or appreciated by the audience. To put it another way, it is the *storyboard*, rather than the *story*, that drives the action of film and dream. The *storyboard* looks like a comic-book, with graphics and captions. It is not at all like a novel.

For filmmakers, both sound and story can, and should be, dispensable. It is not the *plot* that takes center-stage in cinema; it is the imagery. For silent filmmakers, sound and story *had* to be secondary out of necessity: talkies did not come into being until 1927. Even then, the sound was of questionable quality. Furthermore, early musical accompaniments for film did not necessarily relate to the plot, and they often distracted from the story.

To this day, student filmmakers are taught to replay their films without any sound whatsoever, to ensure that their camera shots make visual sense and tell the story without words. That master of mystery, Alfred Hitchcock, used this technique during his own film production, and he was able to switch from silent to sound films in the late 1920s successfully.[3] Many say that Hitchcock's early experience with silent cinema, plus his exposure to German Expressionist film in the twenties, helped make him the master filmmaker, art director, and storyteller that he became.

Yet for Freud the pictorial *representation* of an idea or emotion, through dream or film, was worth less than the *interpretation* of that dream (if it was worth anything at all). Freud was interested in his patient's selective recollection of their dreams, and in the reasons why specific aspects of dreams were recalled, and in the associations that those dreams evoked. In other words, Freud was *not* interested in the *product* of the dream work that Spielberg and other filmmakers admired. Freud was interested in the *process* of *dream work* that *produced* the *product*. Cinema concerns itself with the *product*. These priorities are decidedly different, even if they do overlap.

Given these differences of opinions and priorities, it should come as no surprise that *Secrets of a Soul* (1926) became a subject of intense debate before it was filmed. It is no surprise that Eli Zaretsky's *Secrets of the Soul*—a fascinating twenty-first century book about the historical context of psychoanalysis—appropriated the title of this once controversial, but now neglected, film for the book's title.[4] For the argu-

ments surrounding that Pabst film proved to be more entertaining and more enduring than the film itself. Similarly, the arguments surrounding psychoanalysis took
on a life of their own, and psychoanalysis ultimately made its most indelible mark
on art and culture, rather than in science, neurology, or psychiatry.

Even though *Secrets of a Soul* was meant to spread word of psychoanalysis, the real
credit for promulgating psychoanalytic dream ideas goes to the Surrealists, and to
André Breton in particular. In 1925 (the same year that Hitler published *Mein
Kampf*), the medical-student-turned-poet Breton wrote *The Surrealist Manifesto*.
Writing with the same seriousness as the authors of *The Communist Manifesto*, Breton insisted that dream consciousness should be placed on a par with waking consciousness. When he tried to contact Freud, Freud dismissed him (even though
Freud later welcomed surrealist artist Salvador Dali, who spoke about his "dream
photographs" and his "paranoid-critical method"). Perhaps Freud recognized that a
person cannot survive in the everyday world if his subconscious infiltrates his everyday ideas, as Breton recommended.

It was indeed true that Breton was unable to function in everyday life, in spite of
the fact that he spearheaded an enduring approach to art, literature, and film. He
dropped out of medical school to serve as a medical corpsman in World War I, and
he worked on a neurology ward with brain-injured soldiers. But he could not return
to his medical studies. He devoted himself to poetry instead, and became the leading
spokesperson for his Surrealist movement. Historian of psychiatry Henri Ellenberger
hypothesized that Breton's psychoanalytic theories about dream and waking consciousness could have competed with other psychoanalytic schools that were fermenting at the time. Ellenberger thought that Breton's "surrealist psychoanalysis"
might have become the fourth great school of neo-Freudian psychoanalysis (after the
schools of Jung, Adler, and Sullivan), had he returned to medicine instead of detour-
ing into art.[5]

Having said that, let us look at the Surrealists' approach to dream, and to dream
cinema, and to life itself, so that we can see how Surrealist ideas surfaced in cinema.

In short, Breton and his circle adored cinema. They ran from one theater to
another, catching glimpses of different films, without seeing any film in its intended
sequence, and without watching a film to its end. The purpose of this pastime was to
replicate the dream experience, where logical causality disappears, and time and
place are displaced. As a group, surrealists were especially fond of Buster Keaton and
slapstick comedy, where actors also ran around. Even though they were comedy fans,
they took their theories about dreams and art and film seriously, so seriously that
they literally came to blows during a film screening as they debated about the appropriate role of dream in film.

A fistfight took place, right there in the theater, after Surrealist artist Antonin
Artaud denounced the Germaine Dulac efforts to turn Artaud's script *The Seashell
and the Clergyman* into cinema. Dulac was an early (and underappreciated) experimental filmmaker. Artaud was a Surrealist poet and playwright who sampled mush-
rooms in Mexico and eventually died in a catatonic state in an American mental
hospital. Artaud's influence on theater was enormous. Yet he condemned Dulac,
claiming that she had taken intolerable liberties when adapting his drama for film.

He accused her of "feminizing" his script by making his play into a replica of a dream, when he intended it to be "dreamlike."

Such public demonstrations were standard fare for Surrealists.[6] Other arguments among members of the circle followed (much like the arguments that split early psychoanalysts into separate schools). The Surrealists were dogmatic in their distinction between "dream" and "dreamlike" art. A related debate led to Jean Cocteau's banishment from the Surrealist circle, even though Cocteau's *Blood of a Poet* (1930) is deemed to be one of the most hauntingly beautiful dreamlike films ever produced. Those who do not know "official" Surrealist history are typically surprised to learn that Cocteau was not an "official" Surrealist.

Cocteau's influence persisted, in spite of the Surrealist scorn. Cocteau's *Beauty and the Beast* (1946) stood on its own merit and became a cult classic for the 1960s drug culture. Cocteau filmed a fireplace flanked by faces with moving eyes. It looked like an opium-induced apparition, and probably was, for Cocteau was once an opium addict who took "the cure" twice. He wrote about his experiences in *Opium*, and he emphasized that his great films about opium-induced fantasies were produced *after* freeing himself from "the dragon."

Cocteau's legacy, with regard to dream and film (and with regard to drug and film), lived on through his much younger lover, Kenneth Anger. Anger's *Kustom Kar Kommando* (1965), with its title song, "Dream Lover," became the first music video. Anger's film was clearly Freudian-influenced, as were other "independent" films of this era, such as Stan Brakhage's nightmare series and Maya Deren's *Meshes in the Afternoon* (1943). Deren went on to make other films about altered states, and made her greatest mark through films about Haitian voodoo. Interestingly, Deren's father was a psychiatrist. Of these three, Anger's films were the most sexually transgressive and spoke most directly to the youth culture. Anger's actors straddled muscular motorcycles, and polished and primed their bikes' hardware, as they sang about fantastic and forbidden "dream lovers," suggestively punning in Freudian fashion.[7]

Surrealism's greatest triumph, however, is found in Hitchcock's *Spellbound* (1945). *Spellbound* was produced twenty years before the Freud-inspired experimental film surge of the 1960s. *Spellbound* was perfect and polished and was thus the polar opposite of the amateurish, self-styled dream-themed cinema that gained currency among the 1960s counterculture. *Spellbound* appeared when films noir were coming into their own, although neither this film, nor any other so-called film noir, aspired to be a film noir per se. In contrast to the Surrealists, who detailed their philosophy in a *Surrealist Manifesto*, and defined who and what complied with Surrealist credo, the creators of film noir were not aware that they were creating a new genre.

The film noir genre was invented after the fact, when two French film critics saw stylistic and thematic trends in the dark and dreary American films of the forties and fifties. Film noir directors learned how to make lemonade out of lemons. They labored under complex legal and financial wartime constraints. Forced to make due with low lighting, small budgets, and recycled sets, they used fog and rain and smoke machines to hide the supply shortages and enforced blackouts. Their plots had to conform to government standards, but they took full advantage of relaxed restrictions on screen sex and violence during wartime.

Films noir recycled sets (because of government caps on spending) and also recycled German Expressionism. *Caligari* was their role model, both in set design and in evil character. Films noir were also Freudian-inspired, for they showcased deep and dark psychological secrets. They used voice-overs and flashbacks that mirrored the processes of the unconscious and the process of psychoanalysis. As a genre, film noir produced the best dream scenes ever shown on screen. An entire book could be, and should be, written about night dreams in noir films.

As for *Spellbound*, it is sometimes categorized as a film noir and sometimes not. Its dream scene and psychoanalytic theme, its harsh lighting and bleak plot, make it similar to other noirs of its era. But *Spellbound* transcends categories. Salvador Dali's dream sequence makes this film unforgettable, to the point that many viewers forget the plot or the actors, and walk away with the eidetic memory (recurring visual image) of eye-covered stage curtains, people turned into rabbits, and a melange of melting wheels. *Spellbound*'s dream sequence recollects Dali's painting *Melancholy.* Photographer Matthew Barney's human rabbits, which appeared on the cover of *Art News* (June 2006), recycled Dali's dream scene and turned its animal-human hybrids into a more contemporary collage-photographic format.

Dali's dream sequence is so stunning that few viewers realize that the dream scenes last a mere two and a half minutes. Hollywood legend says that Dali created a half-hour dream sequence, which was cut because of obscenity laws and eventually destroyed. If the story is true, we can surmise that Dali exploited Freudian sexual symbolism to the extreme.

Many other aspects of the *Spellbound* story pertain to dream, hypnosis, and spells in general, as the title implies. Spells can be cast by sorcerers or by Caligari-like psychiatrists. The mysterious story about the mysterious stranger (read the new head psychiatrist who lost his memory) mirrors the Dali dream scenes. The protagonist's profound memory loss reminds us of another dreamlike Dali painting, *The Landscape of Memory.*

In *Spellbound*, a new asylum director (Gregory Peck) arrives, only to learn that the man he believes himself to be was murdered. He has lost his memory, so he cannot recall details of his last contact with the missing man. Naturally, Peck's character, Dr. Edwards, is suspected of murdering the missing doctor whose name he assumed. Another analyst, the sexually repressed Dr. Peterson (Ingrid Bergman), believes in the handsome man's innocence. (Bergman had recently played the romantic lead in *Casablanca*, so she was credible as a proto-romantic in *Spellbound*.) Dr. Peterson is willing to use her psychoanalytic skills, and is ready to risk her professional position, to unearth repressed memories that could clear Dr. Edwards of criminal charges.

Were it not for the secrets revealed by his dreams—and for tantalizing tidbits uncovered during the hypnotic trance Bergman induces—the aspiring asylum director would face murder charges. But, since Hitchcock was Hitchcock, and since Hitchcock was such a master of suspense, he engaged his audience until the end, surprising both his characters and his viewers with a dark and devastating revelation as the film concludes.

Because Hitchcock was more interested in telling a good story than in remaining true to psychoanalytic practice, he added tried and true hypnotic suggestions to free-wheeling free associations about psychoanalytically informed dream scenes. He used the best (and the worst) treatment techniques to enhance the story. Many psychiatrists dislike *Spellbound* because it sends mixed messages about mind-controlling doctors who lose their memory or resort to murder or lose their cool to love. But cinemaphiles adore *Spellbound*'s intricacies.

Plotwise, *Spellbound* is on a continuum with *Caligari* (1919), and its evil imposter doctor who runs an asylum and commits murder (by proxy). If we did not know *Caligari*'s history, and if we did not know that Hitchcock temporarily worked in Germany and studied German Expressionism, we might be tempted to say that *Spellbound* reflects postwar ambivalence about accepting or rejecting more modern methods of psychoanalysis and mental cures. We might be tempted to say that *Spellbound*'s stately Green Manors and its imposter psychiatrists comment on the Jewish refugee psychoanalysts recruited to the stately Menninger Clinic. Maybe that is true. Or maybe Hitchcock was simply a master of suspense and knew how to play upon ambivalence and double meanings, whatever the subject.

If we want to talk about a film that unabashedly deals with the ambivalent attitude toward dream interpretation and psychological treatment, a film that reminds us of the occult origins of dream interpretation and of the carnival-like atmosphere of *Caligari*, we can discuss *Nightmare Alley* (1947). *Nightmare Alley* can be correctly called a film noir, and it can also be called one of the best-made, but one of the bleakest, films around. For the real-life nightmares alluded to in *Nightmare Alley* were far worse than the worst sleep dreams of Miss Lilith's naive subjects.

NIGHTMARE ALLEY AND NIGHTMARE ON ELM STREET

Nightmare Alley fascinates us for many reasons. For one thing, it is a wonderful film, and it is one of the rare films that revolves around exploitative episodes of dream analysis perpetrated by a female "Consulting Psychologist" (as the shingle says on her office door). The consulting psychologist is appropriately named Lilith, a name that recollects the life-draining Lilith succubus of Babylonian and biblical myth. Like the mythical Lilith, this Miss Lilith preys upon her unsuspecting analysands as they sleep and dream. But this suave and sophisticated Lilith teams up with a two-bit carnie (Tyrone Power) who aspires to something better than a secondary role in a third-rate traveling carnival show.

At the carnival, Power plays the stooge for his "clairvoyant" Tarot card–reading partner Zeena (Joan Blondell), who is married to a pathetic alcoholic. Soon enough, Power and Blondell leave the (low-class) carnival, hoping to revive the (high-class) nightclub act that she had perfected with her husband, before his alcoholism progressed and interfered with their performances. At the nightclub, Power dons a tie and tuxedo and meets the sociopathic shrink who leads to his undoing and confirms the ominous prediction of Blondell's Tarot card reading.

Miss Lilith cons the con, convincing Tyrone Power to reveal the secrets of his carnie act. At Miss Lilith's instigation, Power's character Stan leaves his longtime carnie partner in the lurch. In the meantime, Miss Lilith, the consulting psychologist, has been treating her well-heeled patients with dream analysis. She learns their secrets and records their dreams on 78-rpm LPs, then transmits these secrets to Stan, who uses this information in his "mentalist" scenes. His "insight" convinces patrons to pay more money for staged seances.

The crossover between seances and psychoanalysis, and between mentalists and mental health, reminds viewers that twentieth-century psychoanalysts who delve into dreams are little better (and maybe a little worse) than nineteenth-century spiritualists who staged seances and faked rappings and promoted double-exposed trick photography as "spirit photography."

In the end, Miss Lilith betrays her lover, after sucking his lifeblood from him while he lived a dreamlike existence through her dream schemes. Now she leaves him in limbo, just as he left his carnie partner before. Having already abandoned carnie partner Joan Blondell, and having been abandoned by his new partner Miss Lilith, Tyrone Power has no choice: he returns to the carnie and to the only life he really knew. This time around, he has taken to drink. The only available role is the geek, the despised low-life who lives for the bottle and sleeps in a shack. He accepts the part, dives into this role, and lives out his life in a waking nightmare. The roles have been reversed, and the evil woman dooms the gullible man.

If *Nightmare Alley* was brilliant in its subtleties and plot twists and in its ability to make audiences rethink a serious subject matter, *Nightmare on Elm Street* (1984) was the reverse. *Nightmare on Elm Street* was brilliant in its directness and in its ability to tap into the worst nightmares of 1980s-era teens. It was brilliant in its ability to turn an unsavory subject into spectacular commercial success, in spite of many objections. *Nightmare on Elm Street* was intended to revitalize the slasher genre that surfaced in its most embryonic form with *Psycho* (1960), before deteriorating into sensationalistic splatter in the early eighties. Slashers attracted adolescents, offended adults, and enraged social critics, but bestowed box offices with riches. As much as parents and jurists and therapists wanted slashers to disappear, producers who banked on ticket sales wanted to breathe new life into this bloody and grisly film form.

Nightmare on Elm Street did much more than revitalize this moribund genre. *Elm Street* produced seven sequels, along with shelves of toys, Halloween costumes, and a larger-than-life character named Freddy. Freddy was a school janitor who killed the school's children. It was implied that he sexually molested children before murdering them. Irate parents banded together and burned Freddy alive. But Freddy refused to remain dead and returned to haunt children of those parents in their nightmares. Only those who were lucky enough to awaken before Freddy left their dreams had hopes of capturing the psychological-supernatural figure of Freddy.

Even though it is offensive, *Nightmare on Elm Street* is intriguing because of its ability to blend the supernatural with psychoanalytic subtexts. Instead of mocking psychoanalytic dream techniques by paralleling them to spiritualist approaches, as *Nightmare Alley* did, *Nightmare on Elm Street* fuses the two. In doing so, it taps into dream's old-time occult connotations and also reminds viewers that supernaturalism and psychoanalysis were once cousins. *Nightmare on Elm Street* implanted itself in the popular imagination and made Freddy a near-mythic figure.

While psychoanalysts like Freud tried to cleave the psychological psyche from the spiritual soul (*Seele*), cinema merged the two mindsets, without apology. Previously, only Jung (or perhaps Frankl) had seen the psyche and soul on a continuum. By the turn of the twenty-first century, however, a dozen or more films about the crossover between psyche and spirit had appeared, appealing to audiences as intensely as movie magic did at the start of the previous century. *Jacob's Ladder* (1989), *The Sixth Sense* (1999), and *Silent Hill* (2006) are but a few examples of this genre.

Even forward-looking sci-fi films looked to the future by referencing the past. *Blade Runner* (1982) is the best-known of this genre. Based on Philip K. Dick's novel *Do Androids Dream of Electric Sheep?*, *Blade Runner* became a cult classic. It claimed that dreams distinguish humans from machines. Androids that dream are human and cannot be destroyed or decommissioned, as planned. Thanks to Freud's emphasis on dreams and consciousness, the twentieth century came to believe that "I dream, therefore I am." Thanks to *Blade Runner* and other influences, Descartes' compelling concept of "I think, therefore I am" was decommissioned.

CHAPTER 5

HYPNOSIS

POLITICAL PROPAGANDA AND MIND CONTROL

In 1964, Marshall McLuhan coined a phrase that remains with us to this day: the medium is the message. McLuhan became the father of media studies, and a prophet of the "age of information" that arrived two decades later. McLuhan's significance was so great that he popped up in person (like a magical fairy) in Woody Allen's *Annie Hall* (1977). There, he settled an argument between two pedantic movie-goers who were debating his theories as they waited in line.

McLuhan was completely correct concerning the connection between cinema and hypnosis. As a medium, cinema is hypnotizing. So it makes sense that cinema is successful at showcasing hypnosis as a subject. Since the start of the twentieth century, film has molded our mindsets about the help—or the harm—caused by hypnosis and hypnotists. Cinema showed us that hypnosis can be a medical treatment or a carnival act—and that it was equally entertaining, either way!

It is important that films be hypnotizing, or trance-inducing, or mesmerizing. Why would anyone want to make a film that *did not* cast a spell on spectators and sweep them away from the tedium of everyday life? Even documentary filmmakers must ensnare audiences into adopting their points of view. It has been a long time since the early Edison pioneers and the Lumière brothers thought that moving pictures should be scientific tools, and nothing but.

So when audiences or film critics call a film "hypnotizing" or "mesmerizing," they mean it as a compliment. When censors or jurists use the same terms, they are probably making an accusation or a condemnation. When government agents or ministers of propaganda enlist movies' hypnotic effects, they are being, well, Machiavellian. For politicians recognized the utility of mind-control techniques long before movies existed. Totalitarian governments turn to brainwashing techniques, isolation chambers, and repetitive sounds and imagery, on screen or off, when they want to be psychologically persuasive and instill their message in the masses.

How often we hear defendants say that "the movies made me do it." Whether they are serial killers or small-time drug dealers or middle-school students who skip classes, many people lay blame on film (and also on comic books or video games or song lyrics). Whether they are successful at convincing judge and jury that movies exert undue influence is another story. For statistics show that only 1 percent of capital crimes are dismissed through the insanity defense.

As for the number of adolescents who convince their parents that their actions are attributable to the movies, that is a different matter. We have no numbers on that. Yet when we consider how much thought goes into the ratings system (or the Hayes Office codes that predated ratings, or the Catholic Legion of Decency standards), one would think that courts, clergy, and parents alike agree that young minds are indelibly molded by movies.

Social psychologists proved that claims about the influence of media are true, to a degree. The lesser the parental influence, the greater is the grip that movies have on young minds. A skeptic might say that some parents attribute bad behavior to the movies but credit themselves for any good that comes from their children. Skeptics aside, the advertising industry is well aware of media's influence, for advertising would not exist if attitudes could not be altered by media. In 1957 Vance Packard's book about *The Hidden Persuaders* became a best seller, not just because the book was so compelling but also because mass marketing was growing, and the psychology of cinema and media in general was a popular subject of discussion.

Governments took film's hypnotic ability to heart. The U.S. government used commercial movies (along with newsreels) to increase patriotism during World War II. Government censors ensured that films did not sabotage military morale or patriotic spirit on the home front. But the most influential pro-war films were not the mind-numbing B movies that one instinctively links to brainwashing.

Beloved classics such as *Casablanca* (1942) also served government propaganda purposes and boosted popular support for America's decision to join the Allies and enter World War II. The love story with Humphrey Bogart and Ingrid Bergman, and the personal ties between Claude Reins, Conrad Veidt, Peter Lorre, and Sydney Greenstreet, moved Americans' minds and hearts at a time when many Americans still favored "isolationism" and opposed meddling in conflicts across the ocean. Appropriately, *Casablanca* was directed by Michael Curtiz, who himself had fled Hitler.

Casablanca's most influential scene occurs as the film ends, after we have been drawn into the story, and after we have been "hypnotized" into believing that we left our hometown theater seats and are now sitting among the café crowd at Rick's Café in Morocco. We have grown to know Rick (Bogie), who owns Rick's American Café. We also know Sam the piano player by his first name, and will know his name even better after Woody Allen's *Play It Again, Sam* (1972).

Having been psychologically transported to North Africa, we mentally mingle with wartime exiles who pass their time drinking and dancing and dining at Rick's Café while awaiting travel papers. We are entranced by the exoticism of the locale and have been hypnotized as completely as the coiled cobras in the Moroccan market, where Sydney Greenstreet conducts shady wartime transactions. Most viewers believe they are watching a love story. Few realize that the story sets them up to respond to subtle government propaganda.

At the final airport scene, Bergman prepares to depart with Bogart and looks longingly into Bogart's eyes. The hard-boiled Bogart retorts, "The problems of three little people don't amount to a hill of beans in this crazy world." On the surface, those words speak about the life story of this disillusioned drifter who lives out his loveless life in exile. But the words say much more. Bogart—the stateless and shift-less ex-pat—proved that he was prepared to let Bergman—the love of his life—board the plane without him, to send her off into the skies with her patriot husband and Hungarian resistance fighter Victor Laszlo. If Rick could make such a sacrifice so that the Allies could win the war, so could other Americans.

By encouraging viewers to identify with him, Bogie hypnotizes American audiences in a democratic way. Viewers chose to watch the film on their own volition, and not by coercion. Now Bogie was encouraging them to make personal sacrifices to aid the war effort, as Rick did. How much this American approach differed from the Korean Communist approach chronicled in *Manchurian Candidate*, or from the National Socialist (Nazi) approach to movie mind control!

Casablanca was not the only film that was modified to aid the war effort. During the war, censors required many changes in movie scripts. Some films were shot scene by scene, to ensure that each scene passed the censors' oversight. Even before the war, legislators decreed that movie criminals and gangsters could not triumph over government agents, or "G-men." Gangsters or cons who made it to the screen were required to aid the war effort, as happened in *This Gun for Hire* (1942).

In that classic noir film, the hard-core criminal and killer-for-hire Raven subverts an enemy agent and sacrifices his own life in order to aid America. Raven's hand (like his psyche) bears scars inflicted by an abusive aunt during his youth, scars that presumably made him turn criminal. Now he is hunted down by G-men and suspected of kidnapping a detective's "girl" who works as a covert government agent. When Raven accidentally acquires a commitment to a cause—the cause of aiding the war effort—this long-time sociopath also acquires a conscience. Raven is transformed in the film, and the audience is also transformed while watching the incorrigible Raven crawl out of his criminal cocoon and morph into a beautiful human being. As the film ends, Raven is shot as he struggles to protect his country's secrets from enemy scientists.

Casablanca and *This Gun for Hire* aside, America's appropriation of cinema's hypnotic powers was paltry compared to the Nazis' exploitation of hypnotic pageantry for propaganda cinema. Hitler and Goebbels, his minister of propaganda, knew how to hypnotize the masses through media. In recognition of media's influence, the Reich outlawed movies that could compromise their cause. Goebbels was a film fan who watched a movie a night but opposed the use of film as propaganda. Hitler's characteristic mustache was an ode to the movies: he had grown a Charlie Chaplin mustache as a token of his admiration for Chaplin. When Chaplin did not reciprocate this respect, and spoofed Hitler through film, Chaplin's movies were also outlawed.

The Nazis exiled many film industry people, and murdered many more, over their years in power. Yet they subsidized Leni Riefenstahl's *Triumph of the Will* (1935), which starred Hitler as himself and documented a Nazi Nuremberg rally in

1934. Riefenstahl was Hitler's favorite filmmaker, hand-picked by Hitler after Fritz Lang (allegedly) declined the offer that she accepted. Riefenstahl was one of the few top film talents who did not self-exile from Nazi-controlled Germany when 60,000 fellow film workers left. She joined the Nazi party instead.

Triumph of the Will was meant to instill a spiritual (and psychological) sense of unity in Germans. To accomplish this, Riefenstahl added unexpected touches to already-available techniques. By shooting the upwards sky from an unusual angle, she implanted a powerful perception of spirit. By keeping the camera panning and constantly moving, following troops and banners, she invoked a sense of uprooted-ness and disconnectedness at the same time that her imagery promised loftiness and transcendence.

Above and beyond its cinematographic techniques, *Triumph of the Will* capital-ized on movies' ability to mesmerize the masses and turn them into a mindless amal-gam. Riefenstahl's camera captured long lines of swaying arms, synchronized to a rhythmic beat, with banners of swastikas held high, flashing across the visual field. The perfectly timed marching of troops hypnotized viewers as easily as hypnotists' waving wands or blinking eyes or revolving circles (or swaying swastikas, which appeared throughout the film). These repetitive images relied upon the same princi-ples as hypnosis to produce relaxation and increase susceptibility to suggestion.

Considering how easily movies hypnotize audiences, and considering how popu-lar hypnosis was in the eighteenth and nineteenth centuries, it is no surprise that hypnosis starred in films from the start. After all, the medium is the message. There were other equally important reasons to feature hypnosis in film. Hypnosis figured prominently in turn-of-the-century social and scientific shifts. Let us recall, once again, that cinema and psychoanalysis grew up together, and that each was born within a year of the other (with cinema appearing in 1895 and psychoanalysis in 1896). Let us also recall that Freud treated hysterics with hypnosis just before he discovered more modern psychoanalysis and invented talk therapy that encouraged free associations.

Until electroencephalograms (EEGs) proved otherwise, hypnosis was thought to be a form of sleep, and it was named for Hypnos, the Greek god of sleep. Views about sleep and dreams, and about hypnosis, were shifting at century's end, espe-cially after Freud published his landmark *Interpretation of Dreams*. Freud's psychoan-alytic circle was expanding. Fledgling psychoanalysts professionalized themselves and distinguished themselves from other doctors. They published in serious scientific publications. Above all, they needed to differentiate themselves from charlatans, car-nival showmen, magicians, and mentalists who used hypnosis and dream interpreta-tion. The chasm between treatment-focused hypnosis and entertainment-focused hypnosis grew deeper.

When Freud's new talk therapy pushed old hypnosis aside, this "advanced" tech-nique cast extra attention on *all* mental treatments. Psychoanalysis and talk therapy made modern men and women think about the mind, or psyche, in a new way. It spurred debates about the advantages of newer treatment over older techniques and shined a stronger light on hypnosis in the process. Just as Darwin's ideas about evo-lution made his contemporaries reexamine pre-existing ideas about religion, so, too, did psychoanalysis unearth earlier dialogues about free will and destiny, as well as human psychology. H. G. Wells's *Island of Dr. Moreau*, written in 1896 but made into many film versions over the years, dramatized these debates.

Another unrelated event intensified concerns about free will, human control, and the distinction between humans and beasts. In 1920 Ivan Pavlov, who had won the Nobel Prize in 1904, published a book on behavioral conditioning. This Nobel Laureate explained how unrelated stimuli, such as ringing bells, can be paired with reflexive responses, such as salivation (in the presence of meat). This pairing of stimuli produced a learned response to the unrelated paired stimulus. This learned response occurred, regardless of belief, cognition, will, or any other lofty philosophical motivation. Pavlov's discoveries added another dimension to the heated debates about the basis of behavior. Pavlov's studies portrayed humans as beasts, just as Darwin and Freud did. Freud theorized about sexual and aggressive drives that were clearly animalistic. This view of humankind did not rest well with the religious. A year before, in 1919, John Watson had published a related book about behaviorism and the intentional induction of phobias. By then, the world had witnessed the bestial behavior of humankind firsthand and was ready to change the way that it viewed the mind, or psyche or soul, that supposedly propelled behavior.

FROM MESMER TO MÉLIÈS

Cinema, seizing upon these seismic social and scientific shifts, showcased the old and the new and the bad and the good. It showed villains and victims. It showed minds as monsters and monsters as minds. As a thoroughly modern invention that emerged from the womb of the twentieth century, cinema was especially suited to comment on these thoroughly modern debates. Cinema dramatized the skepticism stirred up by new conceptions of the psyche (or of the mindless brain, in the case of Pavlov), and it called attention to hypnosis. But cinema's purpose was not necessarily to editorialize or to pontificate, as a newspaper or a college professor would.

Cinema simply needed a good story with interesting imagery. A story that could be told without words, and a story that did not need dialogue, and a story that employed easily identifiable signs and symbols, as well as gestures and movements that spoke for themselves, was especially useful in the pre-sound era (before 1927). Hypnotists could wave a magic wand. Somnambulists walked stiffly with closed eyes. Each said a thousand words without uttering a sound. Thus they were ideal subjects in the early days of cinema, even without scientific shifts.

After sound was added to cinema, talk therapy and the couch cure added more to the mix. In fact, the popularity of talk therapy increased after talkies pushed silents aside by the thirties. Blending the two techniques together—the couch cure with hypnosis scenes—produced an even richer plot. Later and greater films, such as *Cat People* (1942), *Spellbound* (1945), *The Three Faces of Eve* (1957), *Whirlpool* (1949), and even *The Exorcist II* (1977), combined hypnosis with psychoanalysis, to great commercial success. Yes, they sacrificed clinical truths—as did most interesting films about psychiatric treatments—but they also produced fine and influential films.

The fact that cinema itself was entertaining made it all the more imperative that film highlight the differences—or suggest the similarities—between treatment techniques and entertainment techniques. Ironically, the Lumière brothers never recognized film's entertainment potential and saw it only as a scientific tool. Even the enterprising Edison failed to realize that film could become theater and that audiences would watch films as a group, instead of viewing individual kinetoscopes alone. Later filmmakers were aware of this irony. They played on the confusion between treatment and entertainment, and used hypnosis scenes to remind viewers of this interchangeability. Again, the medium was the message. Fairgrounds and carnivals, with their mentalists and hypnotists and mind readers, were fair game for film themes. For each was a form of entertainment, and each enhanced the other.

Entertainment-oriented filmmakers like Méliès knew that mentalism and mesmerism were carnival favorites long before cinema existed. Filmmakers knew that sideshows drew crowds. They also knew that early films showed in sideshow-like settings and were often just one of a dozen attractions. So it was natural to add hypnotists to early films (and to later films as well), and to highlight the sideshow-like aspects of psychiatric techniques such as hypnotism.

As an added bonus, film technology could finally do justice to fairgrounds. Moving pictures captured the moving lights and whirling wheels of carnival scenes. Movies impressed audiences with these new abilities. Such imagery intrigued spectators and challenged cinematographers. Fairground scenes became standard fare in early film, and they gained great fame through *The Cabinet of Dr. Caligari* (1919). *Caligari* revolved around a hypnotist, a psychiatrist, a somnambulist, and an asylum. Kracauer's *From Caligari to Hitler* chronicles other fairground scenes in cinema.

It is useful to recall that Freud scorned film, dismissing it as second rate (if that). It was only fitting that early film called Freud's hyperbolic claims into question by highlighting the blurry boundaries between charlatans and psychics and psychoanalysts and hypnotists. From its earliest infancy, film reminded viewers that hypnosis was both a treatment technique and an entertainment technique. *Nightmare Alley* (1947) proved that a well-cast, well-written, and well-directed film about those blurred boundaries spoke to mid-twentieth century audiences. In fact, the conflation of the psychological with the supernatural resurfaced as the twenty-first century ended and is now as popular a subject as ever.

Freud certainly deserves credit for drawing attention to hypnosis as a treatment technique, and for setting the stage for literally dozens of silent films about evil hypnotists during film's early decades. Yet he does not deserve full credit, for other individuals and institutions were also treating patients with hypnosis at the same time as he. For Freud went to France to study hypnosis with acknowledged masters of medical hypnosis. It was equally important that Freud veered away from hypnosis fairly early on, even though he wrote a seminal paper about hypnosis shortly before discovering psychoanalysis. The fact that he abandoned this older, authoritarian, despotic, mind-controlling technique in favor of a newer, more neutral, and less controlling approach that involved "free associations" made hypnosis seem all the more evil and outdated and controlling in contrast. This contrast, in turn, made hypnosis all the more appealing to moviemakers who tried to control their audience's consciousness.

Even though Freud was influential in renewing attention on hypnosis at the turn of the twentieth century, we cannot lose sight of the fact that medical hypnosis was used for two centuries before Freud (with Breuer) wrote the historic paper on hypnosis and hysteria. Hypnosis existed long before the neurologist Charcot taught the technique to young Freud in France. Debates about the proper use of hypnosis were particularly prominent in France, where cinema started with the Lumière brothers and Méliès.

A different form of mind control was pioneered by another Austrian doctor a century before Freud. Franz Mesmer (1734–1815) worked in Vienna, where Freud studied medicine and later established his psychoanalytic circle. Mesmer was a "vitalist" who, like his contemporaries, believed that a fluid permeated the entire universe and infused both matter and spirit with its vital force. Unlike his contemporaries, he believed that "animal magnetism" could cure illness.

Thinking that he could control the flow of spirits and thereby disrupt pain and other nervous conditions, Mesmer treated hysterics in group sessions. After his fellow physicians staged a scientific trial of his technique and found no merit to mesmerism or animal magnetism (other than the power of suggestion), Mesmer was forced to move on. He proceeded to Paris, where he and his mesmerism were welcomed in Parisian parlors and by Parisian ladies. Mesmerism disappeared as a treatment technique—although we can argue that recent studies of transcranial magnetic stimulation (TCMS) recollect Mesmer's claims about magnetic healing powers.

Around the same time that Mesmer was practicing animal magnetism, surgeons were putting hypnotic trance to better use. The Scottish surgeon James Braid (1796–1860) used hypnosis in lieu of anesthesia as early as 1843. Chloroform had not yet been discovered, so surgical patients still "bit the bullet" after downing a bottle of alcohol. In Calcutta, another British doctor, James Esdaile (1808–59), used hypnosis and adapted Hindu trance techniques.

Near the end of the century, along came Freud, a Viennese neurologist who studied hypnosis in France and claimed that he could cure hysterics through trance. Freud soon found that hysterics' symptoms disappeared without trance. Words alone worked just as well. Many who studied Freud's early work found his studies deficient in scientific technique, but these critiques were irrelevant to filmmakers, who realized that movies must entertain more than they educate, and that they need not concern themselves with scientific accuracy. Filmmakers were eager to exploit entertaining treatment techniques, such as hypnosis, for storytelling purposes.

Méliès, who began his career as a magician, intuited that whatever worked as a carnival act or sideshow stunt—as hypnosis did—was suited for cinema. As early as 1897, Méliès produced *Le Magnetiseur* [*The Hypnotist at Work*], in which a young woman is put into trance and disrobed. Méliès released another short, *The Hypnotist's Revenge*, in 1909.

Other filmmakers followed suit. The Frenchman Pathe (who put Méliès out of business) was also fond of hypnosis themes. In 1909 Pathe produced *The Hypnotic Wife*, a story about a wife who cast a hypnotic spell on her husband. The revered (but also reviled) American D. W. Griffith's *The Criminal Hypnotist* (1909) appeared in the same year.

In 1910 Lux made *Hypnotism*, a film about a girl who committed robbery while under a hypnotist's influence. The same year, Max Linder made a nine-minute film, *Max Hypnotized* (1910), in which two servants hypnotize their master and order him to murder. A family murder occurs in Eclair's *Convicted by Hypnotism* (1912). Here, a wife is hypnotized by her husband and accidentally kills her father. The year 1914 brought Warner's *The Hypnotic Violinist* (1914), which ran forty-five minutes and revolved around a doctor's wife who is controlled by psychic powers. Many other "primitive" films about hypnosis were made in the first two decades of cinema.

Most early films about hypnosis focused on family matters rather than on medical matters. They suggested that families can entrance their relatives, take control of them, and force them to commit unconscionable acts. These films foreshadowed such psychological thrillers as *Gaslight* (1944), which dispensed with trance entirely and focused on a husband who manipulates the house lights to convince his wife that she is going insane. A decade later, hypnotist-psychiatrists took center stage, overshadowing the diabolical family members of early cinema.

TRILBY, CALIGARI, MABUSE, *AND* CHANDU

Along with cinema, George du Maurier's 1894 novel *Trilby* put the hypnotic eye in the public eye. *Trilby* made it to stage, before resurfacing in several silent cinematic interpretations that predated *Cabinet of Dr. Caligari*'s evil psychiatrist-hypnotist. Trilby's will was usurped by the evil hypnotist Svengali. The name *Svengali* became synonymous for a persuasive person with evil intent. When we speak of someone with "Svengali-like powers," we recollect du Maurier's hypnotist, who, by the way, was *not* a psychiatrist or a physician.

Du Maurier's Svengali invoked another stereotype. Du Maurier's novel characterizes Svengali as an "Oriental Israelite Hebrew Jew." That description is reminiscent enough of Freud to demand comment, especially when we consider that du Maurier's novel appeared just after Freud's paper on hypnosis. Furthermore, Freud was from an *Ostjuden* (Oriental Jewish) family from Moravia (Bohemia) before moving westward to Austria, suggesting that there are even stronger similarities between Freud's real-life persona and du Maurier's fictional Svengali.

Many early filmmakers brought Svengali's character to cinema, but a successful screen adaptation did not arrive until *Svengali* (1931). That version starred John Barrymore and catapulted Barrymore into enduring fame. Around the same time, another memorable movie about a hypnotist appeared. *Chandu the Magician* (1932) was followed by *The Return of Chandu* (1934). Both versions adapted the long-running radio serial about a semi-mystical superhero reminiscent of *The Shadow* and *Mandrake the Magician*. Superheroes were in great demand, as Hitler was gaining power and would soon be named chancellor of Germany in 1933. Comic-book superheroes who could combat the world's worst villain were being born back then.

Horror meister Bela Lugosi played the arch-villain Roxor in the first *Chandu*, but he played Chandu himself in the Roxor-less *Return of Chandu*. This white-skinned

Chandu uses a crystal ball and wears an Oriental-style turban as he gazes into it. Chandu fights evil in general and the evil of Roxor, the would-be world conqueror, in particular. Chandu learned his powers from an Indian yogi, and now creates illusions and makes doppelgänger-like doubles of himself. *Chandu* was popular enough to be serialized for movie matinees. He paralleled emerging comic book heroes. Today, Chandu is largely forgotten, possibly because contemporary society does not have as much need for supernatural salvation as society did from the thirties through the fifties, and possibly because later and greater superheroes with more scientific sources of power (such as nuclear radiation) proved to be more enduring and more entertaining.

The most famous film about an evil hypnotist/evil psychiatrist appeared in the Weimar era, which preceded the Nazis' rise to power. *The Cabinet of Dr. Caligari* (1919) owes some of its everlasting endurance to Siegfried Kracauer's book, *From Caligari to Hitler* (1947). Kracauer argued (not completely convincingly but completely intriguingly) that Caligari and related cinematic characters foreshadowed Hitler's hypnotic-like hold over the German people and the German people's potential to respond to such a despotic dictator. In the last decade, the Holocaust historian Daniel Goldenhagen's widely read book, *Hitler's Willing Executioners*, disputed the long-held belief that the German people were mesmerized by the Nazis. In doing so, Goldenhagen indirectly redirected attention to Kracauer's controversial theories about *Caligari*.

Even if we overlook Kracauer's role in reviving interest in Robert Weine's *Caligari*, we cannot overlook *The Cabinet of Dr. Caligari's* cinematic accomplishments. One glance at this film assures us that *Caligari* the film deserved the recognition it received. This silent classic is often erroneously assumed to be *the* first great film ever made, or *the* foremost example of German Expressionism, or *the* earliest horror film, or *the* first depiction of an evil psychiatrist.[1]

None of those assumptions are true, but that does not detract from *Caligari's* stature. Other great films were made before Weine created *Caligari*. There were evil cinematic psychiatrists galore prior to 1919. Evil hypnotists of all persuasions were plentiful in film's first two decades. Many excellent examples of German Expressionism exist (even though the Weimar era was short-lived). The horror genre was well-entrenched prior to *Caligari*. Even the subjects of sleep, dream, hypnotism, and psychosis were embedded in cinema long before 1919.[2]

Caligari's visuals are unforgettable, even if its convoluted story line is confusing. Its crooked streets, unsettling angles, and mismatched roofs were inspired by German Expressionism and by the art of Edvard Munch and Alfred Kubin and by Max Reinhardt's theater. This imagery entered contemporary set design and children's books. Dr. Seuss books and Seuss's kaleidoscopic *5,000 Fingers of Dr. T* (1953) borrow from *Caligari*, as does Tim Burton's black comedy *Beetlejuice*, which was made before Burton saw the silent film screened![3]

Caligari was written by Carl Mayer and Hans Janowitz. The story is recounted by two gentlemen who sit on a bench, talking in a garden. *Caligari* is supposed to be the asylum director, but he turns out to be a fraud who was a former carnival hypnotist and a current insane asylum inmate himself. As hypnotist, he takes complete control of his somnambulist Cesare (played by Conrad Veidt, who went on to play the Nazi commander in *Casablanca* and related roles, even though he was a fervent anti-Nazi in real life). We must wait until the film's end to learn of Caligari the carnival performer's complex origins.

Early on, we know that Caligari keeps the somnambulistic Cesare in a coffin when Cesare is not assisting Caligari in his sideshow performances of trance states. Caligari secretly commands Cesare to kill, starting with a city clerk who humiliated Caligari when he applied for a permit to perform. The second victim of the somnambulist is the storyteller's friend Alain.

Caligari then cajoles Cesare into taking the life of the heroine, Jane. Cesare tries to stab Jane with a knife, but he cannot carry out Caligari's command because he falls in love with her. After Jane faints from fear at the sight of the knife, Cesare swings her limp body over his shoulder, hoping to save her from Caligari's evil intentions. But Cesare collapses, and drops Jane, before dropping dead himself. Jane escapes, but Cesare lies lifeless in the field. Then the truth is discovered.

By now, Jane's male companion Francis has grown suspicious of Caligari, and has secretly followed him. Francis tracks Caligari to a nearby insane asylum, where he learns that Caligari is more than a carnival performer. Caligari is also the hypnotist who heads the asylum. Francis learns that Caligari has followed the path of a long-dead mountebank named Caligari, who also hypnotized subjects into committing murder when he lived in 1703. Francis learns that Cesare was admitted to Dr. Caligari's asylum and was chosen for Caligari's evil experiments. The asylum staff steps in and discovers that Caligari is insane and must be stopped. Caligari is handcuffed by his staff and stuffed into a cell.

As the story ends, the film returns to its original framing device, where Francis the storyteller sits alongside another man in the garden. Spectators now learn that Francis—who portrayed himself as the story's hero—is also an asylum inmate. This revelation makes us wonder if this story really took place, or if it was a figment of Francis's imagination.

As imaginative as *Caligari's* plot is, it reflected a certain reality. One of the authors, Janowitz, had a good reason to portray the psychiatrist-hypnotist as the embodiment of evil: He received a dishonorable discharge from the military in World War I for psychiatric grounds, and he blamed all psychiatrists for disrupting his dreams, for cooperating with the war machine, and for turning soldiers into killing machines.

Carl Mayer, his collaborator, had other reasons to be bitter. Mayer's father had been a gambler who boasted about his grandiose gaming schemes, much as someone who suffers from bipolar disorder might. Mayer's father never received the help he needed. He lost his life to suicide instead, and Mayer lost a father. To make matters worse, Mayer was walking through a Munich park one day when he saw a child disappear into the bushes. The next day, he read that a little girl was murdered by a madman in that region. Wondering if she was the child he saw the day before, he mined his imagination, presumably unearthed memories of his father's tragic death, and then added details to Janowitz's original idea.

Caligari influenced other Weimar-era film. Shortly after *Caligari*'s premiere in 1919, Fritz Lang started his *Dr. Mabuse* series with *Dr. Mabuse, der Spieler* [*Dr. Mabuse, the Gambler*] (1922). A year after the first *Mabuse* film, an unrelated film about hypnosis debuted in Austria: *The Lost Soul, or The Dangers of Hypnosis* (1923). This aptly titled film never gained the acclaim of *Caligari* or *Mabuse*, but it fortified Kracauer's hypotheses about hypnotists. Lang's *Mabuse* transitioned to talkies, which were dubbed into English. The series continued through 1970. Lang's last *Mabuse* of 1960 contributed to the counterculture's antagonistic attitude toward psychiatry, and it intensified opposition to insane asylums and state control of the mentally ill. *Mabuse* movies (not all of which were made by Lang) turned mind-controlling doctors and other demagogues into objects of suspicion for the 1960s.

Lang's *Mabuse* is almost as famous as *Caligari*, partly because of its merit and partly because *Mabuse*, like *Caligari*, is inseparable from Nazi-era events. Even Lang's life story is intertwined with World War II intrigue. The Viennese-born Lang claimed that Goebbels asked him to head the German film industry after *The Testament of Dr. Mabuse* premiered in 1933. Lang declined this offer, which was later accepted by Leni Riefenstahl. Lang's life story became more complex from that time forward. The story he told of his escape from Berlin was as dramatic as the escapades of his espionage films (and perhaps as fictional).

After this encounter with Goebbels, Lang allegedly boarded a middle-of-the-night Paris-bound train (as his *Ministry of Fear* characters might have done). Because his mother (Pauline Schlesinger) was born Jewish (but converted to Catholicism when Fritz was ten), Lang felt endangered by Nazi policy about Jewish blood. So he left his fortune, his art collection, and his wife behind. He made his way to Paris, where he had studied art after World War I. His wife and former collaborator divorced him and remained behind in Berlin, where she became a Nazi filmmaker.

After Lang reached America, he continued his illustrious cinematic career. His background in German Expressionism added to the film noir style that evolved in the 1940s and 1950s. As popular as film noir is today, some half a century after its invention, and as important as his last *Dr. Mabuse* was to the counterculture's questioning of psychiatric and political authority, it was Lang's *The Testament of Dr. Mabuse* (1933; his second *Mabuse*) that is most important historically. *Testament* expressed Nazi ideology through the mouth of a madman. Creepy references to shower scenes and poisonous gases are eerily similar to actual events that came to pass during the Holocaust, which came to full fruition in 1941. Lang's film was soon banned by the Third Reich, which recognized that the madman-spokesperson made a mockery of Hitler.

Kracauer thought that Lang's evil hypnotist-psychiatrist mirrored Hitler's hypnotic control over the German masses, just as Caligari did. However, we know that *The Testament of Dr. Mabuse* (1933) was made in the same year that Hitler assumed power. We also know that Nazi leaders watched the film *before* they built death camps and gas chambers. Those who view this unsettling film are left wondering if Kracauer was completely correct, partly correct, or if perhaps this film ignited deadly sparks of evil that were simmering in Nazi minds.

Other films that came on the heels of the *Mabuse* movies echoed this dark and debased view of humanity. The original *Cat People* (1942) was one of those. Its plot was powerful enough, and its art direction unique enough, to ensure that it retains a cult following to this day. The original version was directed by Jacques Tourneur, under the supervision of cult horror director Val Lewton. *Cat People* magnified the "smoke and mirrors" effects of early cinema.

In this film, the mysterious, Serbian-accented, cat-featured Irena (Simone Simon) meets her husband-to-be as she sketches panthers in the zoo. Her unassuming suitor does not understand why the park's panthers react so strangely to Irena. He certainly does not suspect that Irena is descended from panther-people who claw like cats and become murderously mean when sexually aroused. He does notice that she is unable to consummate their marriage. When she explains that she suffers from a curse that turns her into a panther during sex, he sends her to a psychiatrist, who hypnotizes her, hears her story, and becomes aroused by her himself.

In the interim, the husband falls in love with another woman, whom Irena trails to a dimly lit swimming pool. In a delicately handled shadow scene that won renown for Val Lewton, Irena the panther-woman stalks her prey. She leaves a shredded bathrobe at poolside, terrifying the swimmer (and the spectator) when she retrieves her robe. When her psychiatrist ignores her bad genetic endowment, and tries to cure her "delusion" through hypnotism, he, too, comes face-to-face with the panther avatar and falls victim to "the curse of the cat people." His attempt to control the beast (or to control his own sexual impulses) fails. The film is one more statement about the shortcomings of psychiatrists and hypnotists and about the perils that await those presumptuous enough to believe that mind control can overpower the biological beast inside.

In spite of its dramatic hypnosis scenes, this film is Freudian theory personified. It highlights the link between sexual, aggressive, and animalistic urges. The plot reminds us of Darwin's influence on Freud, and of his statement that "ontology recapitulates phylogeny." This film can be compared to H. G. Wells's Darwinian-influenced (but pre-Freudian) story *The Island of Dr. Moreau* (1896), which was made into several films. In contrast to Wells's concerns with cognitive, linguistic, and moral differences between human and beast, *Cat People* highlights the psychosexual similarities between animals and humans. It is an ancestor of psychological thrillers of the forties and fifties.

Cat People was remade in 1982, during the heyday of slasher films. The remake was more overtly erotic, as was customary in 1982. It dispensed with the subtle and suggestive shadow scenes that added suspense to the original. The remake starred Malcolm McDowell, who was known for his deranged role in *Clockwork Orange* (1971). McDowell's character and his sister were the last remaining survivors of a now-extinct people who could mate only with one another, even if that meant engaging in incest and shocking audiences via this last remaining screen taboo.

The first *Cat People* (1942) was followed by a largely unrelated sequel entitled *The Curse of the Cat People* (1944). The sequel shows the main character reading a child psychiatry book, *The Inner World of Childhood* (1927), which starts with an introduction by Jung. This book implies that audience and actors are psychologically sophisticated, and reminds us of a parallel scene in Hitchcock's *Suspicion* (1941), where the heroine also reads a book about child psychology.

The Curse of the Cat People retains memory traces of the characters of the original *Cat People*, but little else. Irena, the deceased cat woman, returns from the dead and appears as an apparition to the daughter born to her former husband and his second wife. The husband has completed grieving for his former wife and has almost forgotten the bizarre circumstances surrounding her death. Now he must retell the myth of the cat people, in order to explain his daughter's hallucination.

One year later, Hitchcock directed *Spellbound* (1945). Like *Cat People*, *Spellbound* combines classic psychoanalytic scenes, hypnosis scenes, and dream scenes. As a psychological thriller, *Spellbound* is theoretically worlds away from the supernatural/horror thrillers that Val Lewton and Jacques Tourneur specialize in. Yet both films effectively combine hypnosis and psychoanalysis to push the plot.

KLEPTOMANIA AND EROTOMANIA

Whirlpool (1949) was written by the same man who wrote *Spellbound*: the blacklisted author Ben Hecht, who used the name of Barstow in the McCarthy era, when he and other left-leaning writers were hounded by government inquests and were forced underground.

Like his screen characters, Hecht lived a double life that was riddled with deception and fear of betrayal. Even though *Spellbound* and *Whirlpool* were made by distinctly different directors, both concern themselves with double-dealing doctors, deceptive hypnotists, and healers who kill competitors as effortlessly as they cure patients. In each film, an unwavering love on the part of a secondary psychiatrist drives the quest for the truth and completes the plot.

Although it can be classified as a film noir, *Whirlpool* also exemplifies the melodramas, or "woman's pictures," that became popular around World War II. Gene Tierney plays a beautiful woman who is married to a prominent psychoanalyst (Richard Conte). Unbeknown to her husband, the wife is a kleptomaniac. The action starts when she is caught stealing jewelry from an exclusive department store. A stranger (Jose Ferrer) witnesses her crime and speaks up for her. He persuades the store owners not to prosecute because she is married to a wealthy and respected psychiatrist who pays her store credit. The audience knows that the observant stranger is a hypnotist and astrologer who caters to high society and claims to cure people who suffer from the same sort of psychological maladies that her psychiatrist-husband treats.

The charlatan-hypnotist convinces Tierney that he can cure her kleptomania. Fearful that her husband will learn her dark secret and that his career will be compromised if her kleptomania becomes known, Tierney accepts the stranger's seemingly gracious offer. She meets him at his hotel for hypnosis sessions. Hotel staff note her visits to the handsome hypnotist's suite and presume that they are conducting a clandestine affair.

However, the hypnotist is smarter than the hotel staff and is much smarter than Tierney. The audience is smarter than everyone, thanks to the omniscient narration that tells the audience more than the characters know. It turns out that the hypnotist plans to murder his mistress, who has threatened to turn him in to the police as a thief. The hypnotist knows that his mistress/client was treated by Tierney's psychiatrist-husband, and he suspects that she disclosed his misdeeds to the doctor. Because the psychiatrist records their sessions, he probably possesses proof of the hypnotist's crimes. The hypnotist also knows that he needs an alibi if he wants to murder his mistress.

Conveniently, he can hypnotize Tierney and cajole her into stealing her husband's recordings that contain proof of his crimes. His hypnosis makes Tierney enter the mistress's home on the night that she is murdered by the hypnotist himself, and turns her into the prime suspect, especially since she was seen entering the hypnotist's hotel room repeatedly. The hypnotist expects the police to conclude that she murdered the "other" mistress in a fit of jealousy.

A few glitches must be resolved before the con-man hypnotist can cover up his past and commit future crimes successfully. To make his alibi airtight, the hypnotist feigns abdominal pain and is admitted to a hospital for an emergency appendectomy. The hospital staff chart their visits to his room regularly, unwittingly providing written proof of his whereabouts on the night of the murder. Who would suspect that a postoperative patient could leave his bed, much less leave the hospital to commit a murder, especially since his nurses sign his record each shift?

So when Jose Ferrer hypnotizes himself into feeling no pain, crawls out of the hospital window, drives off to his mistress's home, and murders her moments before the psychiatrist's wife arrives, no one is the wiser—no one except the audience, and the psychiatrist-husband, who is convinced of his wife's innocence no matter what. Yet the psychiatrist's wife is unsure if she committed the murder, for she saw the dead body sprawled in front of her as she awakened.

The suspicious psychiatrist uses his own hypnosis skills on his wife and unearths buried memories of her encounters with the charlatan-hypnotist. He also learns where she hid his records while in a trance. Together, they stake out the psychiatrist's office, and wait for the sham-hypnotist to retrieve the incriminating records.

In the end, good wins out over evil, and the hypnotist is caught in his tracks and shot dead on the spot. The kleptomaniac wife is freed of murder charges, and the psychiatrist husband reclaims his wife, his career, and his professional credibility, to a degree. (His murdered patient, however, does not reclaim her life.) This twisted plot, as incredible as it is, turns into a compelling murder-mystery with twists and turns that remind us of *Spellbound*, and of Ben Hecht's double life.

Whirlpool stands apart from *Nightmare Alley*, which was made two years earlier. Both films concern themselves with showmen-hypnotists and psychiatrist-hypnotists, but *Whirlpool* calls attention to the differences rather than the similarities and casts the medical hypnotist as the hero and the showman-charlatan as the villain. Yet all is not that black and white. Although the psychiatrist comes out ahead in *Whirlpool*, his professional credibility is still contested, just as Ingrid Berman's Dr. Peterson's credibility is impeached in *Spellbound*.

Because we see that the *Whirlpool* psychiatrist is conned as easily as his wife (by his wife), we realize that he is not particularly perceptive. How could he have lived with this woman for so many years without suspecting that she suffers from such serious psychopathology? True, he is a good husband, and a good hypnotist, and he was correctly convinced of her innocence after she was framed for murder. But he is a flawed man, and an unimpressive psychoanalyst, in spite of his impressive credentials.

One cannot help but marvel at the skills of the hypnotist—who hypnotized himself after surgery—just as one cannot avoid smirking at the psychoanalyst's shortcomings. If he is blind to his wife's illness, how much is he missing in his patients? The mixed message about psychoanalysts is not nearly so hard-hitting as the direct messages of *Nightmare Alley* or *Spellbound*, but is present just the same and is readily visible to spectators.

Before proceeding, I should note that cinematic hypnotists and psychiatrists are not inevitably evil. There was a short time, between 1957 and 1963, when psychiatrists were portrayed sympathetically and idealistically. They were saviors who could cure patients and maybe even explain the evil that enveloped the world during World War II, when history's worst genocides were committed by Europe's most cultured nation in the name of "race science."

The Three Faces of Eve (1957) is one of those idealistic films. Joanne Woodward's Eve is cured of her multiple personality via the intervention of an idealized psychiatrist, Dr. Luther (Lee J. Cobb), who combines talk therapy with hypnotic trance. The quiet, mousy, sexually repressed Eve White suffers from headaches and blackouts that prompt a referral to a psychiatrist (rather than a neurologist). By showing that Eve suffers from neurological symptoms that stem from psychological conflicts, *Eve* reifies Freudian ideas about the psychological origins of hysteria and reminds viewers that psychoanalysis upstaged nineteenth-century neurology.

The psychiatrist learns of another personality lurking beneath Eve White's mild demeanor. In a dramatic scene, the wild and racy Eve Black tries to strangle her daughter with a drapery cord. During therapy, a more integrated third personality emerges: Jane. Jane wants to live a life apart from her "alters" and apart from her husband. She initiates an amicable divorce and starts a trendy diagnosis: multiple personality disorder (MPD).

In 1970 Barbra Streisand's *On a Clear Day You Can See Forever* (1970) added to the popular appeal of MPD, which was rarely seen in psychiatry but which was becoming increasingly common in media. A television movie, *Sybil*, was made from a psychiatrist's best-selling but much-contested book. After *Sybil* aired in 1976, a wider audience learned about multiple personality disorder. The public came to believe that pretty young women could behave in dramatically differently ways, without having control over their "alters." It is noteworthy that Joanne Woodward, who starred as the MPD patient in *The Three Faces of Eve*, now played Sybil's psychiatrist.

Until then, multiple personalities were either linked to the likes of *Dr. Jekyll and Mr. Hyde*, or suggested schizophrenia (a very serious psychosis). For the word *schizophrenia* literally means "split brain" and incorrectly implies that psychosis results from two personalities that coexist within one person.

After *Sybil*, MPD took center stage and pushed hypnosis aside. Self-diagnoses of MPD soared, especially among patients previously diagnosed with borderline personality disorder or even manic depression (bipolar disorder). Some psychiatrists used hypnosis or sodium pentothal or sodium amytal (truth serum) to expose "alters." Most psychiatrists remained skeptical of this media–born-and-bred diagnosis, but a few crusaded for it. The diagnosis entered the next *Diagnostic and Statistical Manual* (*DSM*). Some of MPD's most fervent advocates were not medically trained therapists. Some were sued for their overly zealous "treatments." Some psychiatrists say that "alters" often surface after welfare recipients sign other people's names on their checks and afterward realize that they were in an altered trance state.

Horror Films about Hypnosis

The end of the 1950s brought stranger and stranger films about hypnosis. In *The Tingler* (1959), Vincent Price blends hypnosis with LSD. The mere mention of Vincent Price's name tells us that this is a horror movie, and that evil deeds will be done. In this film, women who are frightened to death are found to possess a reptilian-like "tingler" strangling their spines. The premise is preposterous, unless we recall that the Eisenhower era did "strangulate" women psychologically and that mutated monsters were popular movie fare after the nuclear bombing of Japan. Given that this was LSD's film debut, the soon-to-be legendary drug was barely known to Baby Boomers, who were just entering adolescence. Who knew what LSD could do? Hypnosis was too dated to be a show-stopper on its own; it needed to be chemically enhanced.

The Hypnotic Eye (1960) was released a year after *The Tingler*. Like *Whirlpool* and *The Tingler*, *The Hypnotic Eye* is another version of the damsel in distress. In this case, it is not just one woman who falls victim to a hypnotist, but a string of women who suffer unimaginable cruelties. This is a slasher that predated and outdid slashers. It is a *Texas Chainsaw Massacre* made before *Chainsaw*. It is also a film that highlights the dangers of nonmedical hypnosis and shows how charlatans and showmen work wonders or commit crimes, when unsupervised.

Directed by George Blair, *The Hypnotic Eye* incorporates William Castle–style gimmicks.[4] The film stars Jacques Bergerac as the Great Desmond, a Svengali-like stage hypnotist who puts attractive women in a trance on stage. Later, these women mutilate themselves in gruesome home "accidents." One woman rinses her hair in the gas burner instead of the sink. Another lowers her face into an electric fan. A third washes her face with sulfuric acid, and so on.

A police detective and his criminal psychologist partner comb for patterns among the mutilations. The detective's girlfriend grows suspicious when her best friend is disfigured after visiting Desmond. She starts her own investigation and gets hypnotized by Desmond. She is about to be disfigured as she strips naked and prepares to step into a boiling hot bathtub (as the hypnotist instructed her to do). Luckily, her detective-boyfriend arrives in time. He finds her in trance and saves her from harm. We learn that it was Desmond's wife and partner who engineered the mutilations because her own face was disfigured. As the film closes, the evil Desmond tries the same trick that we saw in *The Tingler*'s closing stunt. Desmond stares into the eyes of the audience (via the camera) and attempts to hypnotize his stage audience and film spectators. This same gimmick also appears in *Horrors of the Black Museum* (1959).

The Hypnotic Eye is more than the sensationalistic and sadistic film that it seems to be on the surface. It comments on consumerism and on the advertising industry's hold on 1950s-era women. It references Vance Packard's much-discussed *The Hidden Persuaders*. The pre-credits sequence parodies an often-aired TV shampoo commercial when it shows a woman "washing" her hair in the flames of a gas stove.

Other scenes comment on the belief that buyers are magically transformed by consumer goods. Here, the cosmetics sold through hypnotic television commercials turn into tools for scarification and self-mutilation. We can also read in references to the "willful women" from late 1940s postwar films, who were replaced by enterprising "girlfriends" who solve crimes better than their boyfriends.

Shortly after *The Hypnotic Eye* appeared, history's greatest film about hypnosis, brainwashing, and mind control was made. *The Manchurian Candidate* (1962) is as serious as *The Tingler* is silly. *Manchurian Candidate* compared hypnosis to other psychiatric approaches, such as dream analysis, and behavioral (Pavlovian) conditioning. Behaviorism was invented by Russians, and preferred by the Russian public, but was now advocated by American academicians who found psychoanalysis too unscientific to be taught in psychology classes.

Manchurian Candidate owes its intensity to its plot and its all-star cast (which includes Frank Sinatra and Angela Lansbury, among others). *Candidate* was well-timed—too well-timed, it turned out. It came on the heels of the McCarthy Era, when cinematic paranoia peaked. It also dramatized a real-life event: the capture and brainwashing of American sailors by North Korean communists a decade before. But it also debuted just before John F. Kennedy's assassination, and so was pulled from movie theaters and was not re-released for more than twenty years. This complicated film is discussed in detail in the chapter on "Cold-War Paranoia."

To sum up, let me say that an entire book can be written about hypnosis and mind-control movies. Because we have just one chapter to do justice to this subject, let us end with a mention of Woody Allen's *Curse of the Jade Scorpion* (2001). Allen spoofs two insurance brokers who fall in love, unwittingly, after a skilled but shady hypnotist tells them to do just that. The title recollects films of an earlier era: *Curse of the Hindoo Pearl* (1912), *Curse of the Crimson Idol* (1914), and *Curse of the Scarabee Ruby* (1914). Allen, as always, alludes to psychiatry in his movies. He also proves that his knowledge of film history is unimpeachable, even though his personal life is imperfect.

Like other quality comedians, Allen uses comedy to introduce an unfamiliar idea. Or he spoofs the sunset days of that idea through parody, which is a later stage of comedy that signals the object's demise. Innuendos about Woody Allen's own love life often appear in his films, along with overt references to his neuroses and his thirty-year-long analysis (which he ended when he married the Korean-born adoptee, Soon-Yi, in 1997). Knowing his pattern, we wonder if his allusions to the exotic Oriental hypnotists of the past actually allude to his hypnotic attraction to this much younger woman.

In this film, Allen does not comment on charlatan-showmen hypnotists as much as he impugns the imperceptible forces that push people into love and lust. He tells us that such forces dissipate when the trance fades and the somnambulist awakens to see the light of day. We come away wondering if this hypnotist is just another plot-driving device, or if the film prepares us for the next revelation about Woody Allen's fragile love life, as his other films did.

Whatever the upshot, Woody Allen tells us that hypnosis is a technique of the past that will never fully fade away in the future. We already know that the powers of the mind are always waiting to be tapped—for Woody Allen had already told us so in his previous thirty years of cinema. We will take a closer look at Woody's worries later.

CHAPTER 6

MADHOUSES, HAUNTED HOUSES, AND POLITICAL POLEMICS

CALIGARI TO KING OF HEARTS TO CUCKOO'S NEST

Madhouse movies have been a staple of cinema since its start. Houses in general are cinematic staples, for several reasons. Houses provide scene and setting. They can be background or center stage. Each room in the house is a unique place where action can occur. Houses come in all shapes, sizes, and styles and are interesting for that reason alone. Houses are also familiar to everyone: everyone knows what a house is. Filmmakers need familiar objects—called "fetishes" by film scholars—to make their movies identifiable as a member of its genre and therefore marketable to the masses.

Houses can become unfamiliar—or *unheimlich*, to use Freud's German word—when they become "un-house-like" and inhospitable. To fully understanding mad-houses' function in movies, we would do well to review Freud's essay *The Uncanny* (1919) (or *Der Unheimlich* or "un-house-like"). One need not agree with other aspects of Freudian psychology to appreciate this essay.

Like all of Freud's essays, this piece was written in German and later translated into English. The German title *unheimlich* deserves scrutiny. *Unheimlich* is difficult to translate into English, so difficult that entire academic articles are devoted to this word alone, as Prawar's *Caligari's Children* (1980) demonstrates. *Caligari's Children* focuses on horror films, and examines the concept of *unheimlich* with respect to haunted houses. The literal translation of *unheimlich* is equally applicable to our study of madhouses in movies.

Freud's term alludes to the creepy, crawly psychological sensation that we describe with the English term *uncanny*. Even our English word is difficult to define. But Freud's original word, *unheimlich*, literally means "un-homelike." Without the prefix, *heimlich* means "home." "Mad houses" are both *heimlich* (homelike) and *unheimlich* (un-homey) at the same time, so they serve a special function in film, and in horror film in particular.

Let me explain further. Freud struggled to identify the elements that contribute to the sensation of strangeness or eeriness or uncanniness that German-speakers know as *unheimlich*. He went on for page after page before concluding that a scene or a setting or a sensation that is as familiar as a home will cause a distinctively disturbing sensation when something is slightly out of kilter, but not so out of kilter as to render the setting unrecognizable and unfamiliar.

Freud mentioned marionettes and automatons—or dreams and madness—as examples of the uncanny, or the *unheimlich*. For marionettes and automatons are close enough to real human forms to remind us of humans. But they are different enough to induce a sense of unease and discomfort and a feeling that something is amiss. Similarly, madness is close enough to ordinary human behavior to resemble daily actions, but it is also different enough from average activity to make it uncanny. We can apply this same principle of familiarity/unfamiliarity to "homes" and "mad homes."

Madhouses automatically become *unheimlich* because they are similar to ordinary homes that house ordinary human beings. Yet madhouses have been adapted to house madmen and mad people and mad doctors. Madhouses do not house friends or relatives or even wayfarers. Madhouses are homes to people who are out of kilter and who are themselves *unheimlich*.

Movie madhouses are intentionally "un-homey." High-end sanitariums or rest homes or lodges, as seen in *Now, Voyager* (1942), *Girl, Interrupted* (1999), or *Rainman* (1988), are notable exceptions to this rule. Because madhouses automatically induce a sense of the uncanny, they are perfect settings for the strange happenings of horror films. Horror meisters recognized this quality early on and turned asylum thrillers into a distinctive subgenre of horror films. In recent years that once popular subgenre has largely faded away or has fused with supernatural subject matter. For major political, legal, and even economic shifts changed the way people get committed to madhouses and changed the types of psychiatric treatments they receive in those madhouses. I will elaborate on those political and policy changes over the next few pages.

First, let us turn back to Freud and his original essay. It is odd that Freud wrote his essay *Der Unheimlich* in the same year that *Cabinet of Dr. Caligari* premiered in 1919. Even though records tell us that Freud did not see this specific film (or any other European film), and even though we know that Freud rarely went to the legitimate theater (even though he wrote influential art and literary critiques), one nevertheless wonders if Freud was in any way familiar with *Caligari*, or if he would have discussed *Caligari* in his essay had he seen this famous film before writing his equally famous *The Uncanny*.

For *The Cabinet of Dr. Caligari* is uncanny in the extreme. Not only was it set in a madhouse and in a fairground and in a garden outside of the asylum, but its crooked streets, jagged angles, exaggerated costumes, and stilted postures of its characters made the familiar unfamiliar, causing an extreme sense of unease. Diagonal lines generally induce unease because they lack the stability of horizontal lines and are not grounded like vertical lines projecting from a surface.

Everything in *Caligari* is set at an angle, and at a deliberately disorienting angle at that. One need not understand a single word of the silent film script to sense the uncanniness of Caligari's madhouse or of the carnival. Even the opening garden scene, where two benign-looking men sit side by side talking about the story to follow, instills a sense of the uncanny. Once the film is over, and once we learn that these men are inmates in the asylum behind the garden, we realize that they themselves are mad, and that their recollections of the events may have taken place in their imaginations only. This ambiguity makes us walk away with an even greater sense of uncanniness, wondering if our own perceptions are as distorted as the intersecting angles on the famous Expressionist film set.

For this reason, and for many other reasons, *Caligari* became the prototype of the madhouse movie. Many presume that *Caligari* was the *first* film ever made about a madhouse. Yet that presumption is not true at all: *Caligari* was not even the first film ever made about a "mad doctor" (as doctors who tended to the insane were once called). Nor was it the first film about a mad doctor, or a doctor who went mad himself.

Caligari was simply the most famous of this genre, and maybe even the most memorable. Kracauer's 1947 book *From Caligari to Hitler* turned the sham psychiatrist Caligari into the standardbearer of authoritarian, despotic, diabolical, dictator-like doctors who use their twisted skills to kill rather than to cure. Kracauer claimed that Dr. Caligari foreshadowed Hitler's rise to power and predicted the German people's acceptance of the authority of the Third Reich and the Nazi killing machine.

Kracauer's arguments were not completely convincing to many readers, but they were convincing enough to the anti-authoritarian and anti-psychiatry counterculture that swept across America (and other parts of the world) in the 1960s and 1970s. In those years, activists held rallies against the state, and Yippies deliberately misspelled America as Amerika to evoke associations between the United States and Nazi-like government control. Dr. Caligari provided filmic proof (although not living proof) that psychiatrists were agents of the state. According to that reasoning, psychiatric patients were political prisoners who were held against their will because they behaved in ways that were not socially sanctioned. The asylums that housed such patients served as prisons for those who did not agree with the "establishment's" world view. Such were the philosophical views set forth by the likes of Michel Foucault.

If we examine the events in *Caligari*, we come to appreciate Kracauer's reasoning, and we also see parallels with the 1960s counterculture. The filmic Dr. Caligari was really just a madman who took over the asylum. Caligari was ready, willing, and able to subvert the will of the innocent Cesare, and to force Cesare to kill on command. Finally, Cesare's love for a woman whom Caligari ordered him to destroy brought him to his senses and allowed him to resist Caligari's commands. Cesare dies in peace instead, after rescuing his lady love, Jane.

Dr. Caligari was evil incarnate. He was as evil as the devil but was divested of past centuries' superstitions. Dr. Caligari was a real person, rather than a supernatural entity, even though he proved to be an imposter. Kracauer thought that Caligari was a man of his times: a mortal man who could kill without conscience, who could turn other men into killing machines. That had happened during World War I, which had raged just before *Caligari* was filmed.

By the time the 1960s and 1970s counterculture rolled around, another war inspired rage against authority: the Vietnam War. World War II seemed like a distant shadow to many, but not to all, and especially not to those who had lost loved ones in the war. Yet the anti-authoritarian sentiment inspired by the antiwar activists was strikingly similar to the cynical views expressed in *Caligari*. Anti-psychiatry attitudes were peaking around 1970, even though psychiatry, and psychoanalysis in particular, had enjoyed unparalleled popularity in America a decade or two earlier, and even though more and more young physicians were specializing in psychiatry, according to historian of psychiatry Edward Shorter.[1]

The counterculture credo was clear: psychiatrists could harm patients—rather than help them—when they labeled them as insane or schizophrenic. They caused further harm, perhaps permanent harm, by subjecting patients to painful, disfiguring, or potentially dangerous treatments such as shock therapy (ECT) and psychosurgery. They might not force them to murder, as Dr. Caligari did, but they could incarcerate their patients and detain them in hospitals or commit them to institutions. In other words, these psychiatrists functioned as prison wardens as much as they functioned as medical specialists. By inference, psychiatric institutions functioned as prisons as much as they functioned as hospitals. What a legacy *Caligari* left!

Besides the obvious evil-psychiatrist and fraudulent-psychiatrist theme that runs through *Caligari*, another theme runs through the film: the theme of the inmates who take over the asylum. As we know after watching the film, the man who calls himself Dr. Caligari turns out to be nothing other than a one-time carnival barker who assumed the identity of the real asylum doctor. (How reminiscent of *The Wizard of Oz*, an all-American favorite!)

The fraudulent Dr. Caligari models himself after a mountebank (carnival barker) who lived centuries earlier. Inmates knew Caligari as an imposter. The mentally ill man who tells the tale of Caligari and Cesare while sitting on a garden bench, outside the hospital proper, knows this also. Yet our storyteller conceals the fact that he is also an asylum inmate until the film ends.

This theme of the inmates taking over the asylum appeared in Edgar Allan Poe's pre–Civil War story "The System of Doctor Tarr and Professor Fether" (1845). Poe's story is simple and straightforward. *The Cabinet of Dr. Caligari*'s storyline, however, is as convoluted as the screen sets themselves. Poe's original premise about Dr. Tarr and Professor Fether found its way into films that predated *Caligari* by a decade. Edison's comedic *Lunatics in Power* (1909) and Eclair's *The System of Dr. Tarr and Professor Fether* (1912) are truer to Poe's story. We encounter a different take on this theme in *King of Hearts* (1966), another counterculture classic that is far more light-hearted than many counterculture cult films.

MADHOUSE MOVIES AND PRISON FILMS

Some academicians say that madhouse movies are a subgenre of prison films because both prisons and asylums are institutions that impose outside control on those who live inside. Insane-asylum and prison films are distinctly different from hotel films (or general hospital films), because hotel guests (or medical patients) stay voluntarily and are free to leave when they please—unless they are held hostage by intruders (to push the plot) or are too sick to move (to add to the drama).

For sure, there is some cross-over between asylums and prisons, but the overlap is imprecise. More importantly, this appealing argument overlooks the fact that madhouse movies, or sanitarium cinema, predated prison films by decades. It is patently incorrect to claim that madhouse movies evolved out of prison movies. Madhouses in movies are very old indeed, whereas prison films and gangster films came into their own in the 1920s, during the Prohibition era, when crime became commonplace, and when gangs, criminals, reform schools, and penitentiaries become sources of public concerns. It is more correct to say that prison films are a subgenre of crime films, but that leads into another subject.

The argument that equates madhouse movies with prison films is not completely illogical, even if it is incorrect. This theory evolves out of the groundbreaking sociological theories of Erving Goffman, whose book *Asylums* (1961) was a must-read for all social psychology courses of the sixties. This book remains important to our understanding of behavior changes that occur in institutionalized persons. For people who remain in hospital settings too long (or in concentration camps or other forms of detention) are known to alter their behavior, sometimes consciously, sometimes unconsciously, so that they can please their caretakers or their guards and make life in the institution more bearable. Often, inmates identify with the aggressor and emulate the mannerisms or mode of dress of their captors, no matter how much they despise their captors. Sometimes they become placid and docile and incapable of making any decisions of their own and need to have their controlling captors make all decisions for them.

Goffman made prisons and mental institutions sound similar when he listed each as examples of asylums that shape inmates' behavior. By assessing the *end effects* that asylums exert on behavior, rather than focusing on the behavior that lands people in prisons or hospitals in the first place, Goffman cast attention on the similarities between these institutions and deflected attention away from the differences of their inmates. Admittedly, criminal behavior and mental illness often co-occur. It is not at all uncommon for persons with psychiatric disorders to find themselves in the hands of the police before they find their way to medical care. The concept of "criminalizing" the mentally ill is an important issue to psychiatric patients, psychiatric practitioners, and the criminal justice system, and to cinematic subjects as well, although filmmakers deal with this issue very differently than psychiatric policymakers do.

Goffman wrote decades before criminalization of the mentally ill became a catchword. (Ken Kesey's novel, *One Flew over the Cuckoo's Nest*, which was written just a few years later, took the opposite approach, and revolved around a criminal who *pretended* to be insane, rather than about a psychiatric patient whose bizarre behavior is mistaken for criminal intent.) In the 1960s Goffman and his colleagues cast doubt that mental illness existed as an "essential" entity. Many intellectuals of his era deemed this concept to be a social construction that maintains social order and controls politically dangerous people.

Goffman's book helped seed the anti-psychiatry movement of the mid-sixties. This anti-psychiatry movement was not the first to surface in America, but it gained momentum because it paralleled important political shifts that were occurring simultaneously. Goffman's research fortified theories of the French philosopher Michel Foucault, who wrote *Madness and Civilization* (1961) as well as *Discipline and Punish: The Birth of a Prison* (1975) and *The History of Sexuality* (1984). As his choice of research topics suggests, Foucault perceived similarities between mental institutions, criminal behavior, and "sexual transgression" (such as homosexuality and other atypical sexual expressions that he himself engaged in).

The anti-psychiatry movement that emerged from these sociological, philosophical, and historical studies opposed institutionalization and proposed the closing of asylums. This attitude was advocated by renegade psychiatrists such as Thomas Szasz, and R. D. Laing, and David Cooper. Some former mental patients joined the bandwagon and broadcast their views on the Madness Network News of counterculture radio stations such as WBAI in New York or the Pacifica Corporation. Such programs capitalized on the counterculture spirit of the times, and cinema followed suit.

Even "establishment" psychiatrists read and reread these anti-psychiatry theses, weighing the merits of these arguments before dismissing such ideas outright. Many anti-psychiatry or anti-establishment ideas filtered into mainstream psychiatry, especially because so many psychiatrists and psychiatrists-to-be were young enough themselves to be swayed by the anti-establishment youth movement. Older psychiatrists and psychoanalysts who arrived from Europe's Old World were part of the Old Guard that maintained the authority of outdated, fin-de-siècle Freudian ideas. Freud and Freudianism, once at the vanguard, shook the establishment in their day, but, like all avant-garde movements, even psychoanalysis was growing old and stale.

Freud's Victorian-style sitting room in his second home in London looked outdated compared to Laing's Kingsley Hall in London. The well-publicized and over-romanticized Kingsley Hall was the anti-institution that allowed psychotic patients to experience psychoses without intervention. There, they could work through their hallucinations and delusions. Laing's free-spirited approach to psychosis came into question decades later, when ex-patients alleged that they suffered abuses in this alternative environment, which supposedly shielded them from institutions and asylums of the establishment.

Long before these allegations against Laing and Kingsley Hall came to light, Laing himself concluded that his treatment plan caused more harm than good. He closed Kingsley Hall in 1970, but not before igniting the counterculture, and inspiring Laingian films such as *King of Hearts* (1966). Ironically, Freud's house is now a museum in North London, but Laing's Kingsley Hall is all but forgotten, except perhaps by film fans and historians of psychiatry, who recall that Kingsley Hall was used as a set for the *Gandhi* film in the 1980s.

Laing never denied the concept of insanity (which is a legal rather than medical term). He never claimed that psychosis was exclusively a social construct (as some of his counterculture contemporaries did). Rather, he maintained that society was insane, and made its members insane, so that one cannot distinguish between an insane society and insane citizens.

Curiously, both Laing himself and the soldier hero (Alan Bates) of *King of Hearts* were Scottish, even though the film was made in France and subtitled in English. Because *King of Hearts* was set during World War I, this war-themed film became an easy parable for Vietnam and for the cultural and generational conflicts that colored the late sixties. It invites comparisons to the dark-spirited *Cabinet of Dr. Caligari*, which can be read as a commentary on World War I, and which was directly influenced by its co-writer's wartime clashes with military psychiatrists.

In *King of Hearts*, however, the protagonist rejoins the asylum inmates once he concludes that the nicest people live inside the institution and that life on the outside is insane. At the end of the film, Alan Bates sheds his clothes and holds a bird cage in his hand (using a symbol that would be reused in *One Flew over the Cuckoo's Nest*). Stark naked, he knocks on the asylum door and is invited to re-enter this special world.

The film begins in late World War I, when a French army private (Alan Bates) is sent to a small French town to defuse a bomb planted by Germans. Chased by Germans before completing his mission, he seeks refuge in a local insane asylum. Not knowing that everyone else has fled the town, he sees only asylum inmates and assumes that they are typical townspeople. The psychiatric patients do not panic like ordinary citizens; they remain in town and take it over. The inmates, in turn, believe Alan Bates to be the King of Hearts and welcome him warmly. Their allusion to the Queen of Hearts of *Alice in Wonderland* is telling.

Wanting to save the inmates from the Germans, the private tries to lead them out of town. But they play in the street instead, wearing colorful costumes that recollect 1960s-era hippie clothes. Their unusual names are equally colorful and allude to wild flowers. Like many 1960s-era students who feigned insanity to get draft deferments, the soldier-hero of *King of Hearts* has thoughts about the virtues of insanity. When he realizes that he must leave the town as the film ends, he chooses insanity over sanity. This classic late-1960s film was an important and popular antiwar allegory about the antiwar era.

A film that came on the heels of *King of Hearts*, and shook up the psychiatric establishment even more, was Milos Forman's film version (1975) of Ken Kesey's novel, *One Flew Over the Cuckoo's Nest*. This film shaped society's attitudes toward psychiatric treatment and institutions as much as did academic theory. Both public and professionals shifted attitudes toward ECT, lobotomy, and involuntary institutionalization after viewing this film. It was partly in response to *Cuckoo* that California outlawed *all* ECT treatment.

In *Cuckoo's Nest*, Ken Kesey's writing skills merge with Jack Nicholson's acting abilities to stir the social unrest of the seventies. What results is an alchemical mix of the vicious and vindictive Nurse Ratched (Louise Fletcher), an abject American Indian asylum inmate, and small-time criminal and con man McMurphy (Jack Nicholson). *Cuckoo's Nest* made film history when it became one of only four films ever to capture *all* major Academy Awards.

With several assault convictions already on record, McMurphy (Nicholson) lands in jail again, this time for statutory rape. He claims his girlfriend lied about her age and never told him that she was fifteen. No matter, because the inept con man decides to con the prison authorities into believing that he needs psychiatric treatment that will send him to cushier conditions on the mental ward.

But his plan backfires, as the hospital proves to be deadlier and more destructive than a prison cell. He locks heads with Nurse Ratched, who controls the ward and the inmate-patients with an iron first. Unlike the snide and sneering male nurse who heads the detox ward in *Lost Weekend* (1945), Nurse Ratched oozes power and control. She is an emblem of everything that can go wrong with the newly formed feminist movement. Even in her crisp white nurse's uniform, she is deadlier than any black-garbed, spike-heeled film noir femme fatale.

When McMurphy tries to liven up the ward by playing card games and basketball with fellow inmates (and even succeeds in making some of them a little better), Nurse Ratched retaliates, locking McMurphy in solitary confinement, in straitjackets, and in a Thorazine-induced stupor. He ends up nearly comatose, an involuntary victim of shock therapy and lobotomy. By the time the psychotic "Chief" takes Nicholson's life, Nurse Ratched has already taken his spirit and left only a dead shell anyway. Nicholson now dies a peaceful death. His dead body is carried out by the inmates, as if they were carrying Christ on the cross. He is the sacrificial lamb of the counterculture, a man who sacrificed his life to combating social control.

It is important to note that politics and psychiatric policy were inseparable in the sixties and the seventies. This film is testimony to that connection. To understand the reasons behind the rise and fall of asylum cinema or madhouse movies, we must step back in time to see the dramatic changes in psychiatric policy that occurred during the French Revolution—or even earlier, when church doctors, rather than medical doctors, took charge of behavior changes.

ANCIENT ASYLUMS AND MODERN DAY ADULT HOMES

For the greater part of history, the psyche was believed to be spiritual or supernatural. The soul (or *Seele)* morphed into the "psychological" relatively late in time. The concept of the unconscious was the brainchild of the Romantic philosopher, obstetrician, and anatomist Carl Gustav Carus (1789–1869). The field of psychology was an outgrowth of natural philosophy and a late nineteenth-century invention. For most of humankind's history, mental illness was imputed to demons, djinns, or dybbuks and was the province of church doctors rather than medical doctors. This history shows us why madhouse movies, which were once so popular, faded from the picture by the late seventies and then resurfaced with supernatural subthemes at the turn of the twenty-first century.

Psychology, or the study of the psyche, was intended to be an improvement over occultism. Ironically, the founder of America's first psychology lab, William James, returned to religion in later life, and is better remembered for *The Varieties of Religious Experience* (1902) than for his Harvard psychology lectures. Carl Gustav Jung, Freud's one-time heir-apparent, devoted himself to occultism from the start and gained a loyal following because of his odd inclinations. Freud's atheism, and his musings about *The Future of an Illusion* (with religion being the illusion), was just one point of view among many competing sentiments.

Setting aside these prominent examples, history shows us that psychology and supernaturalism were locked in perpetual struggle. Efforts to free the study of the mind, or psyche, from the stranglehold of superstition seemed to have been won in late nineteenth-century Europe, but only temporarily. The tug-of-war endured. The very fact that the word *psyche* means "soul"—and that the term was a holdover from the Romantic Era, when philosophers and poets believed that the immaterial spirit existed apart from the material world—is testimony to this struggle.

M. H. Abrams, the esteemed scholar of the Romantic era, referred to Romanticism as "natural supernaturalism" because Romantic poets imputed the same lofty properties to the psyche and to nature that superstitious and religious people ascribed to totems and fetishes. Psychoanalysis emerged from Romantic thought and added Darwinian ideas about evolution from animals. The Romantic era was diametrically different from the Age of Reason, which preceded it. During the Age of Reason, it was unfashionable to attribute mental disturbances to ghosts or spirits or reincarnated souls. Naturally, not everyone was enlightened during the Enlightenment, and folk beliefs persisted, which was fortunate for filmmakers, who realized that silly superstitions were perfect plots for screen and stage. The popularity of the different versions of *The Dybbuk* proved that!

The Enlightenment was not a good time to be insane, however, because in this era that overvalued reason, it was felt that a madman who had "lost his reason" was not valuable to himself or to society. Ergo, mad people were somewhat subhuman and were denied basic human dignities. By mid-eighteenth century, most mental patients in the Western world were confined to prison-like asylums. They were chained to walls, barely clothed, poorly fed, and subjected to bodily cruelties. Considered incurable by caretakers, few received treatment.

When the French Revolution arrived in 1789, all prisoners were freed from prisons. To show sympathy with the political spirit of the day, and support for the New Regime's *Liberté, Égalité, Fraternité*, psychiatrists such as Pinel in France and Chiarugi in Italy unchained their patients. Their decisions were *not* based on clinical criteria, as would be done today. This political revolution paved the path to the Romantic era in the next century.

By the late 1800s, medical doctors had assumed more responsibility for mental symptoms and combated supernatural explanations for strange behavior. The mere fact that psychiatry once shared a heritage with superstition cemented the connection forever, at least in the minds of filmmakers. The link between the psychological and the supernatural never fully disappeared and is resuscitated for cinema whenever the opportunity arises or the social climate supports it.

For instance, *The Exorcist* (1973) was popular enough to spawn three sequels. This story about a psychiatrist-priest who sacrifices his own life while exorcising Linda Blair's demon was a good story when it first appeared in film in the seventies, at a time when the counterculture and the anti-psychiatry movement were questioning the authority of psychiatry. Experimental psychologists were calling psychoanalysis's broad, sweeping claims into question and were suggesting that psychoanalytic speculation was no better than superstition or a new religion.

The cinematic link between psychiatry and superstition was in no way limited to Catholic ritual. The perennially popular Yiddish play *The Dybbuk* predated *The Exorcist* by decades and was made into two film versions long before William Blatty wrote the novel that inspired the *Exorcist* film. *The Dybbuk* was based on the writings of S. Ansky, who lived around the time of the Russian Revolution and later wrote in Paris.

The Dybbuk tells the tragic story of a migrating spirit (*dybbuk*) that causes symptoms of mental illness in a young woman. She is "inhabited" by the unsettled spirit of a young yeshiva student who hoped to marry her, but committed suicide when their engagement vow was broken. His soul was caught in a spiritual limbo because of this suicide, and because of his dabblings in forbidden studies of mystical kabbalistic texts. She is eventually freed from his *dybbuk*, and freed from her symptoms of possession, after a rabbinical folk healer exorcises her *dybbuk* with rituals and incantations. She nonetheless dies of exhaustion, but presumably rejoins her lover after death.

The Dybbuk was made into a silent subtitled version and then into two Yiddish-language films that are each important in their own right and are also important because of their uncanny relationships to pivotal points in film history. The first film, *A Vilna Legend*, arrived in 1924, as the silent era was about to end. Two other versions (*The Vow* and *The Dybbuk*) were made in 1937, shortly before Yiddish filmmaking in Poland came to a halt after the 1939 Nazi invasion. The Nazis eventually exterminated most of Poland's Jewish population. Freud also died in 1939.

As anachronistic as such supernatural-psychiatric stories are, they never grow old. Cinematic stories about the supernatural inhabitation of asylum inmates became more appealing after asylums grew less scary. Asylums and state hospitals were emptied because of public policy changes, reimbursement problems, and shifts in psychiatric treatments. Many out-of-the-way institutions closed their doors when community-based care became the norm. The de-institutionalization movement seemed like a humane solution for asylum inmates, but it turned out to be a naive solution, as filmmaker David Cronenberg shows in *Spider* (2002), which is the sad tale of a schizophrenic man who lives out his days in a drab adult home.

Historical films such as *Quills* (2000), with Joaquin Phoenix, go several steps beyond *Spider* and remind us of horrors that were commonplace in pre–French Revolution asylums and in the asylum where Marquis de Sade was imprisoned. For the most part, *Quills* acts as an artistic excuse for showing sadism on screen. It graphically depicts Marquis de Sade's tongue excision, which is carried out on the order of a priest (Joaquin Phoenix) who later goes insane himself and ends up in a cell of the asylum. Even after the French Revolution, horrors still occurred in asylums, institutions, or mental hospitals, whatever they were called. The infirm, the impecunious, and the insane were housed with petty criminals. The settings were scary and the treatments brutal. Patients were dunked into water, were spun around while suspended, and were shocked, beaten, or simply starved. In short, filmmakers did not have to invent horrors for their asylum thrillers. They only needed to turn the pages of the history books to find horror films.

When nickelodeons opened in 1905, such abuses were rife, in spite of reformers' efforts to prevent them. Relatives could commit vulnerable people to mental institutions and leave them with little recourse for appeal. Rest cures and "taking the waters" were also common, but were reserved for the well-to-do, as seen in Charlie Chaplin's comedy *The Cure* or in that classic "woman's picture," or "weepie," from the forties, *Now, Voyager* (1942), in which Bette Davis's character received compassionate care from a psychiatrist portrayed by Claude Rains. Others endured experiences that mirrored Olivia de Havilland's *The Snake Pit* (1948).

Long before *The Snake Pit* appeared in 1948, other reformers had spoken out about mental illness. Clifford Beers's autobiographical book *The Mind That Found Itself* (1908) was the most influential of this ilk. Beers probably suffered from manic depression (bipolar disorder). He was tireless in his campaign against abuses and indignities inflicted on mental patients and was instrumental in founding the mental hygiene movement, which had its counterparts in film. Some 1930s movies about the social causes—and cures—of criminality are believed to reflect Beers's efforts.

Likewise, Beers gained support because of such films as Jimmy Cagney's *The Mayor of Hell* (1933) and *Angels with Dirty Faces* (1939). These films increased opposition to reform schools and gained support for psychiatry and social work instead. A decade later, when we see an orphan boy sent off to "boy's school" in *Gun Crazy* (1948), we see this sentence as excessive, and understand that the judge's lack of understanding drove the young boy to worse crime.

By the end of the thirties, drastic procedures such as lobotomies arrived in America. First discovered in Portugal by Antonio Egas Moniz in 1935, lobotomies were imported when European psychiatrists emigrated to America. As horrific as this procedure sounds, some patients found welcomed relief from lifelong suffering through this simple surgery. Unfortunately, it was not long before such surgeries were overused and abused.

One would expect that lobotomies scenes went hand in hand with so-called asylum thrillers, and that such surgery would be common in these films. But the fact is that "brain exchanges" were featured in the very first decade of film, long before lobotomies were invented. Furthermore, most lobotomies were performed in doctor's offices and were done with ice picks. Psychosurgery was simple enough to schedule during lunch. Lobotomies are so easy that they rarely make for good movie scenes, with Hannibal the Cannibal's kitchen-table lobotomy on Ray Liotta (and his gourmet sauté of Liotta's forebrain) being a notable exception to this rule.

Of course, we know that filmmakers do not follow the same regulations that physicians follow, and we know that moviemakers often bend the rules of reality to add to the drama, to push the plot, or to accentuate the art direction. As an example, the psychiatrists at the stately old mansion in *Spellbound* (1945) are shown performing surgery, even though "real" psychiatrists never operate in a "real" psychiatric rest home (nor do they commit murder-suicide).

When Universal Studios made their classic horror films in the early thirties, they did not need asylums or brain surgery or even shock therapy to scare spectators. *Frankenstein*, *Dracula*, and *The Mummy* stood on their own merits, without institutions, although Count Dracula's sidekick, Renfield, made it known that he had spent time in an asylum before becoming the count's chauffeur. *Frankenstein* was reanimated through ordinary electricity that was available when Mary Shelley wrote the story upon which it was based. It just so happened that shock therapy arrived soon after the classic *Frankenstein* film appeared, so that the frightening Dr. Frankenstein inadvertently added to the fears that surrounding this new electroshock treatment.

By the late thirties, ECT had replaced the earlier and more dangerous insulin coma therapy and the chemically induced comas. The invention of the electroencephalogram (EEG) in 1929 made it possible to monitor brain waves and administer electricity more safely. Both ECT and EEGs were good for film scenes, because they are visually graphic and enhance the art direction and general drama. EEGs show interesting patterns, and ECT causes dramatic thrashing. ECT was even more visually striking before muscle relaxants were invented, with patients flailing about during seizures, often breaking limbs.

Shock therapy became a film staple for many years, and was used in serious films as well as B movies. One example is Joan Crawford's portrayal of a wronged woman who was found wandering around, nearly catatonic, in *Possessed* (1947). *Shock Corridor* (1963) is another. *Shock Corridor* revolves around a reporter who ventures into a mental ward to get a story but sinks into a state of catatonia instead. It plays upon unconscious fears of contagion and implies that those who come too close to the mentally ill might catch it themselves. The list of shock films goes on and on.

Horror films and melodramas alike exploited ECT themes. *Shock* (1946), with Vincent Price, describes an unhappily married psychiatrist who accidentally murders his wife during an argument. His neighbor witnesses the murder, in *Rear Window* style. She goes into shock in response, and is brought to a sanitarium by her well-meaning husband, who hopes to cure her condition. Unfortunately, the asylum is run by none other than the murderous Dr. Cross (Vincent Price), who plans to administer an overdose to silence her forever.

Vincent Price's name on a film was a buzzword for horror. He was also associated with evil psychiatrists. In the late 1950s, he played a psychiatrist who administers both LSD and hypnosis in *The Tingler* (1959).

Not all films about ECT or institutions are horrific. *Fear Strikes Out* (1957) is a (relatively) true-to-life story of a real baseball player who suffers a breakdown, presumably because of pressure from his overbearing coach-father, who never made it to the majors himself. The catatonic ball player is partly cured through compassionately administered ECT and went on to play ball, coach, and become a broadcaster (before he was fired for making inappropriate comments that are now believed to be symptomatic of his bipolar disorder). The ballplayer is played by Anthony Perkins, who later achieved cinematic immortality as *Psycho*'s terribly troubled transvestite, Norman Bates. This same year brought another pro-psychiatry classic, *Three Faces of Eve* (1957).

As late as 1982, the shock value of shock therapy was too much for filmmakers to resist, and shock therapy found its way into an action-adventure film, *Death Wish II* (1982). In *Death Wish II,* the ECT machine became a convenient killing machine. When Charles Bronson chases the villain through a hospital and sees the villain stuck in an ECT machine, he throws the switch, sends the villain into seizures, and causes film's first ECT fatality.

When *Cuckoo's Nest* appeared the same year, with its riveting scenes of Jack Nicholson subjected first to ECT and then to a lobotomy, audiences were primed to see ECT as evil. They reacted rashly to the political polemics of *Cuckoo's Nest*. Electroconvulsive therapy was repeatedly portrayed as bad, and talk therapy as good, even when ECT was the only treatment that saved someone from suicide. *Good Will Hunting* (1997), a film that portrays the rule-bending nonmedical psychologist Robin Williams positively, and the medically oriented MD negatively, was the classic of this kind.

One would think that ECT and surgery were the most gruesome psychiatric treatments in history. Not so. Some treatments never made it to the silver screen, did not achieve the widespread public notoriety, and are subjects of academic study only. A particularly horrific (but effective) treatment was fever therapy, which caused convulsions that were induced by injections of malaria-infected serum. This discovery won psychiatrist Julius Wagner-Jauregg a Nobel Prize in 1927, and it cured some patients of neurosyphilis-induced psychosis.

Hydrotherapy (which was vaguely reminiscent of the witch dunkings of the Middle Ages) was also employed, and it appeared in early silent cinema shorts. Leather restraints, straitjackets, and a variety of other uncomfortable devices were once common currency in mental hospitals. These devices are rarely used today and are governed by many legal restrictions, but they are still useful for film scenes that sublimate sadomasochistic impulses of audiences or actors.

The big shift in treatment came in the early fifties, with the invention of the "major tranquilizer" Thorazine (chlorpromazine). Thorazine could stop hallucinations and delusions without putting patients to sleep. Previously violent psychiatric patients became placid. Unfortunately, some twenty years after its discovery, Thorazine was found to cause serious movement disorders after long-term use. It eventually fell out of favor. However, for the generation that grew up just after World War II, Thorazine was a miracle drug that freed paranoid patients from imaginary persecution. This "chemical restraint" substituted for physical restraints and rubber rooms.

For the first time in years, some seriously schizophrenic patients could leave institutions, return to their families, and live out their lives, quietly and relatively comfortably. And thus the de-institutionalization movement began. As Thorazine decreased the need for lengthy stays in scary mental institutions, mental institutions became less scary. Unfortunately, Thorazine also "zombified" patients: it made them move stiffly, robbed them of facial expressions, and stripped them of signs of human will. The advances brought about by Thorazine did not bring nirvana. What they did bring was a rash of zombie movies, which just happened to coincide with the McCarthy era and the Cold War paranoia that accompanied the House Un-American Activities committee (HUAC) investigations. Films such as *Invasion of the Body Snatchers* (1956) were intended as covert political commentary about HUAC and McCarthy and "communist plants," but this film and others of its ilk could also be seen as commentaries on the so-called Thorazine shuffle.

Once patients started returning home, at least for short stays, and once relatively few patients needed the lengthy hospital stays that hallmarked the pre-Thorazine era, psychiatrists grew overly optimistic. By the 1960s, psychoanalysts were taking over institutional psychiatry and pushing the old asylum doctors aside. More and more, asylums were replaced by mostly office-based private practice. Psychoanalysts and psychoanalytically informed psychiatrists typically opposed institutionalization or used it as a last resort. When confinement was necessary, it took place at high-class, high-price, home-like places such as the Menninger Clinic in the Midwest,

Stoney Lodge in Vermont, Austin-Riggs in Baltimore, or McLean's outside of Boston. Green Acres in *Spellbound* epitomized such institutions, and Bette Davis's art classes in *Now, Voyager* showed such long-term, *Magic Mountain*-type of rest homes at their best.

The idea of committing a relative to a public institution like Bellevue or Bedlam was abhorrent to anyone who could afford otherwise, especially after Boris Karloff starred in a film called *Bedlam* (1946), or after Olivia de Havilland's performance in *The Snake Pit* (1948). In the interim, several riveting films about shock therapy and asylums made their way to the screen. Such films as *Shock Corridor* (1963) played on fears of entering a locked psychiatric ward and never leaving.

The fifties turned into the sixties, and the social unrest and opposition to authority that struck the mid-sixties made its way to psychiatrist institutions. Even psychiatrists who believed in the concept of mental illness and disagreed with Szasz's ideas about *The Myth of Mental Illness* (1961) nevertheless rode the political waves and took up the banner of deinstitutionalization, much as Pinel and Chiarugi had during the French Revolution. Their hopes buoyed by the early successes of Thorazine, many prominent psychiatrists pressured politicians to close large institutions and move mental patents back into the community.

Films such as *King of Hearts* and *David and Lisa* (1962) played into the romantic ideal of insanity. Oddly enough, there are similarities between *King of Hearts* and *Caligari*, even though the light-hearted and colorful comedy of *King of Hearts* seems worlds away from the dark and dismal German Expressionist *Caligari*. But *Caligari* can be read as a reinterpretation of Poe's story about Dr. Tarr and Professor Fether, where inmates take over the asylum. In *Caligari*, the result is evil because the inmate is evil. In *King of Hearts*, the result is positive because mental illness is seen as a superior state and psychiatric patients are inherently superior in a world that has been corrupted by war and crime and capitalism.

Years after policies for deinstitutionalization were put into place, the psychiatrists who pushed for this policy admitted that this was the worst decision that could have been made. Many mental patients did worse, rather than better, without trained staff to care for them. Mental hospital movies were worse for wear, also. With more and more legal constraints against involuntary commitments to hospitals in place, and with more safeguards against sadistic treatments, asylums were no longer the threat that they once were. So the fear induced by asylum thrillers grew weaker. The genre would either disappear, or it had to be reinvented.

In the meantime, a few updates of the old-fashioned romanticized rest homes appeared. Besides *King of Hearts* and *David and Lisa*, there were *Lilith* (1964) and *I Never Promised You a Rose Garden* (1977). The much later movie, *Girl, Interrupted* (1999), occurs in an upscale sanitarium (Austin Riggs) that is now an endangered institution because of managed care cutbacks on reimbursement. If it is any recompense, it should be said that Angelina Jolie's award-winning performance in *Girl, Interrupted* is worlds away from *David and Lisa*'s love story. *Girl, Interrupted* is a hate story rather than a love story. It evokes no emotional sympathy for Jolie's sociopathic character, although her appearance provokes sexual responses from those so inclined.

The best of the latter-day "good" mental hospital movies was *Rainman* (1988), which starred Dustin Hoffman as the autistic older brother Raymond. Tom Cruise is the "normal" but narcissistic son of a controlling father who leaves his fortune to Raymond's mental hospital and leaves Cruise with only a car. *Rainman* chronicles the younger brother's struggles to accept his autistic brother's limitations. Hoffman won an Oscar for his portrayal of the stilted autistic savant who must eat pancakes on Mondays and avoids all eye contact. The psychiatrist who heads this upscale institution is surprisingly capable of communicating both with impaired patients and with relatives who need "psycho-education." He does not get flustered when Cruise abducts Hoffman and takes him on a cross-country joyride in his inherited car. For he is confident from the start that Cruise will recognize Raymond's limitations and return him.

Most mental patients do not spend their days in upscale residences like *Rainman*'s. More of the de-institutionalized wander the streets, live in homeless shelters, or are confined to "adult homes" or halfway houses. Their living conditions are often squalid, and may not be any better than the living conditions in the old-time insane asylums or "funny farms." It is not uncommon to read about scandals occurring in adult homes. Sometimes psychiatric patients are subjected to unnecessary (but not unprofitable) operations. Other times, their money is stolen by unscrupulous home operators. It is not rare to hear of deaths in adult homes that burn to the ground because bad wiring or overcrowding interfered with emergency evacuations during fires.

Few films deal with this disturbing and comparatively undramatic setting and subject matter. David Cronenberg's *Spider* (2002) is one film that does, but it features a halfway house in the United Kingdom rather than in the United States. Made by a Canadian director who specializes in mining odd mental states and strange behavior and weaving them into futuristic sci-fi–like tales, *Spider* is uncharacteristically realistic for Cronenberg. It is based on the novel by Patrick McGrath. *Spider* follows the footsteps of a schizophrenic man who is poignantly played by Ralph Fiennes. The film enters his chaotic mind and unfolds it, scene by scene. The opening sequence warns about the gravity of Spider's plight when it says that "the only thing worse than losing your mind is finding it again."

The protagonist lives a joyless, loveless, useless life that centers around a squalid adult home that is run by an embittered, older, unmarried woman (Lynn Redgrave). Redgrave shows none of the idealism of volunteers who put in unpaid shifts to help the homeless. She shows none of the professionalism of nurses, nuns, or social workers. Redgrave is indifferent at best and insulting at worst, but she is not as malevolent as *Cuckoo's Nest*'s Nurse Ratched. Spider heeds her real-life put-downs at the same time that he hallucinates his mother's contemptuous chastisements, heard courtesy of an endless tape loop that plays in his schizophrenic head.

Unlike *Cuckoo's Nest*, which invoked anger and aroused people to political protests, *Spider* merely makes us feel the pain of the protagonist. This film is difficult to watch, in spite of the stellar performance by its cast. *Spider*'s low lighting and simple set design recollect German Expressionist details, but they also remind us that *Spider* sets are not an affectation. *Spider* is for real, and an ugly reality is never as charming as a contrived nightmarish vision like *Caligari*.

One might think that the decline of asylums would have stopped production of asylum thrillers once and for all, but this once tried-and-true theme was too good to abandon. It simply needed to be spiffed up a bit, and made scarier, even if that meant adding supernatural elements to realistic details. Hollywood producers mined the distant past, and produced a new sub-subgenre: supernatural asylum thrillers. This achievement was relatively easy, and it was also credible, considering that demonic possession, psychosis, and seizures were once considered to be one and the same. The success of the *Exorcist* (parts I, II, III) proved that even educated audiences could be convinced that ghosts and spirits and demons lurk in the minds of the mentally ill.

House on Haunted Hill (1999), the remake, is an excellent example of the supernatural asylum thriller. This turn-of-the-millennium remake tells the story of an eccentric millionaire who offers guests $1,000,000 to spend the night in a so-called haunted house (this was a cost of living increase from the original's offer of $10,000 in 1959). It just so happens that this house was once an insane asylum where inmates were mercilessly killed by an insane doctor who conducted unspeakable Nazi-like experiments them. We witness room after room of concentration camp–type horrors that were inflicted on mental patients before we (and the dinner guests) realize that the mansion is haunted by their spirits.

The original 1959 William Castle classic was much campier and less philosophical than the remake. It starred Vincent Price as the millionaire playboy mansion owner who hates his gold-digging, philandering wife enough to stage her murder. In the original, one of the greedy guests is a psychiatrist who scoffs at the house's haunted history. In the opening scenes of the gimmick-laden 1959 version, guests receive party favors: loaded handguns, packed in tiny coffins. Blood drips from the ceiling as zombie-like apparitions float through rooms. Severed heads and skeletons appear out of nowhere—before a guest is found hanging in the stairwell. To compete with TV, which appeared in most households in the 1950s, Castle used gimmicks galore.

As the twentieth century drew to a close, and as the millennial spirit captured film audiences and filmmakers alike, the abstract concept of the liminal (the betwixt and between state) found its way into film. Films such as *Jacob's Ladder* (1990) and *The Jacket* (2005) focused on the bardo state, which occurs during the transition between earthly existence and the other world, whatever and wherever that world may be. Psychosis has a prominent feature in such films, since the borderline between sanity and insanity is a "betwixt and between" state in its own right.

In *The Jacket*, Adrian Brody portrays a beleaguered mental patient who is confined to a straitjacket. He is subjected to cruel hospital experiments and locked in a morgue-like chamber in his last moments of life. It is not until the last few minutes of film that we realize his "hallucinations" of cruelties and indignities occurred in actuality. His recollections are real, even though he experiences his life as a series of flashbacks as he lies dying. For he has suffered head trauma and subsequent amnesia and confusion after stopping by the roadside, as a good Samaritan, trying to protect a child from a drunk-driving mother.

The debate about asylums and institutions is yet completed. Today, some politicians and the public (but not psychiatrists), want to commit sex offenders to mental hospitals *after* their prison terms are completed. What bad psychiatric practice this is, but what good movies it will make! We know how popular Freddy was! Freddy the burnt child molester appeared in the many *The Nightmare on Elm Street* films. Given the current political climate, we should not be surprised if we see Freddy or his ilk again, resuscitated in a brave new breed of asylum thrillers.

CHAPTER 7

PSYCHOLOGICAL THRILLERS AND SERIAL KILLERS AND THE MOTIF OF MADNESS

NOVELS TO FILMS

The very existence of the term *psychological thriller* testifies that psychology seeped into cinema. Almost everyone has heard this term, yet few can define it. In a book called *Movies and the Modern Psyche*, it would be unthinkable to omit mention of psychological thrillers, or to devote anything less than a full chapter to this subject. Yet it is exceedingly difficult to define psychological thrillers with certainty.

Many genres are identified by icons or fetishes associated with the genre. Westerns show spurs and saddles, and noirs have slinky dresses and spiked heels. But psychological thrillers cannot show the mind on screen, although they can depict dream scenes.

One can look to literature or radio, which also include psychological thrillers as a category of novel or broadcast. Theoretically, we could borrow literary definitions of psychological thrillers, as was done when literature departments spawned the first academic film departments and adapted literary theory to film studies. Before resorting to such tactics, I prefer to find film-specific characterizations of this genre.

Because of my own difficulties with delineating psychological thrillers, I decided to do an informal survey of those in the know—or those who should be "in the know"—namely, managers of high-end video stores and former film majors. For here I was, an author of an academic book about *Dreams in Myth, Medicine, and Movies* who once taught media studies classes, and I could not offer an exact answer. This subject obviously required research.

When asked to define psychological thrillers, some say, "I know one when I see one." Others retort, "Isn't that a way of saying that the film is boring and slow?" One video store owner said that "psychological thrillers" are "more intellectual" than ordinary "action-adventure" movies or "mystery-suspense" stories. Others think that this is an outdated term used for marketing purposes only, since the prime time to market psychological thrillers has come and gone, especially now that serial killers are a separate subgenre.

Had I not seen an ad for a "psychological thriller" in the *New York Times* in August 2006, I might have agreed that this expression is obsolete, or that films that could be characterized as psychological thrillers now fall under different or more fashionable headings. Many films—especially successful or memorable films—cross genres well enough to be marketed or shelved as something more striking or sensational than psychological thriller.

For instance, high-end video stores, such as Kim's in New York, shelve films by directors rather than genre. Hitchcock has a section, as does Fritz Lang. We all know that Hitchcock was the master of mystery-suspense movies and of psychological thrillers, whatever they are. German Expressionism and French New Wave and Japanese manga movies merit their own shelves in some video stores, but psychological thrillers have disappeared from category headings. Luckily, top video stores preserve the original box art from 1940s and 1950s favorites, so we sometimes see "PSYCHOLOGICAL THRILLER" splattered across the covers.

Indeed, when we search the current determinants of genre—mainly Moviephone, Videohound, or Fandango—we find no heading for psychological thriller whatsoever. Videohound, that humongous compendium of films available on video or DVD, has a single category that sounds vaguely similar to psychological thriller: "psycho thriller." Those words tell us how this term has mutated over time, possibly because the word *psychological* is hardly as cutting-edge as it was in the forties and fifties. The expression *psycho thriller* suggests that the motif of madness has more cache today.

Alternatively, this term may have mutated into psycho thrillers because serial killers came into their own after the Manson murders (which claimed the life of Roman Polanski's actress-wife, Sharon Tate, star of *Valley of the Dolls*). Neither we (nor the producers of the *Hannibal* series) can forget the fact that we live in a post–Jeffery Dahmer era that makes Leopold and Loeb's single murder in Hitchcock's *Rope* (1948) look charitable in comparison.

Before then, the movie world made do with the gruesome deeds depicted in Fritz Lang's *M* (1931). In a world that regularly witnesses serial killers and multiple murders, the loss of a single life is less shocking than it was when Richard Speck severed the lives (and breasts) of eight Filipino student nurses. Speck killed in the same city (Chicago) where two wealthy young boys committed the homoerotic murder that inspired Hitchcock's psychological thriller.

Given the problems with characterizing cinematic psychological thrillers, let us see what the literary world says about this subject. According to an amateur reviewer on Amazon.com, "psychological thrillers are different from any other type of literature. They go deeper than the average crime novel. They are more sinister than the average general fiction novel. They create chills, but not with blood and guts and gore and serial killers (well, okay, sometimes there ARE serial killers)."

Most importantly, "they mess with your mind." The reviewer then says that "you can't help turning pages, desperate to find out what will happen next but at the same time almost dreading the next twist. There is no one definition for a psychological thriller—everyone has his own opinion . . . a psychological thriller is a 'slow burner,' where the tension builds inexorably. There is no escape, no cop-out, no cavalry riding to the rescue. The characters are also carefully, delicately constructed. Even the most monstrous serial killer is fleshed out artfully. Some psycho-thrillers also fall under the umbrella of crime novels, while others do not."

The general consensus is that psychology figures into the narratives of novels that are termed psychological thrillers. Consistent themes pertain to reality, perception, mind, questions about existence or purpose, issues of identity, and deliberations about death. Characters often try to determine what is true and what is not. Perception is distorted, because they misperceive the world around them or because their perceptions are altered by outside factors. The mind itself is a powerful force in the psychological thriller, and it is often used as a location for narrative conflict. Characters often battle their own minds to reach a new level of understanding or perception.

Alternatively, characters concern themselves with questions of existence or life's purpose and use the narrative's conflict to discover the reasons for their existence. Other characters are preoccupied with identity, because they are either confused about their identity or have forgotten it due to amnesia or brain injury or a drug that was administered to them. Death is also a prominent theme in psychological thrillers, either because characters are threatened with death, or cause someone else's death, or ruminate about—or even fake—their own death.

When literary types try to distinguish between psychological thrillers and general thrillers, they claim that thrillers focus on plot, whereas psychological thrillers focus on characters. This distinction poses a problem for film. For film's greatest virtue is its ability to capture action and movement. Critics such as David Lodge see this quality as film's greatest fault. In *Consciousness and the Novel*, Lodge laments that films that translate novels for the screen typically omit internal dialogue for the sake of "showing" rather than "telling."

Of course, film fans admire the medium's ability to animate. Many movie lovers admire Alfred Hitchcock above all because he can tell a story without words. It is curious that Hitchcock is the director most closely associated with psychological thrillers. Hitchcock insisted on storyboarding his films, and replaying films without sound, to ensure that the plot was apparent without any dialogue at all. (Some say that Hitchcock's start in the silent cinema enabled him to make this transition, while others claim that Hitchcock's alcohol-induced memory lapses demanded that he storyboard scrupulously, lest he forget last night's work).

Whatever the reasons behind Hitchcock's amazing abilities, it is generally accepted that Hitchcock's abilities were amazing. *Spellbound* (1945), *Psycho* (1960), *Rope* (1948), *Strangers on a Train* (1951), *I Confess* (1953), and *Dial M for Murder* (1954) testify to his skills in this murky genre of psychological thriller. The mere fact that comedian Mel Brooks, Woody Allen's contemporary, saw fit to satirize Hitchcock thrillers in his hilarious *High Anxiety* (1977) further proves Hitchcock's impact on several generations of spectators. I will talk about Hitchcock's psychological thrillers after we examine the first psychological thriller, from 1931.

M IS FOR MURDER, AND MUCH MORE

M (1931) was the brainchild of Fritz Lang and his then-wife, Thea von Harbou. *M* was Lang's first sound film, although he had directed over a dozen films before *M* and many after. Some of his films are clear-cut psychological thrillers, and others are classic cloak-and-dagger mystery-suspense. His early endeavor, *Metropolis* (1927), is a forerunner of sci-fi. Many consider *M* to be Lang's greatest achievement in his large body of work. This film borrows from opera and uses a musical leitmotif—*In the Hall of the Mountain King*—to give the film score depth and definition.

M is the story of a child-molester and murderer who roamed the streets of Berlin. It is believed to be based on the real-life case of serial killer Peter Kürten, the "Vampire of Düsseldorf," whose 1920s crimes still resonated when the film premiered. Peter Lorre played the loner, schizotypal murderer. His raspy voice, bulging eyes, and emotive acting (a holdover from the silent screen) always make him memorable, whatever his role.

Lorre's character roams the shadowy streets. Lang's camera catches his lonesome meanderings, with a sensitivity that many talkie producers lost after sound evolved. Later, we watch Lorre offering ice cream cones to an unsuspecting little girl whom he later abducts and strangles (and presumably molests prior to her death). Lorre eludes the police, the detectives, the entire city. His acts are so unconscionable that even the criminal underground is shaken up, first by the police who suspect them of these sinister acts, and then by their own disgust at the thought of being mistaken for something so contemptible as a child murderer and molester.

As the film opens, a circle of girls play a game that revolves around a rhyme about a child murderer. This foreshadows the appearance of Hans Beckert (Lorre), the serial killer who terrorizes Berlin's children (and their parents). The audience is not allowed to see the face of the would-be murderer at this point. We see only his shadow and long shots of his body, and we hear him whistle the theme from *In the Hall of the Mountain King* as he buys a balloon from a blind man. He gives the balloon to the little girl he intends as his next victim.

The next scene shows the little girl's mother frantically searching for her daughter. The audience watches the balloon fly into the air. The audience's privileged view intensifies the tension, and makes spectators more uneasy, because they know that something sinister is about to happen. Yet they, like the girl's mother, cannot intervene.

The police are as powerless as the audience. The murderer eludes their efforts. Still, they stage raids and round up the usual suspects and use modern criminological methods, such as fingerprinting and handwriting analysis. Soon the criminal world starts to compete with the police in the race to capture the child killer.

Eventually, the murderer reappears and makes the mistake of whistling near the same blind balloon salesman. The blind man is hypersensitive to sounds. He takes note of the tune and confides his suspicions to one of the criminals. The criminal tails the killer, but first marks his hand with chalk so he can tag the man, should he elude him again. When Peter Lorre tries to skulk away, the criminal marks a large letter M on the killer's top coat in chalk.

The gothic letter M, which appears in bright white, induces a chill for reasons that extend beyond the plot. This M appears in the gothic print that became the Third Reich's trademark. When *M* was made, Hitler was two years away from taking command in Germany. One cannot view Lang's *M*, and see such emotion-laden gothic lettering, without seeing signs of the coming of Hitler and the Holocaust, and the world's worst mass murder of children and adults alike.

At least that is what Siegfried Kracauer saw when he looked at Lang's film, and when he wrote *From Caligari to Hitler* in 1947, after he had arrived in America.

But the film is not over yet, and its links to the Third Reich have just begun. For the criminals capture the child murderer Beckert and bring him to a kangaroo court. There, Beckert delivers an impassioned plea to the jury. He claims that he did not want to commit these crimes, and that he should be acquitted because he is insane. The monologue ends when Lorre screams, "Who knows what it's like to be me?"

Lorre's climactic speech was appropriated by Joseph Goebbels for the Nazi propaganda film *The Eternal Jew* (1940), which blamed Jews for bombarding German culture with "degenerate" art. The propaganda film prepared Germans for the genocide that began in 1941. Noting that Lorre was Jewish, *The Eternal Jew* used Lorre's speech in *M* as further "proof" that Jews transmit inheritable criminality and therefore deserve to die.

Today when we watch *M,* many of us are mindful of the movie's political implications and of its eerie connection to the Holocaust. We can also look to Lang's masterpiece, and Lorre's masterful acting, for parallels with contemporary culture. For twenty-first-century America singles out child molesters, or sex offenders, as society's most evil villains. We tend to think that the pursuit of child molesters is a construction of contemporary American culture, and that Megan's Law and the push to imprison molesters in mental hospitals after they complete prison terms are recent ideas. This film proves otherwise. It highlights the power that the child molester/murderer holds for the popular imagination, especially when depicted by a director of Fritz Lang's talents.

Lang had no way of knowing that twenty-first-century psychiatric research would prove that persons with schizotypal personality disorders are more prone to paraphilias, or sexual perversions, than the average person. Such odd and isolated people fall short of being diagnosed as schizophrenics because they do not develop delusions or imaginary dialogues. Instead, they have peculiar perceptions and live lonely and loveless lives, like Peter Lorre's character in *M.* Nor did Lang have any way of knowing that his worst fears about child murder, or murder in general, would come to pass after the Nazis took power and Hitler became chancellor, two years after *M* debuted. For child murder (specifically, the murder of Jewish children) would be officially sanctioned by the state a decade later.

One might say that Hitchcock's 1954 psychological thriller *Dial M for Murder* plays upon the title of Lang's *M.* One can also say that Hitchcock's *Rope* (1948) continued a current that Lang put in place when he made *M* in 1931. Many may argue with these theories, but few disagree that Hitchcock perfected the psychological thriller, and carried it to its finest extremes.

HITCHCOCK'S CONTRIBUTION

Hitchcock's *Rope* is lean and mean. It lacks the twists and turns of many psychological thrillers. *Rope* was based on a play about a true crime committed in 1924: Leopold and Loeb's murder of fourteen-year-old Bobby Franks in a mansion-studded neighborhood on Chicago's south side. Meyer Levin's highly publicized novel *Compulsion*

(1956) called more attention to Hitchcock's thriller. The Leopold-Loeb case itself was called "The Trial of the Century."

The trial, and the events leading up to it, became a legal landmark when the wealthy college boys were defended by Clarence Darrow, who was already sixty-seven. A lifelong opponent of the death penalty, Darrow gave an impassioned twelve hour plea to the jury that saved the boys from the death penalty. Loeb, however, died in prison at the age of thirty, killed by another inmate in an attack that was less gruesome than that suffered by serial killer Jeffrey Dahmer.

Darrow claimed that both boys learned to kill at the University of Chicago, where they received the finest education. A college education, and a law school education, which Leopold obtained, was a privilege reserved for the wealthy in 1924. Darrow pointed out that the boys studied Nietzsche and learned about his concept of the *Übermensch* [*Superman*], who lived above ordinary morality. They emulated Nietzschean ideals by murdering young Bobby Franks.

The murderers were more than mere friends. One was believed to be a paranoid schizophrenic who had grandiose delusions that were reminiscent of the delusions that Nietzsche developed in the late stages of neurosyphilis. The other, it was hinted, was secretly homosexual, and followed the lead of the stronger partner. Both boys strived to commit the perfect crime, even though they lived in luxury and had impressive academic achievements. Their "perfect crime" was uncovered by a Polish immigrant who found Leopold's eyeglasses, left near the boy's body.

Plotting the crime and winning the case were complicated, but Hitchcock's execution is striking in its simplicity. The film is shot in one location, and it looks like a single camera shot (even though several editing seams are apparent to the skilled observer).

In the film version, two brilliant aesthetes, Brandon Shaw (John Dall) and Phillip Morgan (Farley Granger) plan the perfect murder based on lectures given by their former housemaster, Rupert Cadell (James Stewart).

The young men in the movie (who are older than Leopold and Loeb were when they committed their crime) invite a former classmate to their apartment for drinks. They then strangle him, and hide his body in a chest, to show their innate superiority. Immediately afterward, they host a party in their apartment and set candelabras on the chest that contains the body. The guests include the victim's father and aunt, his fiancee and her former boyfriend, and Rupert (Stewart).

Intending to impress the older, sophisticated, and inspirational Rupert, Brandon drops hints about David's murder and starts a discussion on the art of murder. The conversation focuses on David, the murdered man, his connection to the guests, and his unexplained absence. As often occurs in psychological thrillers, spectators have privileged information that they are "dying" to share with actors on screen. The spectator grows uncomfortable because of this privileged information: tension mounts internally, and the psychological impact increases.

Spectators are not the only ones who experience distress. Unlike Brandon, Phillip gets more anxious during the party, especially when his former headmaster Rupert (Stewart) interrogates him about David's absence and uncovers inconsistencies in his story. Throughout this time, Brandon fingers the rope used to strangle their unfortunate friend. He parades this evidence in front of everyone, but no one suspects, not yet.

The clincher comes at the end of the party, as Rupert prepares to leave. While standing near the hallway closet, he is handed someone else's hat by mistake. He looks inside, and sees the initials D.K. (for David Kently, the name of the missing friend). Rupert grows uneasy but departs nonetheless, only to return a little while later, his suspicions having increased. The audience's tension also increases. The hat reminds us of the lost eyeglasses that linked Leopold to the murder.

Rupert reenters the apartment, saying that he misplaced his cigarette case somewhere in the house. He plants his cigarette case, and then finds it himself, but has bought himself time to theorize about David's disappearance. Brandon encourages his speculations, seemingly enjoying the repartee. When Rupert lifts the chest's lid and sees the body inside, he realizes that his former students murdered David. He is horrified, rather than impressed as Brandon anticipated. He is also ashamed that his lectures led to this horrific act. He grabs Brandon's gun and fires shots into the air, hoping to attract police attention. The audience is relieved when the police arrive and solve the crime.

In 1951 Hitchcock directed another film that deserves comparison—or contrast—to *Rope*. That film was *Strangers on a Train*. As the name implies, *Strangers* is the story of two strangers who meet on a train. Superficially, the plot is the polar opposite of *Rope's* story about close companions who commit murder together. Yet the psychological impact is similar, and some of the same cast resurfaces in each. *Strangers* stars Farley Granger, the lead murderer in *Rope*, along with Leo G. Carroll, who was *Spellbound's* murderous M.D. and is a supporting character here.

Strangers is based on a novel by Patricia Highsmith, who also wrote *The Talented Mr. Ripley*—which was made into a popular film in 1999, proving that psychological thrillers were not extinct, even when *not* advertised as psychological thrillers. In *Strangers*, a successful tennis star named Guy Haines (Farley Granger) wants to divorce his unfaithful wife Miriam so he can marry the woman he loves. That "other woman" is the daughter of a senator who can further his career.

While riding a train, in traditional Hitchcockian fashion, Haines meets the unstable Bruno Anthony (Robert Walker). Bruno is a handsome but seemingly harmless playboy who hates his father. The two strangers share secrets—but Bruno already knows Guy's secrets. Bruno tells Guy about his plan to exchange murders between two strangers, so that neither would be suspected. Bruno will kill Miriam if Guy kills Bruno's father. Then each will be free to proceed, undetected.

Guy does not take Bruno seriously, but Bruno, it turns out, is very serious. Bruno kills Guy's wife (and her unborn baby) and then demands that the horrified Guy honor his part of the bargain. He sends Guy a pistol to kill his father but suspects that Guy is reluctant to act. So Bruno lies in his father's bed (like the Big Bad Wolf who lies in Grandma's bed). When Guy enters the room (as Bruno expected) and says, "Mr. Anthony, I've got to speak to you about your son," Bruno rises, grabs the gun, and retorts, "Don't worry Mr. Haines, I won't shoot you. It might disturb mother."

Strangers on a Train is one of many Hitchcock films that explore the theme of the doppelgänger, or double. In *Strangers on a Train*, we find verbal puns and visual metaphors about double-crossing and crossing one's own double. The multiple references to double-crossing in the dialogue are obvious enough, and standard enough for Hitchcock, who is expert at foreshadowing and at mirroring the overall plot through incident props.

Other visual touches alert us to double-crossing and to the doubling of identity. For instance, as the film begins, and as Bruno sits on the train, he orders two double drinks. Guy's cigarette lighter is decorated with two crossed tennis rackets. They start their conversation when they make contact by crossing their legs in their train seats.

The cigarette lighter plays an important role in this film (like the lighter in *Spellbound*). The double-crossed lighter connects Guy to the murder after Bruno steals it and plants it at the murder scene, and literally double-crossing him. A murder committed early in the film is seen doubly reflected in both lenses of the victim's glasses. Railroad crossing signs appear repeatedly, along with crossing train tracks. Then there is Hitchcock's signature cameo appearance, where the director's double appears in a double bass fiddle case that resembles Hitchcock's own portly profile.

The action advances, as do the intrigue and the audience's tension. We expect something sinister. When the promiscuous wife's corpse is discovered, strangled, at a local carnival's Isle of Love, Guy's motives make him the police's prime suspect. He must prove himself innocent. That task becomes more difficult as Bruno makes more appearances to remind Guy about the murder. As usual, the audience knows the truth, and wants to share the secret with the police, but spectators cannot talk to actors on the screen. So the audience suffers, also.

Guy claims to have been on another train when the murder occurred. But the professor who shared his compartment was too drunk to recall their conversation or Guy's face and so cannot be a credible witness. Meanwhile, Bruno stalks Guy, pressuring him to fulfill his part of the bargain. The film concludes at the fairground where the wayward wife was murdered. That scene recollects the fairground scenes of German Expressionism and *The Cabinet of Dr. Caligari*. We know that evil acts occur in innocent fairgrounds, where whirling wheels and roller coasters make for a rocky ride, and where spinning strobe lights alter perception and impair cognition. It is fitting that the final scene, where Guy proves his innocence to the police, and where Bruno is crushed under a merry-go-round horse, takes place in this otherworldly, out-of-kilter world that was intended to amuse innocent young children. Yet until the very moment when Bruno succumbs, we the audience clutch our seats, wondering who will win, as Hitchcock captures our consciousness and pulls us into this suspenseful psychological thriller.

We would need a complete book to catalogue each of Hitchcock's psychological thrillers. For the sake of brevity, let us turn back in time and take another look at *Spellbound* (1945). One of Hitchcock's lesser known works, *Spellbound* is remembered because it was the first film to use a psychoanalyst—rather than a detective— to solve a murder mystery.

Spellbound's arch-villain turns out to be Leo G. Carroll, who appears in later Hitchcock films and who also played Topper (a man who sees ghosts) on TV. With his craggy looks, mangy mustache, and walrus-like wrinkles, Carroll's face is as recognizable as it is distinguished. He should look distinguished, for he previously headed the elegant sanitarium known as Green Acres, where the action begins.

We must wait until the final scene to learn that Dr. Murchison (Leo G. Carroll) murdered the would-be hospital head who was meant to replace him. In the final scene, Carroll points a gun at Ingrid Bergman (Dr. Peterson) and at the audience. When he realizes that his deception has been uncovered, and that he has no chance of escape, he points the gun at his own head and fires. His final act is suicide, the act that his rest home prevents in patients.

Just as significantly, Dr. Edwards (Gregory Peck) is vindicated by Carroll's confession. Dr. Edwards is the handsome younger man who plans to head the hospital but who loses his memory instead. Yet he has not lost his sex appeal, for he wins the affections of the overly-serious and sexually repressed Dr. Constance Peterson, who is the only female analyst among the all-male medical staff.

Unable to remember his own name, Dr. Edwards believes that he is the man who was murdered. So he is suspected of murder himself and must be cleared of the charges. Dr. Peterson, played by the comely Ingrid Bergman, who had recently appeared as the romantic lead in *Casablanca*, believes in Edwards's innocence. Using hypnosis and dream interpretation, she excavates repressed memories of ski slopes and wagon wheels and criss-crossed lines that stand for ski tracks. In this way, she traces the days that Dr. Edwards spent on the ski slopes with the missing doctor, before that doctor died in a skiing accident.

It is useful to look at the background behind this film, because this landmark movie was the first mystery-suspense film to use a psychoanalyst as a driving device in place of a detective. Freudian psychodynamic theories were fashionable when *Spellbound* was made. It was widely known that neurotic symptoms result from psychological shocks and that memory of the shock may be banished from conscious recall and repressed. Today, we would call this process post-traumatic stress disorder (PTSD), and we expect flashbacks and intrusive memories rather than repression. In the forties, however, Freudian theory about "repressed memories" reigned.

Significantly, *Spellbound*'s producer, David Selznick, entered analysis in 1943 because he was stressed by his relationship with an actress and stressed by being an independent filmmaker without big studio backing. He often spoke of his analysis but sometimes claimed that he was analyzing his analyst, May Romm, rather than the other way around. Either way, this personal experience gave him the idea of making a film based on his own experiences. He even brought his psychotherapist to the set as a technical advisor. Selznick had worked with Hitchcock before, was eager to collaborate with him again, and eventually wrote a book about "Hitch."

Until then, Hitchcock was better known for thrillers. *Spellbound* moves away from his traditional plots. Hitchcock remained aware that the film was a fantasy. At the film's beginning, he announces that the film is simply a story taking place in a Freudian world and that it should therefore be seen as such. Hitchcock was more interested in making a good movie than in representing psychoanalysis or Freudianism factually. When Selznick's analyst disputed a fact about the way therapy works, Hitchcock is said to have told her, "My dear, it's only a movie."

In spite of his dismissive attitude, Hitchcock explores themes that are central to Freud's work, such as the unresolved tension between material reality (what actually happened) and intra-psychic reality (what our ego leads us to believe happened). The

Spellbound fantasy is a version of the Oedipus myth, with incestuous desire and repressed guilt, along with a few other riddles.

The idea of the old making way for the new is also significant in *Spellbound*, in the abstract sense and in the actual. *Spellbound* deals with the abstract aspect of how old ideas about treating the insane were being replaced by newer, psychoanalytic approaches. It also deals with the concrete concept of the old giving way to the new, in that older professionals, such as the murderous Dr. Murchison (Leo G. Carroll), was being replaced by a younger psychiatrist.

Hitchcock's plots are convoluted, and they require an agile mind and good memory to recall their twists and turns. But one of the key points of this film, and of many Hitchcock films and other films of its era, is the issue of amnesia and loss of identity.

AMNESIA, MEMORY, AND *MEMENTO*

Amnesia was a common cinematic theme immediately after World War II, when there was so much that so many men and women wanted to forget. Amnesia once again because an important movie MacGuffin (or driving theme, to use Hitchcock's own term) at the turn of the twenty-first century, when Alzheimer's disease appeared in headlines, and when anxiety about memory loss increased as Americans aged. The fact that the second millennium was coming to a close made people more aware of fading memories, the passing of time, and the inevitability of change (and possible apocalypse). Several films about amnesia and memory loss were made at that turning point in time. One of the more memorable of those memory-loss films (which were also dubbed mindf**k films) was *Memento* (2000).

In *Memento*, Leonard (Guy Pearce) is an insurance investigator whose short-term memory was damaged by a head injury incurred while trying to prevent the rape and murder of his wife. He cannot compound new memories, so he lives through flashbacks or "in the moment." He recalls his wife's murder, which occurred just before he lost consciousness. He remembers his tragic insurance client who suffered similar memory loss, but whose claim was denied because Leonard could not believe that such specific brain damage could occur.

Leonard can barely function in daily life because of his memory impairment. But he is not an ordinary amnesiac, like Larry Cravat in *Somewhere in the Night* (1946), or even like Dr. Edwards in *Spellbound*. He tattoos important dates and reminders on his skin, as though it were an Outlook calendar. He takes incessant Polaroid pictures. The movie is told in forward flashes of events—as opposed to the flashbacks that Freudian psychoanalysis and film noir made famous.

Leonard wants to avenge his wife's murder, and he lives for the moment when he can confront her killer. He also relives the memories of his former client, who has no one left to avenge either him or his wife. His revenge motive is timeless, but his tale is told in postmodern fashion, with the broken narratives and disrupted time zones. This film captures the experience of those born into the electronic era, where time is displaced by pushing fast-forward or backward buttons on videos or cellphones.

The human aspect of the narrative is key, not so much through Leonard, but through his client's sad love story. Because Leonard doubted his client, he tested him by telling him that he had not yet injected his beloved diabetic wife with insulin. Leonard expected his client to refuse to inject insulin, because he believed that the client could remember what he did that morning, even though he claimed that he could not.

Instead, the claimant proved himself worthy of his insurance claim. He injected his wife again, this time killing her unintentionally when her blood sugar plummeted from the extra insulin. When she died, he lost the love of his life. He also lost the only person in the world he could rely on, for she cared for him in his memoryless state. No wonder that Leonard, the man who cannot compound new memories, is doomed to living hell. His world is populated by memories that he has already collected, including the memories of his client, whose wife he killed indirectly, and memories of his own wife, whose murder he could not stop.

Memento is a strange film in more ways than one, and it is not exactly a psychological thriller. It makes us feel little remorse for a man who pushed another man into killing his wife. One can say that it is a psychological thriller because the mind and the memory (or lack thereof) push the plot. But the popular (and offensive) label of "mindf**k film" that is usually applied to this film and others like it describes this genre better than the now-dated rubric psychological thriller. It is a credit to the filmmaker and editor, whose brilliant pastiche of flash-forwards and flashbacks makes an otherwise unappealing subject matter and unlikable protagonist both engaging and enthralling.

ROBERT MITCHUM MOVIES: *CAPE FEAR* AND *NIGHT OF THE HUNTER*

Since we are on the subject of flash-forwards and flashbacks, let us flashback to another kind of psychological thriller. *The Night of the Hunter* (1955) starred Robert Mitchum, that ugly-handsome man who often portrayed war heroes wearing metal helmets, but who got his start as a villain in psychological thrillers like this one and like *Cape Fear* (1962). *Night of the Hunter* was the only film ever made by its director, Charles Laughton, who had greater fame as an actor.

Robert Mitchum's evil character wears a telling tattoo. A letter is emblazoned on each knuckle: L-O-V-E on one hand and H-A-T-E on the other. Such tattoos are the trademark of sociopaths who have no conscience and no ability to tell right from wrong. For sociopaths, love and hate are alike. There is no distinction, as we see in this story.

In the film's opening scene, a man named Ben Harper has committed murder for the sum of $10,000. He hides the money in his daughter Pearl's stuffed toy. He departs hastily, but before he leaves, he makes young Pearl and her older brother John promise not to tell anyone where he hid the money, not even their mother Willa, who is played by a beautiful young Shelley Winters.

Ben is apprehended and put in prison. As he awaits hanging, Ben is approached by his cell mate, the Preacher, who tries to goad Ben into revealing where he stashed the cash. When Preacher (Robert Mitchum) is released from prison, he heads for the Harper home, intent on finding the money. Preacher charms the lonely widow Willa and cajoles her into joining him in marriage. Throughout this time, he sings a haunting hymn, "Leaning on the Everlasting Arms." "Leaning, leaning, leaning," he bellows out, in a bass-baritone voice that signals his approaching presence. The music reminds us of Peter Lorre's equally ominous tune from *The Hall of the Mountain King.*

Willa's children see through him, and distrust him, even though he is supposedly a preacher. But the children are just children and their opinions are dismissed. When Willa finally realizes what kind of man he is, and confronts him—after he refuses to share their marriage bed, and berates her for her "unholy" desires—he kills her and leaves her children orphaned. The scene of Willa floating in a pond, face down, her blonde hair billowing out of the car that she drowned in, is one of the more eerie scenes and eidetic images of this disturbing film.

The children escape and find refuge with Rachel Cooper. She is an earnest woman who lives on a ranch and raises abandoned children as if they were her own. She is wary of the attention that men are showing to one of the other children, the peripubescent Ruby. One of the men who woos Ruby turns out to be the conniving Preacher, who tracked down the children after they rowed away from him on the river. The Preacher makes Ruby feel guilty about her lustful desires, and she eventually tells Rachel that she has been spending time with the town boys rather than attending sewing lessons, as she said. She also admits that she revealed the whereabouts of young Pearl and John to a man who claims to be a preacher and their father.

Ruby's confession prepares Rachel for the climactic encounter with the Preacher. When the evil Preacher arrives and attempts to coerce the children into revealing the whereabouts of the money, he is shot by the good Rachel Cooper, played by Lillian Gish, who previously starred as the abandoned and abused young woman in *Broken Blossoms* in her youth.

The story of *Night of the Hunter* may sound fanciful on the surface—or it may sound like a made-for-TV movie about the recent rash of sexual abuse by priests and other clergy. Yet it was based on actual events that took place in the 1930s. During the Great Depression, a criminal named Harry Powers seduced widows, and then stole from them before killing them. All the while, he pretended to be a preacher, like Harry Powell, the pseudo-preacher played by Robert Mitchum.

The opening scenes of *Night of the Hunter* are strikingly similar to another, even better-known psychological thriller that would be made in 1960. That thriller was *Psycho*, the first slasher film, and the film that many consider to be Hitchcock's masterpiece. *Psycho* begins when the blonde-haired Marion steals money from her trusting boss at the bank. She stashes the cash in a luggage bag, then hurriedly stuffs her belongings into her suitcase and races off in her car. She does not stop driving until she reaches the Bates Motel many hours later. There, she meets Norman, the meek-mannered hotel desk clerk who turns into a transvestite murderer at night, and who gives her more than she deserves for her dark deeds, in true Deuteronomy eye-for-an-eye style. The real action of this famous psychological thriller film starts *after* Marion commits her crime, in much the same way that the *Night of the Hunter* action starts *after* Harper stashes the money.

The year after *Psycho* appeared, another classic psychological thriller starring Robert Mitchum made its way to the screen for the first time. The first *Cape Fear* appeared in 1961. It was popular enough to merit a remake by Martin Scorsese in 1991.

Like *Psycho* and *Night of the Hunter* and so many other films of this ilk, the wronged character does wrong before the story starts. Retribution, although not necessarily divine, is often the MacGuffin in the psychological thriller. In *Cape Fear*, the young family man-attorney withholds evidence that could have freed an otherwise despicable rapist from prison. The lawyer takes the law into his own hands—and he pays for it, dearly. On the side, this self-righteous lawyer carries on a clandestine affair with a single woman in his office.

In the first version, the single woman is a secretary. In the postfeminist remake, the young lover is an attorney who works with the protagonist. Either way, the lustful woman who lures the married man from wife and family gets her comeuppance, suffering more than the man who led her astray.

When the sinewy-muscled rapist, Max Cady (first played by Robert Mitchum and later by Robert De Niro) is released from prison, he pursues the man who sent him behind bars (or who could have prevented him from incarceration, had he presented all the evidence to the jury). Like any self-respecting sociopath, the rapist never holds himself responsible for his own act and invariably blames others for his downfall, including the attorney.

Cady begins his revenge by seducing the attorney's young lady lover. The would-be seduction turns into a savage rape in which she is beaten and bitten and spends weeks in the hospital, before returning home to New York, scarred forever in both body and mind.

The rapist moves in closer, poisoning the family dog. The peaceful, flowered, whitewashed southern villa that the attorney and his family call home turns into a place of mayhem and madness. The home becomes a makeshift fortress once the family senses the presence of the rapist, be it Robert Mitchum or Robert De Niro. Unfortunately, the attorney's teen-age daughter is intrigued by the would-be rapist, and is lured by him when he stakes her out at school.

When all else fails, and after the attorney (first played by Gregory Peck and then by Nick Nolte) comes close to losing his law license because he breaks the law to pursue his pursuer, he sends his family off on their houseboat. He plans to use them as bait. They sail to Cape Fear, off the Carolina coast, where craggy mountains and raging waters mirror the razor-sharp edges and avenging rage of Max Cady. Using more brainpower than his attorney-opponent believes he possesses, the repulsive yet resourceful Cady attaches himself to the bottom of the boat and then resurfaces. He and the attorney are locked in a death battle that holds our attention to the end. In fact, the action in this film is intense enough to merit a listing not just as a psychological thriller, but as an action-adventure (even if it lacks the high-speed boat chase).

Like many memorable films, *Cape Fear* falls into more than one category and cannot be categorized as one genre only. One wonders how Movie Phone, or Fandango, or whatever movie distribution device will follow, will categorize *Cape Fear* in the future.

Regardless of what we call it, the psychological thriller is here to stay, even if it goes by another name at a later date. The mysteries of our own minds will always be with us. When there is no identifiable enemy or opponent out there, we can create our own terrors, and moviemakers will follow suit, seeking to scare us out of our anxiety, at least temporarily.

Curiously, psychological thrillers intrigue us—and even addict us—because they operate on a timeless principle of "doing-undoing" that Freud identified. By experiencing the anxiety of the thriller, we achieve a catharsis at the end of the movie. We feel relief once we realize that the action occurred only on screen, and that we ourselves (or the characters we identified with) are no longer at risk. A sense of peace sets in and we breathe easy.

I am not being facetious when I suggest that the adrenaline, noradrenaline, and dopamine release that occurs during exciting events (such as riding roller coasters) may actually induce some of us to seek out more and more psychological thrillers, much as some thrill seekers seek out cocaine. For there undoubtedly is a neurochemical component to the movie-going experience—just as there is a neurochemical component to every other aspect of experience. And we know that dopamine release can be addicting, very addicting, as the experience of cocaine and amphetamine addicts proves.

Luckily, watching too many psychological thrillers does not cause the serious side effects that those dangerous drugs do. Nor are there legal repercussions. But we will probably never know just how much dopamine each of these movies makes us release. For I doubt that moviemakers will ever need to conduct the costly and time-consuming medical tests used by pharmaceutical manufacturers or medical researchers. The only proof of a positive effect required by film studios is a boost in box office receipts. And the only proof that we, the spectator, demand from our future films is the foreknowledge that we enjoyed other films of its genre.

CHAPTER 8

FREUDIAN WESTERNS AND FILMS NOIR

FATHER FIGURES AND FEMME FATALES

On the surface, it seems strange to link Westerns to films noir. The settings of these two genres could not be more different. Westerns, by definition, occur in the American West (even when shot somewhere else). Westerns take place on the wide, open range. Movement, action, and adventure, set against craggy mountains, grassy plains, winding trails, and bright blue skies, are Western trademarks.

Films noir, on the other hand, are urban. They are shot on city streets or on deserted docks. Noirs take place in claustrophobic, confined spaces. Noir action occurs in alleyways, or dark cars, or tenements flanked by fire escapes. Films noir are dark, by definition, and are almost always black and white, whereas Westerns evoke images of intense color contrasts, even if made before Technicolor.

The reason we link these two genres together, in this single chapter, is that the films noir of the forties influenced Westerns in the fifties, producing a subgenre known as Freudian Westerns, or psychological Westerns. Both films noir and Freudian Westerns were turning points in the modern psyche's evolution in movies. Furthermore, both noirs and Westerns fetishize film symbols that become the genre's trademark. Those nonsexual film fetishes stimulated true sexual fetishes among those so inclined and become fodder for the Freudian imagination, with its preoccupation with psychosexual symbols. To understand the significance of these genres in "movies and the modern psyche," let us look at Westerns, which surfaced in the film industry's infancy.

TRADITIONAL WESTERNS AND FREUDIAN WESTERNS

Westerns were known as horse operas or oaters. They appeared early on. Edwin S. Porter's *The Great Train Robbery* (1903) was a Western, and an American-made movie—made in America, by an American, about an American subject. (That issue was important to Americans in pre-Hollywood days, before anyone imagined that the United States would dominate the film industry later in the century.)

Because Westerns take place in the American West, it is often assumed that Westerns were exclusively American productions. That is not true. The French were the first to film Westerns, but World War I halted their efforts. Then "spaghetti Westerns" appeared in the sixties, when Sergio Leone teamed up with Clint Eastwood to film Westerns in Italy.

Silent Westerns (accompanied by music) of the pre-sound area played on a theme that was important to the early twentieth century: civilizing untamed civilizations. In the visual arts, themes revolving around the return to the primitive became popular at the turn of the century, as seen by the public's embrace of paintings by Gauguin, Rousseau, and others. Gauguin's paintings of primitive colors and primitive ceremonies seen during his voyages to Tahiti, and tales of personal indulgence in primitive sexual urges with young native girls from his Eden-like existence in Oceania, appealed to Europeans and Americans. Urbanization was rapidly encroaching, and industrialization was stripping landscapes of their pastoral appeal, so relief was sought through art, film, and literature.

The Western represented the West as the last untamed place in America. The genre played upon this romantic image that was already in place—even though land rushes and homesteading pushed herders out of the picture decades before moving pictures appeared. The great migration westward had closed off the open range by the turn of the century. Cowboys were all but defunct, and the West was totally "civilized" when cinema was invented.

But truth didn't matter to spectators, who were more interested in fantasy than fact. It was irrelevant that classic Westerns portrayed an era spanning a mere fifteen years in time: between 1865 and 1880. During those years, the beef industry expanded. Cowboys were needed to drive the cattle westward, for slaughter, no less (to the horror of today's animal rights activists!).

What mattered were the myths embodied in this genre, along with the fetishes: the cowboy boots, the silver spurs, the ten-gallon hat, and, most of all, the low-slung gun that was easy to identify as a phallic symbolic, once Freudian interpretation of films was adopted. And I should remind you that my use of the word *fetish* is not a slip of the tongue. Nor is it an intentional reference to psychoanalytic terminology. For this word is standard among film scholars, who note that Westerns are especially rich in fetishes that immediately identify the genre. And, yes, cowboy-boot fetishes also appear in the "real" fetish world patronized by those who seek "specialty sex" in waterfront bars that demand patrons to wear "leather or western."

Apart from speculating about the purposes of these obvious fetishes, many other opportunities for psychoanalytic readings of traditional Western symbolism and archetypes exist. The contrast between civilization (urbanization) and the wilderness's open range fits the Freudian paradigm. The wilderness where the cowboys roamed is a place where instinctual desires have free reign, as they did before the fall, when Adam and Eve were banished from the Garden. Let us not forget that Freud himself wrote *The Ego and the Id* (1923) and wrote about the control that the ego and superego wield over the instinct-driven id.

Curiously, the first (and only) film that Freud saw was a Western, and that was while he was touring in America, when he was invited to lecture at Clark University in 1909. He was accompanied by his younger colleague and then heir-apparent, Carl Jung. It is well-known that Freud dismissed the significance of film (and of America) after that single viewing.

Still, it is curious that one of his philosophical books of his later years, *Civilization and Its Discontents* (1930), addresses the same themes that Westerns address. According to Freud, civilization cannot proceed unless citizens suppress instinctual desires and sublimate baser urges. Westerns deal directly with this conflict, and with conflicts between outlaws and lawmen. Outlaws, by definition, defy laws and follow urges of their ids, whereas lawmen represent the superego, which produces guilt that prods them to pursue outlaws who defy society. Like the punitive superego that punishes with guilt, lawmen bring outlaws to justice.

However, Westerns do not follow the typical Oedipal trajectory of classical drama and of Freudian theory. In other words, in the Western, the triumphant male does not get the girl, even though he rescues her before the story ends. Instead, he heads off alone, and asserts his independence, having made the land safe for the arrival of more virgins.

What the Western *does* demonstrate, par excellence, is the classic "Madonna-putana"/mother-whore dualism. The pure and idealized woman (the untouched Madonna) is pitted against the degraded and defamed woman (the putana or vagina) who satisfies men's baser appetites, like a prostitute. The dichotomous roles of men and women, and the distinction between the mother-Madonna versus the putana-whore, are as important as the distinction between the outlaw-lawman in Westerns. In pre-1950s Westerns, there are two kinds of women: the good and the bad (school teachers and barmaids), just as there are two kinds of men (lawmen and outlaws), and two kinds of land (town and frontier).

It has been said that the woman represents civilization, whereas the man represents the frontier that must be conquered so that civilization can progress and so that the United States (and humans) can expand. The frontier equals individual freedom. The frontier and individual freedom must be sacrificed for the sake of civilization and for the sake of family life. The rugged individualism of the cowboy was a paradigmatic American value, but it was also at odds with the national unity needed to incorporate the West into the United States. Westerns dramatized this political and psychological dichotomy.

So it is especially interesting that the mythical cowboy typically rode off alone into the sunset, spurs and guns and horses and lassos and all. He typically rescued the pure and pristine woman who ventured west (usually to spread civilization by teaching school to unwashed, ill-mannered, and unlearned men who panned for gold or herded cattle). Usually she was abducted by Indians (who represented pure id, pure desire, and pure savagery). But the cowboy never claimed the woman as his own or took her as wife.

The good guy–cowboy thwarted attacks on virtuous woman, but left her untouched and untarnished as he headed off on his own. What he did when he was alone was never discussed. In the forties, sex seeped into the Westerns. Jane Russell and Mae West appeared in *The Outlaw* (1943) and *My Little Chickadee* (1940), respectively. But the Legion of Decency objected, blocking their release until cuts were made.

When these films were released, sexual temptresses were usually hot-blooded Mexican women (another version of "the other") rather than white bread, beef-fed, all-American types. A few films deviated from this formula, most notably Barbara Stanwyck's *Annie Oakley* (1935) and Jean Arthur's Calamity Jane in Cecil B. DeMille's *The Plainsman* (1936). Jean Arthur played opposite Gary Cooper, who was Wild Bill Hickock. Barbara Stanwyck went on to play "wicked women" or ruthless women in sex role stereotype–smashing roles that foreshadowed the feminist era. Gender bending in general and cross-dressing became important sub-themes in the Freudian Westerns that appeared in the fifties, when psychology permeated film.

There was good reason for this shift in Westerns. Earlier, "classical" Westerns were based on popular dime novels from the 1860s. These books, reworked into films, proved to be equally popular as cinematic subjects. The fact that their social concerns were outdated and outmoded was hardly important to spectators who were content to romanticize the past.

By 1950 psychoanalysis and general psychology entered mainstream film. Audiences expected psychological depth to characters. They would not accept cardboard cut-outs who acted out mythical roles that did not derive from their personal past or their inner turmoil. Exactly how and why psychology infiltrated film at this point is a curious question, especially when we recall that psychoanalysis and cinema grew up together in the final years of the nineteenth century. Although the French surrealists of the twenties and thirties saluted Freud, and used his dream theory in their films, the surrealist-inspired films were anything but mainstream. For one thing, they required far more theoretical and philosophical understanding than was available to the average man or woman who sought cinema as a source of entertainment.

The world was different by the fifties. World War II had just concluded. The experience of this war brought three things: first, the GI bill sent more men to college than ever before. Second, it sent many European intellectuals and filmmakers and psychoanalysts into the United States, in desperate attempts to escape Hitler's death camps, or even just to avoid financial devastation or artistic censorship. These people introduced the public to psychoanalysis. Third, the horrific events of the Holocaust demanded psychological, sociological, or even economic explanations. The unparalleled need to explain the depravity of human behavior demonstrated by the Nazis, by the Vichy government, by some Polish nationals, and others pushed people to look for insights from psychologists and psychoanalysts, who claimed expertise in understanding human behavior.

Freudian Westerns were also directly influenced by film noir, which had proliferated in the forties. With their dark and disturbing themes, and their nightmarish visions depicted in stark black and white, films noir increased interest in the motivations *behind* the action. What drove a man to be an outlaw? What made a man—or a woman—"gun crazy"? Why would someone lay down his life to protect another? Did early life experiences mold a lawman and force him to forsake his own safety for the sake of righting a wrong? And why would one man want to right one particular kind of wrong, when another lawman demanded a different kind of justice? Was it because one lawman witnessed his mother's rape by an Indian—or by a white out-law? Did that memory make him want to defend women's honor, even if it drove him to his death? Or was he an orphan, without a male figure to model himself after, so that he became a gunslinger instead? So many questions about what drove the psyche! So many more motifs for filmmakers to mine!

Freudianism became more fashionable in the fifties, and sexual symbolism associated with Freudianism became better known as well. Topics such as family dramas or Oedipal conflicts or latent homosexuality attracted audiences. Westerns were well established and could add Freudian insights. No film is more flagrant in this respect than Howard Hawks's *Red River* (1948).

Hawks is considered the consummate Western director, with Ford as his only serious competitor for first place in this genre. In *Red River* John Wayne and the much younger Montgomery Clift join forces before drifting apart. Their parting initially looks like a biblical rift and reminds the viewer of Abraham's words to his son: "You go your way, and I'll go mine." But that is just the beginning of this camp classic.

Monty Clift is a handsome young man who wears his holster slung low, perhaps too low, emphasizing his slender yet muscular torso. His character's family was killed during an Indian attack, and he is the sole survivor. He is left with a cow when he meets John Wayne, who is a herder who owns a bull. Their animals mate. This actual and metaphorical mating becomes the film's MacGuffin. Queer studies scholars observe that the film's homoerotic overtones are foreshadowed by this heifer/bull match.

Father-figure John Wayne invites the orphaned Clift to join the cattle drive. Wayne is an experienced cowboy who has spent years on the range. His weathered skin attests to his experience outdoors. The family-less Wayne plans to make Clift his heir. He treats him like his son, until the inevitable showdown. But before the classic cowboy showdown, even more memorable events occur.

In what may be the most comically homoerotic scene ever screened as a serious cinematic scene, a young gun named Cherry arrives and challenges Clift's shooting skills. They do some leisurely shooting. Cherry eyes Clift's gun, and then Cherry and Clift exchange guns, and Cherry spews out lines like "Can I see your gun? Would you like to see mine?"

This symbolism eluded the average 1950s spectator (or maybe not). However, those who watch reruns of this film decades later, and who have heard that Montgomery Clift's personal life was marked by uncertainty about sexual preference and by drug use that maybe masked his discomfort with his socially unacceptable same-sex attraction, the symbolism is so shallow as to evoke laughter (or tears, depending upon one's persuasion). John Wayne, as we know, was the quintessential man's man, the war hero, the heroic he-man, and the epitome of masculinity.

Gender-bending women appeared in a few memorable post-1950s Westerns, although such films were nowhere as common as films with standard male cowboy stars in mostly-male films. Joan Crawford's gun-toting, leather-clad Vienna in Nicholas Ray's *Johnny Guitar* (1954) became a cult classic in its own right. This film is often cited as a comment on McCarthyism, partly because it was shot in Spain, where director Nicholas Ray was in self-imposed exile. Also, its theme of isolation-ism and of hiding behind the law to rid a town of "outsiders" who do not fit in mir-rors McCarthy tactics and outlooks.

But it can also be read as a commentary on traditional gender roles, and a spoof of those roles, at that. Watching this film replay in art houses, and listening to mostly gay male cult audiences chuckling as Vienna challenges her "isolationist" lover, convinces the viewer that the gender-bending trend of this film is timeless, even though the political connections to McCarthyism and American isolationism during the Cold War have cooled off.

Anyone who views, or reviews, these Freudian Westerns from the fifties comes away convinced that gender-bender themes in Westerns emerged half a century before *Brokeback Mountain* (2005) broke trends in the twenty-first century. Con-versely, those who never saw Monty Clift and John Wayne in *Red River* were entitled to think that homoerotic themes in cowboy films were something new. True, *Broke-back Mountain* broke ground when it tackled same-sex attraction openly and sensi-tively, without camp or comedy or cryptic allusion.

Gun Crazy (1950), starring Peggy Cummins and John Dall, is both a Western and a film noir, but most of all it is a low-budget B movie that plays upon sensation-alism, simple set design, and great camera shots of car chases and getaways that are shot from the backseat of a speeding car. Even the cover of the recently released DVD looks like a pulp fiction cover, with its bright yellow letters splattering across the cover, spelling out "thrill crazy," "kill crazy," and *Gun Crazy.*

The woman on the DVD cover does not wear Western garb, as she does in the film, where she is a carnie. Rather, she dons a standard noir split skit, with spiked heels, tight sweater, and bountiful blonde bangs that bounce off her face. She holds not one gun, but two, one in each of her hands, as she shows a three-quarter view of her torso and a partial profile of her face, implying that she has more secrets to share than are permissible for a novel or movie box cover.

The story is fairly straightforward: Annie Laurie Starr literally stars in a sideshow sharp-shooting act, where she dresses like Annie Oakley, save for the tight black pants. She defies anyone in the audience to outshoot her. She wins, almost always . . . until a man named Bart Tare takes her up on her bet and outshoots her. Not only does he humiliate her before her loyal carnie fans, but he also bankrupts her because she bets more money than she possesses. Needing money himself, he joins the carnie with her, and the two stage their act together, until . . .

As it turns out, we already know more about Bart and his past before we meet Annie, because the film opens with a scene from his youth that explains the origins of Bart's gun obsession. He is an orphan who is preoccupied by guns because they symbolize manhood and masculinity, and because he lacks a male role model in his own, having lost his own father. The Freudian formula, as well as the film formula, is easy to understand, once one learns to read the fetishes. (How odd that film scholars use this sexually charged term for symbols in films!)

The film's opening foreshadows the fate that will befall Bart, again in true Freudian fashion. The boy is father to the man, as the Romantic poets said decades before Freud. Freudian-style psychological determinism is hard at work in this film, as it shows us how Bart's formative childhood experiences shape his adult behavior and set him up for failure, because of repetition-compulsion even more than the gun mania that a judge will soon allude to.

Bart is an otherwise ordinary young boy, save for the fact that he is orphaned and lives with his older sister. He has friends, attends school, and shoots guns whenever he can, because, he explains, guns make him feel like a man. Then everything changes, after the fateful event occurs.

On a dark, rainy night on a shadowy street where a neon HOTEL sign blinks on and off (using film noir chiaroscuro conventions of shadows and fog), the rain-drenched Bart walks out of the rain and up to a hardware-store window. He spots an ivory-handled gun on display. Unable to resist temptation, and intrigued by Western sharpshooters (in a foreshadowing of his encounter with Annie), he hurls a rock through the glass, breaks the window, reaches in, and grabs the gun.

But then he tumbles into a puddle, and soon finds himself lying on the wet ground, looking up at a law officer who arrests him for breaking and entering and for petty larceny. Soon after, he finds himself facing a judge, who refuses to listen to his sister's and his friend's pleas. The judge sends Bart off to a boy's school, hoping to cure him of his "gun mania." Some years later, Bart is free and looking for work when he runs into Annie at the carnival.

Bart sees that he and Annie go together "like guns and ammunition." But Bart is haunted by his past and is determined to avoid anything that would send him back to the "boy's school" or the adult equivalent: prison. He regrets his youthful misdeeds, yet he is still doomed to suffer for his latest sins. For he committed a different kind of transgression when he outshot this deadly femme fatale.

After the pair is cast away from the carnival, they set off together to make their way in the world. Needing money (and not knowing about Annie's past history of bank robbery plus manslaughter), Bart is goaded into robbing banks with Annie. Together, they race off in the getaway car after she sets up the teller. Eventually, something goes wrong. She—not he—shows her true colors, mercilessly shooting a man who pursues her after a foiled holdup. The two set off on the lam, with Bart lamenting the death of the man while Annie shows no remorse. One can guess the ending, especially if one knows the film noir formula. Both are shot dead in the end.

But there is a little more to the story. After staging holdups, first in Western gear with fringe and buckskin and cowboy hats, the pair turn to more mainstream criminal costumes: dark glasses and long trench coats. The license plate number on their getaway car gives them away, and they are traced to the carnival. The carnie owner, who was Annie's lover before Bart arrived and splattered his face, alerts the police to their whereabouts.

As a last resort, the two return to Bart's childhood home. The sheriff is in hot pursuit. They forge through the marshes, but Annie goes insane and threatens to shoot Bart. Bart shoots her instead, committing the only murder of his life. When the sheriff's party hears the gunshots, they presume that the shells are meant for them, and they shoot into the reeds, leaving Bart dead, with his body straddling Annie's corpse. Music plays mournfully in the background.

To understand this film noir formula and see how femme fatales and Freudian-style "phallic women" fit in—and how film noir Freudianism influenced Freudian Westerns (or vice versa), let us look closer at the film noir genre.

FILM NOIR: DEFINITIONS AND EXAMPLES

Film noir is an ambiguous term that was coined by French film critics in 1946. The French had not seen American films during the war because of a ban imposed by the German Occupation. After France's liberation in 1944, the ban was lifted and France was flooded with Hollywood films. The French immediately identified a new and unique type of thriller. They named this new style film noir, but not because of the harsh, dark shadows of black-and-white films made under wartime constraints, and not because of poorly lit, low-budget, recycled sets camouflaged by rain, fog, or smoke. Rather, these movies were based on hard-boiled detective novels that the French called *romans noirs*, or, literally, "black novels."

Film scholars debate whether film noir is a specific genre, a subgenre, or just a style that became a successful marketing term. Most agree that film noir is a subgenre of crime thrillers or gangster films. Most are B movies that were intended as double-features. Film noir characteristics appear in other genres, such as Freudian Westerns and melodramas.

Film noir producers never aspired to start a new movement. They never joined a cohesive collective, as the Surrealists did, and they never identified themselves as "film noir directors." Still, these films emerged during a time of intense political instability and paranoia (1941–58), and their subject matter shows it. Most noirs (apart from 1990s "neo-noirs") were shot between the start of World War II and the height of the Cold War. In the United States, the American dream was in tatters: American national identity was strained as the United States toyed with the idea of abandoning its isolationist policy and joining the Allied forces to fight off fascism and defend the country against Japanese attack.

The war pushed American women out of the home and into the workforce. World War II witnessed the gender-bender poster child, Rosie the Riveter. Men, in the meantime, left home and went to war. Men's influence on domestic life was diminished, and their presence in movie theaters was nearly nil. Films were made for women, and showed their tensions and aspirations.

Rosie the Riveter's costume was unmistakable: she flexed a well-muscled arm, and wore a bandana. Likewise, the "phallic women" of film noir needed to be just as easily identifiable. High heels, pointed like daggers in full-Freudian phallic style that was the rage in those days, made the noir neo-female just as identifiable as Rosie. This new woman retained Rosie's strength, but she was as obviously female as Rosie was a factory worker.

When the men returned from the war, they not only returned with war wounds or psychological traumas, but they also returned to a changed world, to a changed home life, and to changed wives, daughters, and even mothers. Women had won unprecedented independence during the men's absence. Masculine identity was called into question after the war, and was bound up with the question of national identity.

National identity was called into question once the war ended, when returning soldiers finally had the wherewithal to ask themselves what they had fought for.

Film noir reflected these psychological and sociological concerns, even if those films did not plan to deliver a particular political message, as occurred during the war years, when government pressure, as well as patriotism, produced such pro-Allied films as *Casablanca*. Film noir was also a visual style that evolved out of wartime constraints. Most noirs were shot via night-time photography, which was necessary because of wartime blackouts and low lighting on Hollywood sets. Hollywood lights had to be dimmed to avoid attracting Japanese attention. After all, California-based studios were dangerously close to the coastline and could invite attack.

The high-contrast lighting produced deep shadows and oblique angles, similar to the style seen in German Expressionism, which also evolved out of the constraints of World War I. In addition, film noir was directly influenced by European émigrés who had once worked in German Expressionism before fleeing Hitler's reach and resettling in Hollywood. The oblique angles created a sense of uncertainty and instability. The shadows and fog made spectators wonder what evil lurked beneath. The war years proved that unimaginable evil hides in the most cultured of places. Who knew what other evil lurked? Film noir shadows hinted that worse awaited.

As Hitler gained power in Germany, and as his forces marched eastward to Poland and Czechoslovakia, and westward to France, psychoanalysts, filmmakers, and actors headed across the Atlantic. Fritz Lang, Josef von Sternberg, Billy Wilder, Richard Siodmark, Otto Preminger, Douglas Sirk, Max Ophuls, and Peter Lorre are a few of the most famous film names who made their way to the United States.

The gritty city streets of American film noir, the dimly lit interiors, the tightly framed shots, and the extreme camera angles recollected German Expressionism. The pessimism, the gloom, the suspicion, even the guilt, were part and parcel of the European émigré experience and the so-called guilt of the survivor that cast a shadow over those who escaped Hitler. Film noir cityscapes are fraught with danger and deceit. Moral boundaries are blurred. Bodies are blurred by shadows, so that spectators are unsure of their physical form. Sometimes, only the voiceover narration (which acts as the consciousness) is clear. Protagonists are often shot in half-shadow, implying that every person has a "shadow side" (to use Jungian terms). Every man and woman is capable of committing the worst evil, or maybe even great good.

It is noteworthy that the psychoanalyst Carl Jung imputed the Nazi savagery to the "shadow side" that exists in all humans. Jung was Freud's one-time heir-apparent who later accepted chairmanship of the Nazi-led Medical Committee for Psychology and wrote bitterly anti-Semitic diatribes in the Nazi-sponsored newsletter. He obviously had his own "shadow side." While it is doubtful that Jungianism held the same sway over the Jewish émigré filmmakers and other dramatists after the war as it had before the war, it is quite conceivable that this concept of the "shadow side" was sufficiently well-known to the European émigrés—and maybe even to some of the more sophisticated Americans—to resonate through film noir.

It is also curious that films noir sometimes shifted stereotypes to make for more moral ambiguity. For instance, the noir film *Woman in the Window* (1944) cast

Edward G. Robinson, an actor identified with stereotypical gangster roles, in a respectable role as a professor. The professor falls asleep in his armchair and dreams that he committed murder. Because audiences recognize Robinson from gangster films, they automatically assume that the character in the film does indeed possess such a sinister side, and are surprised when he awakens and learns that the film's action occurred in a dream. This dream theme reminds us of Freudian influences on film noir, and of other dream scenes that recur with regularity in this genre.

Much has been written about film noir femme fatales, to the point that film students come away convinced that *all* females in film noir are evil and that *all* women are fetishized as femme fatales. That is not so. Although evil women abound in film noir, and superficially nice women often harbor hidden evil intentions—Ms. Wanderly in *Maltese Falcon* (1941), for example—it is just as common to find gender-neutral "gal pals" pushing the plot in film noir.

Vertigo's (1958) character of Midge (Barbara Bel Geddes) exemplifies the benevolent female film noir friend. Jimmy Stewart's on-again, off-again, glasses-wearing girlfriend/gal pal remains a true friend, and puts her own romantic inclinations aside, when Kim Novak's double-identified character deceives her pal. Novak's beautiful blonde character convinces Stewart that he failed to stop her (faked) murder. She leaves him riddled with self-doubt and at risk of losing his already shaky sanity.

Similarly, not all evil characters in film noir are female. In *Fear Strikes Out* (1957), it is the overbearing father figure who (supposedly) orchestrates his son's undoing. Based on a true story of a major league ball player who suffers a psychotic break, *Fear Strikes Out* highlights how the character's frustrated father, who wanted to play in the majors himself but ends up as a small-time community coach instead, pressures his son to the breaking point. The son ends up in a mental ward, where he receives shock therapy (ECT) in one of the screen's more compassionate ECT scenes. He recovers better in the movie than he did in real life, but this movie is not documentary.

It is interesting that both film noir and cowboy Westerns contribute to film fetishes and to real-life psychosexual fetishes. In film studies, fetishes refer to symbols that make the genre or the character immediately identifiable. Paraphilias (or sexual deviations) are defined by the fact that their fetishes are essential (rather than optional) for completion of the sexual act or for achieving sexual arousal. The high heels, slinky dresses, and black stockings of film noir, and the leather chaps, studded spurs, and cowboy clothes remain common sexual fetishes today and probably owe their origin (and their perpetuation) to these Freudian-inspired films of the fifties.

Interestingly, it is said that both film noir and cowboy films are sadomasochistic, apart from the fetishistic accoutrements. In both, someone is either being beaten up or is beating someone else up. Or they are tied to a tree, skinned alive, branded, or lassoed, in bondage fashion. It makes sense that sadomasochists are aroused by these films, to the point that they adopt these film fashions as their own.

The fact that dream scenes play such prominent roles in film noir further adds to the Freudian overtones. Not only are sleep scenes suggestive of sexual acts, but dream scenes borrow directly from Freud. Psychoanalysis taught us (correctly or incorrectly) that dreams reveal deep meanings and dark secrets. Because film noir is shot in black and white and is dark by its very nature, it is an ideal genre to dramatize the dark secrets of the night, and to suggest sexual secrets that are not directly revealed during light of the day, at least not between 1945 and 1955, when noir peaked. Because our psyches remain the same from decade to decade, some of the psychological themes of noir films—such as dreams and sleep, sex and aggression— are eternal.

It is interesting to note that anti-Freudian feminist scholarship about film noir actually preserved Freudian psychoanalytic theory long after Freudianism became unfashionable in psychiatric circles. American film departments came to fruition in the seventies, shortly after the women's movement of the late 1960s burgeoned and flowered into university-based women's studies departments in the 1970s. Film theorists such as Laura Mulvey and E. Ann Kaplan wrote about film noir females, producing must-read books and articles for film majors and women's studies students. Their writings inspired later film scholarship about "spectator theory," which focuses on the spectators who watch films and who are coerced into following the (male) filmmaker's (phallic) "gaze" and view the objects in the film from a male point of view.

These highly politicized film theories stimulated feminist sentiment of the 1970s. These ideas also fossilized the very same Freudian theories that were denounced for undermining women and for accusing achievement-oriented women of "penis envy." Regardless of whether one agrees or disagrees with these ideas, it is nevertheless intriguing to see how one idea begets another, and how the proverbial Ouroboros (the snake that swallows its tail) perpetuates itself, both in film theory and in psychiatric practice. We can thank film noir femme fatales for re-cementing the link between psychoanalysis and cinema that began some seventy years earlier.

CHAPTER 9

COLD WAR PARANOIA AND POSTWAR PTSD

PUBLIC PARANOIA

The Cold War began in 1947 and escalated in the 1950s, especially during the Korean War (1950–53). The Cold War peaked with the Cuban missile crisis of 1962, when the world narrowly averted nuclear war. During the Cold War, the "Free World" worried. It worried to the point of paranoia. That paranoia seeped into films produced during those strange years.

Hollywood had more to worry about than the rest of the country. As television sets appeared in more and more American homes, movie-going dropped dramatically, so Hollywood had financial worries. But Hollywood's legal worries, delivered by Senator Joe McCarthy, were worse than any worries previously encountered by this high-risk industry. McCarthyism, the House of Representatives' Un-American Activities Committee (HUAC), and the witch hunts for communists hounded Hollywood more than any other American city.

Hollywood had only recently recovered from its World War II worries, when there were realistic concerns about Japanese submarines sneaking near the shore and bombing the Pacific Coast, attracted by Hollywood lights. But Hollywood could cope with those threats: Hollywood lowered its lights and complied with wartime laws requiring blackouts and gray-outs.

A distinctive film noir photographic style evolved in response to the material constraints of war. Cinema's response to World War II is described by such scholarly books as *Blackout*.[1] Cinema's response to the Cold War was equally intense and could be summed up with a single word: paranoia.

During the Cold War, Americans built bomb shelters in their backyards. They worried about communist invaders and Soviet infiltrators. They wondered when enemy radiation would cook their skins and contaminate their crops. They believed government propaganda about the "Red Threat." Schoolchildren were forced to squat under desks during air raids and were taught about nuclear holocaust and radiation sickness.

Dr. Strangelove (1964) parodied this paranoia, while such films as *Failsafe* (1964) intensified the paranoia. *Failsafe* was the story of an accidental attack on the Soviet

Union that could not be stopped, in spite of many "failsafes" that were built into the system. Those films feel dated today because they focus on time-specific social situations. Films that deal with timeless psychological traits, such as *Peeping Tom* (1960), are more enduring.

In *Peeping Tom* a voyeuristic photographer lures unsuspecting women into his studio. As he snaps close-up shots, he stabs them with a saber that emerges from his otherwise ordinary camera equipment. This disturbing film lends itself to obvious Freudian interpretations about phalluses and dangers of penetration, male aggression, and female victimization. The backstories about the perpetrator's sadistic father provide symmetrical psychoanalytic explanations for his sadism.

Peeping Tom can be read as an allegory about serial killers (who did not appear en masse until the 1970s) or about sexual deviates and sadists in general (who have always existed). It can even be seen as an ancestor of Hitchcock's *Psycho* (1960), which is considered to be the first slasher film. But this gruesome film was, first and foremost, a reflection of the paranoia that prevailed in the 1950s, when Americans were writhing under the suffocating surveillance of the McCarthy era.

Americans were also projecting their own guilt about the bombing of Hiroshima and Nagasaki. They assumed that others would do unto them as they had done unto others, not an unreasonable assumption, given Deuteronomy's demand of "an eye for an eye." This projection of personal guilt onto others is a classic example of paranoia.

Let us look at paranoia for a moment, to see how this defense mechanism operates. Paranoia is first and foremost a form of projection. Paranoid people *project* their personal fears and hates by attributing their *own* thoughts or emotions onto others. They may not be aware of the hateful feelings or evil intentions that they impute to others. So Americans as a whole *projected* their country's responsibility for bombing Hiroshima and Nagasaki onto new enemies, namely Soviet Russia, Red China, North Korea, and Indochina.

True, there were good reasons to fear destruction, especially during the Cuban missile crisis (1962), but it was also true that American politicians and the American public needed collective enemies to project their guilt onto, lest they have to experience such guilt themselves. They grew especially fearful of communist countries that had been their allies during World War II.

Knowing that an atom bomb could level large cities in seconds, and snuff out millions of lives in less time, intensified fears of nuclear holocaust. Knowing that Germany, a nation that was once among the most civilized on earth, had only recently annihilated millions of people with Zyklon B gas alone—without the aid of atom bombs—made Americans even more concerned about mass destruction. America had done nothing to stop the murder of 6 million Jews, so who would stop someone from murdering them? In Hollywood, this threat of mass destruction was even more immediate, for many filmmakers had fled Hitler.

This rabid postwar anticommunism was not merely a manifestation of the mind. Attitudes reflected real-life political changes. After World War II ended, the world was split into two sides: East and West, the "Communist World" and the "Free World." Russia was communist. China and North Korea were communist. The United States was the stalwart of the "Free World."

Other events of the fifties further inflamed American fears of communism. In the Soviet Union, Stalin had massacred hundreds of millions of his own countrymen, implying that he would show less mercy on other opponents. Losing 50,000 Americans during the Korean War, between 1950 and 1953, further fueled anticommunist attitudes.

By the fifties, many displaced persons (DPs) from Nazi concentration camps had arrived. Their accents were unfamiliar. Some heavily accented European émigrés had already resettled in Hollywood and resumed work in film. Actors with exotic accents—such as Peter Lorre—were perfect for playing spies and smugglers. Their accents added mystery to movies but linked foreign accents with double-dealing and sinister intent.

Other postwar social stresses increased tension and produced paranoia. For one thing, American society was in transition. The economy was different, as always happens after war. On the home front, gender (and even race) "wars" were fermenting. Men were returning from combat, having seen sights and done deeds that they never imagined themselves capable of. Women were returning to the home after having done "Rosie the Riveter" jobs while the men were away. Women wondered about their old roles, their future roles, and about the impact of those roles on their families. Baby boomers were conceived during this shifting social order. The social turbulence of the 1960s was seeded in these postwar social shifts, and it came to full fruition when boomers reached adolescence.

Fortunately, the worst fears of the fifties never came to pass. The Cuban missile attack never took place. However, Hollywood suffered a different attack when Senator Joe McCarthy surfaced.

McCARTHYISM AND AMERICAN MOVIES

The McCarthy era was one of the more bizarre episodes in American history. No city was as hard-hit by McCarthyism as Hollywood. Left-leaning movie people were subjected to blacklists, public trials, self-imposed exile, or prison terms. Fear of betrayals by friends and enemies alike became commonplace when film people were forced into testifying against colleagues to protect themselves from imprisonment. These personal paranoid experiences penetrated films produced during that era.

HUAC was convened to do the dirty work. Because some Hollywood studios made pro-Soviet films during World War II (at the government's behest), so as to increase confidence in the USSR after the Soviets joined the Allies, Hollywood as a whole was suspected of spreading communist propaganda. To make matters worse, some facts fueled these fears. Some screen writers were Communist Party members or sympathizers. Most of those writers were Jewish, and most began writing for the New York Theater of the 1930s. Most had studied at City College of New York when communism was chic.

Those who testified against others were granted immunity from prosecution for libel. "Friendly" and "unfriendly" witnesses testified on televised trials, at a time when TVs were appearing in more and more American homes. Ayn Rand, of *Fountainhead* fame, was a "friendly witness" who denounced Louis B. Mayer for being "not much better than a Communist," because MGM produced *Song of Russia* (1944), with its smiling post-Revolutionary Russian peasants. Oddly enough, MGM was the least political of the majors, although it was the first studio to protest the Nazi control of Germany and stop production in Germany before the United States entered the war. Rand was a credible anticommunist, since her best-selling book (and subsequent film) focused on an icy architect who advocated the virtues of selfishness.

Ten witnesses (the Hollywood Ten who refused to cooperate with HUAC) were imprisoned for contempt of Congress. After their release, they and 400 others were blacklisted. Many writers went underground, using assumed names or front men to sell their scripts surreptitiously. They received but a fraction of their former pay, and got none of the credit.

Just as personal psychopathology, public psychopathology, and political psychopathology were merging in response to the Cold War and McCarthyism, psychology in general was entering the mainstream mentality and was making its way into the movies. There were many reasons for this emphasis on the psyche in cinema. For one thing, film noir from the forties had prepared audiences for psychological themes through its emphasis on dark secrets, dream scenes, voiceovers, flashbacks, and first-person narration. One psychological thriller begat another, and whetted the taste for more. The detective themes of film noir were perfect for presenting paranoia.

In addition, soldiers were returning from the war with "shell shock," or post-traumatic stress disorder (PTSD), as it is now known. Their families saw the psychiatric casualties of combat. Yet the idea that fearless soldiers could experience psychological, as well as physical, trauma was still not socially acceptable. In fact, the U.S. government found it so offensive to show psychologically damaged soldiers on screen that it suppressed release of John Huston's beautifully photographed documentary about soldiers' psychiatric treatments for thirty years. *Let There Be Light* (1946) was not released until 1980, although Huston's film *Freud* appeared in 1962.

More men took psychology classes through their GI bill–subsidized education. Women, who rarely benefited directly from the GI bill, were nevertheless inundated with magazine articles and advice columns by psychologists. Television shows, which women watched from home while rearing baby boomer children, talked about psychology, as did the Freudian-themed women's films of the forties. The horrors of the Holocaust also increased interest in psychological and sociological explanations for bizarre human behavior. The bestial behavior demonstrated at concentration camps, and televised through newsreel footage, made Freud's theories about the interplay between sexual and aggressive drives more plausible. The influx of refugee European psychoanalysts into American academic psychiatry and into private psychoanalytic practice and into Hollywood suburbs also made the study of psychology and psychoanalysis more accessible.

Then, during the Korean War, many Americans were captured and "brainwashed," and some appeared on public television and described their new pro-Communist political views. Curiosity about psychology—and brainwashing and behavioral conditioning—surged, and the movie *The Manchurian Candidate* emerged.

Another 1950s-era innovation found its way into film: Thorazine, the first "major tranquilizer" entered U.S. markets in 1954. Thorazine freed many schizophrenics of their delusions, but also turned patients into zombies because it slowed movements and erased facial expressions. Thanks to Thorazine, people who were sequestered away in asylums were returning home, thereby increasing public interest in psychiatric conditions. Psychology went mainstream, and into movies.

Technological advances also made it even easier to show psychology and to produce paranoia in cinema. When zoom lenses for still cameras went into mass production in 1959, the public was even more aware of the possibility of being observed from afar. Paranoid plot lines intensified.

Filmmakers turned public (and personal) fears into films. The Red Scare increased interest in spy films, which are paranoid by definition because spies search for hidden secrets. Ian Fleming's novels from the fifties became blockbuster Bond films in the sixties. *Our Man Flint* (1966) and *In Like Flint* (1967) were popular. *The Ipcress File* (1965), with Michael Caine, showed communist agents brainwashing Western scientists, turning them into blundering idiots, until Caine's Bond-like hero discovered that their brains were drained while on lecture tour. The television series *Man From Uncle, Secret Agent, The Prisoner,* and *The Avengers* compounded these themes.

Pick-Up on South Street (1953), with Richard Widmark, said it all when he said "better to be a criminal than a Commie." A year later, in 1954, public sentiment shifted, and the Senate censured Senator Joe. As the fifties ended, the blacklist eroded when Otto Preminger and Stanley Kramer openly defied these policies. Both Kramer and Preminger had escaped Hitler and were each committed to personal political ideals. Kramer produced social realist films about racial prejudices, including *The Defiant Ones* (1958), *Pressure Point* (1962), and *Guess Who's Coming to Dinner* (1967), all starring Sidney Poitier. Kramer's *Judgment at Nuremberg* (1961) was a powerful film about Nazi war crime tribunals. Preminger once played the German officer in *Stalag 17* (1953), a black comedy about Nazi infiltrators in a World War II POW camp, and later produced socially probing films such as *Anatomy of a Murder* (1959), *Exodus* (1960), *Carmen Jones* (1954), and *Porgy and Bess* (1959), along with such psychologically oriented films as *Laura* (1944).

After the blacklist ended, screen writers like Ben Hecht got credit for films. The twists and turns, and unexpected endings, of Hecht's stories were as convoluted as his own life under McCarthy. He specialized in paranoid films, such as *Spellbound* (1945), *Rope* (1948), *Whirlpool* (1949), *Where the Sidewalk Ends* (1950), and *Strangers on a Train* (1951). One wonders if his brilliance would have been subdued, or if it would have shone brighter, had it not been for the fact that he, like his characters, had to assume a double identity during the McCarthy era.

Before the blacklist ended, Hollywood tried to prove its loyalty to the country, and to Congress, by producing anticommunist movies. Most of those films bombed at the box office. Other films had veiled references to McCarthy witch hunts and "communist plants." Some of those films became cult classics and were even remade decades later, after their political poignancy had evaporated. Two such films—*Invasion of the Body Snatchers* (1956) and *Manchurian Candidate* (1962)—deserve extra attention.

POD PEOPLE AND PARANOIA

On the surface, the first *Invasion of the Body Snatchers* (1956) looked like state-of-the-art sci-fi. That genre blossomed after *Sputnik* (1957) and the race to space turned space travel into a reality rather than a fantasy. The zombie-like townspeople of *Body Snatchers* could also be seen as members of the recently arrived "Thorazine generation." *Body Snatchers* also parodied McCarthy's belief that invaders and infiltrators were everywhere, even in small-town American cornfields.

The film told of alien invaders who planted seeds in basements years before, intending to take over earthling bodies upon their return. When clones hatched from the pods, they displaced human psyches and possessed their bodies, like dybbuks. They inherited the humans' memories, but not their emotions, and so could pass undetected by almost everyone. Then the day came when the small-town family doctor grew suspicious when he noticed that his patients were robbed of their emotions, and realized that they were being replaced by pods.

Invasion of the Body Snatchers (1956) was remade at later dates. Donald Sutherland, Jeff Goldblum, and Leonard Nimoy (*Star Trek*'s Mr. Spock) starred in the 1978 remake, which followed two spectacularly successful sci-fi films: *Star Wars* (1977) and *Close Encounters of the Third Kind* (1977). Until then, everyone presumed that sci-fi had a small and select following. Suddenly, sci-fi appealed to far wider audiences, so that some Hollywood's highest-grossing films turned out to be sci-fi. Such financial success encouraged more sci-fi films. *Body Snatchers* was remade in this spirit and was stripped of its political message and McCarthyism.

Theoretically, the *Body Snatchers* remake might remind radicalized viewers of the "Thorazine shuffle" and the zombification produced by Thorazine. It might have fortified the anti-psychiatry movement that sprang from the writings of such psychiatrists as R. D. Laing and Thomas Szasz, who said that "schizophrenia" was a reasonable response to an insane society or that it was a socially constructed concept rather than a real illness. But it did not. Still, *Body Snatchers* (1978) turned into a teaching tool about a rare psychiatric syndrome that leads psychotics to believe that family or friends were replaced by impostors.

Manchurian Candidate, in both its original and its remade versions, can be compared to and contrasted with *Body Snatchers*. *Manchurian Candidate* (1962) appeared after the McCarthy era, but it preserved the pervasive political paranoia, partly because it reflected a real Cold War event that occurred between U.S. sailors and Korean communists. It also contrasted "Free World" free associations and dream themes with Soviet-style behavioral conditioning and brainwashing.

Eerily, the initial release of *Manchurian Candidate* foreshadowed John F. Kennedy's assassination. It was pulled from movie theaters immediately afterward, for fear that it might provoke more political assassinations. This uncanny correspondence turned it into a cult classic years before it was re-released in 1987. *Candidate* deserves cult status on cinematic merit alone. The spectacular performance of its all-star cast, with

Frank Sinatra and Angela Lansbury as one of the most toxic screen mothers of all times, is complemented by Laurence Harvey and Janet Leigh, remarkable black-and-white cinematography, and an exceptional screenplay.

Directed by John Frankenheimer, *The Manchurian Candidate* was adapted from Richard Condon's book by the same name. It begins with a title, "Korea 1952," to remind audiences of the highly publicized brainwashing experiments during the Korean War a decade before. Viewers knew that North Koreans had captured Americans, subjected them to sleep deprivation, re-education, and brainwashing, and then broadcast their "confessions" on live TV. To the astonishment of Americans, these previously patriotic prisoners publicly denounced American policy and promoted Korean communism instead. Real events like this lent credibility to Joe McCarthy's paranoia.

The first scene of *The Manchurian Candidate* introduces us to Captain Bennett Marco (Frank Sinatra) and Sergeant Raymond Shaw (Laurence Harvey). The younger Sergeant Shaw is the son of an incredibly evil mother (Angela Lansbury) and the stepson of an aspiring, self-serving, slimy vice-presidential candidate (James Gregory). Shaw has returned home from Korea and is about to receive the Congressional Medal of Honor for an act of heroism that he cannot remember.

Shaw's commanding officer, Captain Marco, describes Shaw's heroism: Shaw saved the lives of platoon mates after their capture by Manchurians (read North Koreans). The nine surviving members of his patrol parrot Marco's words. The president secures Shaw's pin to his lapel in a publicly staged event that was orchestrated by Shaw's publicity-seeking stepfather. The unpleasantries exchanged between Shaw and his parents foreshadow future developments.

The scene shifts to Major Marco, now reassigned to a cushy post in Army Intelligence in Washington, D.C., partly because he suffers from recurring nightmares and panic attacks, as do many PTSD patients. These dream scenes, described below, are among the most famous in film.

In the dream, Marco and his men sit together at a ladies' auxiliary meeting. The scene swiftly shifts, as dreams do, and shows the brainwashing scene in Manchuria. Knowing that Marco is asleep, we initially assume that the quick, disjointed scene shifts are standard jump-cuts, cinematic shorthand for dream scenes. We soon realize that these jagged juxtapositions tell truths that are not accessible to the conscious mind, just as dreams do.

The camera returns to the garden meeting, where an elderly white woman speaks to twenty club members about "Fun with Hydrangeas." Soldiers look on from the sidelines as she speaks. Then the camera shifts to an Asian-featured doctor who stands in the same spot where the garden lady spoke. Captive American soldiers sit behind posters of Stalin and Mao while twenty uniformed communist soldiers look on from the sidelines where the club ladies stood.

The doctor says that he will demonstrate the powers of hypnotism. He points to the American soldiers and states that "I have conditioned them—or brainwashed them, which I understand is the new American word. They believe that they are waiting out a storm in the lobby of a small hotel in New Jersey where a meeting of the ladies' garden club is in progress."

Sinatra's dream scene shifts back to the garden, where Shaw simulates a game of solitaire. He goes through the hand motions of dealing himself cards, even though he has no cards in his hands. When Shaw is asked if he has ever killed anyone, he replies that he has not. The evil Asian doctor disagrees, telling Shaw that he will demonstrate his ability to kill on command. He instructs Shaw to choose the platoon member whom he dislikes the least. When Shaw chooses Captain Marco (Sinatra), the doctor objects, stating, "That won't do, Raymond. We need the Captain to get you your medal." So Raymond names a second choice, Ed Mavole (Richard La Pore). Obediently, Raymond strangles Mavole with a scarf as Captain Marco yawns and the platoon members sit by, bored. Mavole dies in the dream.

At this point, Captain Marco abruptly awakens from this nightmare. Distressed by these recurring dreams, Marco consults an army psychiatrist, who happens to be African American (even though there were, and still are, very few African American psychiatrists in America). *Candidate* appeared before the Civil Rights Act of 1964, so blacks were still disenfranchised from the American establishment. A black cinematic psychiatrist sent the audience a message: he represented an alternative "establishment," even though he was an Army officer in full uniform.

Marco tells the "good" American doctor about his dream, explaining that Shaw was honored for saving the lives of all but two of the men in the platoon. The two men whom Shaw did not save were presumed to be missing in action (MIA). One MIA was Mavole, the man murdered in the dream. After recounting the dream's details, Marco repeats a phrase that will be pivotal to the plot: "Raymond Shaw is the kindest, bravest, warmest, most wonderful human being I've ever known in my life."

After this psychiatric consultation, Captain Marco is reassigned to a less stressful post. When another platoon member has strikingly similar dreams about his wartime experiences, the plot thickens. This time around, the dreamer is black, and the dream characters are black, but the storyline is the same. When Corporal Al Melvin (James Edwards) dreams of the garden party, he dreams of a garden club of equally boring black ladies who dress in their Sunday best, like African American churchwomen of that era.

Corporal Melvin's dream shows Sinatra stating that his first duty upon return will be to recommend Raymond Shaw for the Congressional Medal of Honor. Melvin also sees Shaw kill Mavole. When he sees Mavole's blood splatter on Stalin's portrait, Melvin awakens, screaming and awakening his wife. Melvin repeats the same line as Sinatra: "Raymond Shaw is the kindest, bravest, warmest, most wonderful human being I've ever known in my life."

Corporal Melvin is just as disturbed by these dreams as Captain Marco, but he drafts a letter about the dreams to Shaw instead of consulting a psychiatrist. When Shaw reads the letter, he shifts into playing solitaire, as he did in the dream. To contemporary psychiatrists, these recurring nightmares are typical of the disturbing dreams and disrupted sleep of post-traumatic stress disorder that Vietnam vets describe. Fortunately for the film, *The Manchurian Candidate* was made before this diagnosis appeared in the *Diagnostic and Statistical Manual*, 4th edition (DSM-IV)—and before any DSM existed—so clinical diagnoses do not distract from the story. Fortunately for Frank Sinatra's character, he starts to suspect that something is amiss and heads for New York, where he calls upon Shaw.

When Sinatra arrives, Shaw is busy with Chinese agents in his Manhattan apartment. A furious fight scene erupts between Sinatra and Shaw's Chinese employee. Shaw then reveals to Sinatra that he has the same recurring dream that Corporal Melvin described in his letter.

From then on, the plot gets more complicated. Now that Sinatra and the audience have seen the truth through the dream scenes, they will learn that their wartime experiences were engineered through the evil Russian Pavlov Institute, which specializes in the kind of behavioral conditioning that won Pavlov a Nobel Prize.

The Pavlov Institute reprogrammed the entire platoon into believing that Shaw was a hero, when he was really a killer who killed at the communists' command. Moreover, Shaw can be commanded to kill again on cue. He is preprogrammed to enter a "twilight state" of hyper-suggestibility whenever he sees the red Queen card (which reminds spectators of the Red Queen's irrationality and insanity in *Alice in Wonderland*).

As the film concludes, we learn that it is not the communists per se who commit the ultimate evil. Rather, it is Shaw's own mother (Angela Lansbury). She is a secret communist operative and a very real "Red Queen." She and her commie cronies are plotting to kill the presidential candidate so her husband can win the vice-presidency, then ascend to the presidency, take over the country, and hand it over to the communists. In the end, even the evil mother, who cooperates with the communists, is shocked to learn that the communists chose her son to complete the murder that leads to the communist takeover.

In the meantime, Marco (Sinatra) has been struggling to unravel the mystery about Shaw. He wants to test his theories, and to rid Raymond of his irresistible urge that overtakes him when he sees a red Queen in the cards. Sadly, a tragic act occurs before Marco can intervene: Shaw enters an "altered state," engineered by his evil mother. Entranced by the red Queen card, he kills his fiancee and her father at his mother's command. He destroys the love of his life and the only person worth living for. He is unable to cope.

The grand finale occurs at the political convention, where Shaw, now painfully aware that he is programmed to kill on command, aims his rifle at the stage. Unable to rid himself of either the communist or the parental control, and unable to accept his complicity in the killings, Shaw the sharpshooter shoots each of his parents just before turning the trigger on himself. (This final scene is an homage to Hitchcock, who used a similar closing in *The Man Who Knew Too Much* [1956].)

The enduring appeal of *The Manchurian Candidate* is manifold. Many think that it was a wonderful way to show off Sinatra's talents as an actor as well as a singer. Aside from this commercial consideration, *Candidate* provides sophisticated political commentary about McCarthyism, and current concerns with brainwashing and recent U.S. involvement in the Korean War. It also touches on the social roles of African Americans in pre–civil rights society. It comments on the evolving role of women in 1960s post-Eisenhower society, and it predicted potential evils that could befall society, should women become more empowered.

Above all, *Candidate* details a distorted and destructive Oepidal relationship between an unassuming son and a narcissistic mother who will stop at nothing— not even the sacrifice of her own son—so that she can achieve her own ends. Like many mother-son relationships portrayed in 1960s-era film and literature, this relationship shows that over-involved mothers poison their sons. *Candidate* is also a Cinderella story told in reverse, where the evil stepparent is the stepfather and the hapless victim is the son.

One can argue that the dream theme in *Manchurian Candidate* is not about dreams at all, and that dreams merely unfold the drama, revealing the plots and subplots, and so should be read as dramatic devices and nothing but. However, the director's use of dreams is deliberate. For dreams denote alternative realities and thereby allude to duplicity and double-dealing. The dream subplots make themselves manifest at night and thereby mirror the dual reality of human experience. The film also comments on the American concept of dreams, and Americans' belief that free associations to dreams can override communist brainwashing control and lead to a "free world" for all.

The Manchurian Candidate was even more appealing when re-released in 1987. The complexity of its plot and subplot, which is achieved through the dream scenes that contrast with behavioral conditioning, gives *Candidate* an endless life. (Its uncanny correspondence to the Kennedy assassination added to its allure.) Long after it ceased to speak to contemporary social concerns, and long after the glory days of its all-star cast, the plot is still a classic fairy-tale story about an evil stepparent, with traditional gender roles reversed.

Four years later Frankenheimer directed another film, *Seconds* (1966). Starring Rock Hudson as a middle-aged man who wants to start life over, and who is "doubled," this film retains the same paranoid flavor as its predecessor, and reminds us of mid-1950s "pod people." It also comments on the youth culture of the mid-sixties. But *Seconds'* plot is much too disturbing for most viewers (just as *Peeping Tom* is too disturbing for most). So it remains an undiscovered classic, known to film aficionados and to those who attended Cinema Classics' Paranoid Film Festival in the late 1990s. Curiously, its handsome star, Rock Hudson, lived a double life himself. When Hudson died of AIDS in the eighties, he made the world aware of secret lives lived by romantic leads who played heterosexual lovers on screen.

John Frankenheimer, director of *Seconds* and the first *Candidate*, was not involved in the 2004 remake of *The Manchurian Candidate.* The remake omitted the hypnosis, brainwashing, and behavioral conditioning scenes of the original and retained only the dream scenes. The remake lost the paranoid flavor and the political context and capitalized on the original's cachet and on the box-office draw of Denzel Washington. The remake pushed the original's race-related subplot into prominence when it substituted Washington for Sinatra as Captain Marco, and drew attention to the fact that Washington gained fame by playing the slain civil rights leader and radical black activist, Malcolm X.

The subtlety of the original spoke louder than the direct message of the second. In the first *Candidate,* the African American soldier's dream about a garden party populated by black women makes the dream scene credible and convincing, for Marco (Sinatra) dreamed an identical dream about white women in the same garden.

The original portrayed two African American actors in nontraditional roles and challenged stereotypes of black actors and black people in general. Adding an African American psychiatrist who was an Army officer was also a first, for very few black physicians were featured in film and even fewer were represented as psychiatrists. By highlighting racial factors in this film, the director called attention to racial issues in society. When the remake makes racial issues central rather than peripheral, it also obscures the real event that the original recollects: the televised brainwashing of Americans by communists. That brainwashing event made Joe McCarthy's paranoid accusations credible.

The brainwashing scene was especially credible in the sixties, when college psychology classes taught about behavioral conditioning (or Pavlovian conditioning). But the psychosurgery scene in the 2004 remake was not believable. Psychosurgery *does not* parallel Russian-discovered Pavlovian conditioning, which was a threat to Americans because of its *Russian-ness*. The Pavlov Institute of the first film spoke to the Cold War communist threat.

The second film deserves *some* credit for attempting to update the movie by referencing neuroscience—but not much. Furthermore, when the second *Candidate* was made, invasive techniques such as vagal nerve stimulation (VNS), deep brain stimulation (DBS), and transcranial magnetic stimulation (TCMS) were still experimental (as they still are!). These cutting-edge techniques were neither common enough nor effective enough to provoke debate about use *or* misuse. Sci-fi must make spectators suspend disbelief, provided that the science is relatively credible. Mixing social critique with incompletely credible neuroscience sends a muddled message—not a mixed message. A muddled message is the same as *no* message.

Thus, the remake comes closer to second-rate science fiction than to political polemics. It loses steam as a psychological thriller. It looks like a rip-off of *Total Recall* (1990), which was based on Philip K. Dick's amphetamine-induced paranoid tale of a "brain bolus" implanted into government agent Arnold Schwarzenegger's brain. This intranasal "brain bolus" implants false vacation memories of a trip to Mars and ablates his real memories.

The second *Candidate* reminds us of Robin Cook medical thrillers, such as *Coma* (1978), and vaguely conjures up another sci-fi film based on a Dick story, *Blade Runner* (1982). At times, Denzel Washington's soldiers look like *Stepford Wives* (1975), stripped of their wills.

The first *Manchurian Candidate* was significant for other historical reasons as well. Not long after *Candidate*'s 1962 premiere, the United States got involved in the Indochinese War. That turned into the Vietnam War, which became the defining event for postwar baby boomers. Vietnam was a political touchstone. Unlike the Cold War, which produced paranoia and a subtle sense of distrust, Vietnam's consequences were overt. Public protests, student strikes, draft dodging, Kent State killings, and self-immolation by Buddhist monks produced Cecil B. De Mille–style spectacle off-screen.

The Vietnam era did not result in many war movies, either during or after the war. Antiwar protests morphed into media events unto themselves. "Live from Saigon" televised news, images of rioting National Guards, napalm bombing of babies, and Chicago's YIPPIE convention obviated the need for staged battle scenes on screen. There was no need for cinematic spectacle when public spectacle was so accessible.

The Vietnam era left many legacies, one of which is the concept of PTSD. For decades, Vietnam veterans lobbied to gain public and professional recognition of PTSD (and to increase combat-related disability and medical benefits). Their approach was polar opposite of World War I vets, who suffered in silence or abandoned careers to pursue the arts (as some Surrealists did). Like the Vietnam war itself, the quest to legitimize PTSD became a highly publicized political issue. The PTSD war was waged in Congress.

Before the concept of PTSD was coined, *battle fatigue* and *shell shock* were standard terms for soldiers' psychological distress. Interestingly, Freud's theories gained steam because his contention that World War I "war neuroses" were more psychological than physiological proved true. Soldiers who were closer to the front were no more likely to suffer shell shock than those stationed farther away. The idea that atropine-based nerve gas alone caused psychosis lost steam when soldiers recuperated with the rest cure and talk therapy.

Still, as late as 1946 it was unacceptable to show soldiers' weaknesses on screen. When John Huston made *Let There Be Light* (1946)—a documentary-like film about a soldier seeking treatment from an army psychiatrist for psychogenic amnesia—the government forbade its release. The film was finally released in the 1980s and added credibility to Vietnam vets' PTSD claims.

MEMORIES, AMNESIA, AND MURDER

While realistic films about wartime trauma were unacceptable, fictional films apparently were acceptable. In the same year that Huston's film was blocked, Joseph Mankiewicz's *Somewhere in the Night* (1946) appeared. Starring John Hodiak, Nancy Guild, Lloyd Nolan, and Richard Conte, *Somewhere in the Night* made psychogenic amnesia its central theme. By default, it also deals with the loss of identity and sense of displacement induced by World War II.

One can argue that World War II and the military uniform were simply convenient framing devices for a film whose main MacGuffin (or driving device) was generically psychological. As a film about the quest for identity, *Somewhere* is also reminiscent of Hitchcock's *Vertigo* or *Spellbound*, which revolve around confused identities, assigned identities, and self-accepted identities. Related themes played out in racial terms in films such as *Pinky* (1949).

However one reads it, *Somewhere in the Night* is intriguing, and it even rivals Hitchcock. It begins when a serviceman awakens in a Honolulu hospital, only to discover that his face was reconstructed and that he has no memory of his identity. He is told that his name is Taylor because his civilian sports jacket has a lapel label that says "Taylor." Besides the sports jacket, he possesses only three personal items: his wallet, a scathing letter from an ex-lover, and a note from "Larry Cravat."

When his bandages are removed and his physical health returns, he leaves the hospital, wearing his soldier's uniform and a Purple Heart received for battle wounds. Bereft of any memory of himself, his associates, or his activities, he sets out to find Larry Cravat, hoping that Cravat will help him learn who he is himself.

The missing memory, lack of identity, and personal and social displacement of this so-called George Taylor (John Hodiak) is a metaphor for post–World War II society. Like the fictional Taylor, returning servicemen had to combat and overcome changing social circumstances. Often embattled by their own consciences, they needed to come to terms with acts they had committed during the war. A committed family man could commit murder on the battlefield, while a heartless murderer could pass unnoticed in an army of murderers. No one knew who was who, or who was what, or what or whom they were returning to.

The importance of Taylor's memory loss also tells us about the growing importance of psychoanalytic psychology in postwar America. A man was not known for his soul, his spirit, or even his social or family connections. A man was a distinctive and special human being because he possessed personal memories. His childhood memories, his repressed memories, his individualized memories separated him from others in the crowd, from others in uniform, and from other servicemen who were stripped of their individual identities while in the service. Without individual memories, any man—including "Taylor"—was just any other soldier.

There were many reasons why *repressed memories* became a psychoanalytic buzzword by the fifties. In Europe, Freudian analysts stressed transference and the relationship between analyst and analysand. But American analysis concentrated on excavating repressed memories, possibly because depicting repressed memories was so much more cinematic, so much easier to display to film and television audiences, and so much better accepted by Americans.

In the coming decade, women would also learn about their concealed pasts, just like these male soldiers. *Three Faces of Eve* (1957), *Bridey Murphy* (1956), and the television serial *Sybil* (1976) dramatized "split personalities" that were supposedly caused by repressed memories or even past life regression, when recollections of so-called "past lives" come into consciousness. Each film was spectacularly influential, not just as a film, but in terms of influencing patients' and even professionals' perceptions about controversial diagnoses such as multiple personality disorder and dissociative identity disorder.

Unlike the male soldier in *Somewhere*, most women who searched for their previous identities asked for the assistance of a (usually) male psychoanalyst or perhaps a male detective. In contrast, George Taylor starts his search in soldierlike fashion. He is kicked unconscious by an assortment of goons, hoodlums, and unsavory detectives. He escapes through a military-like maneuver.

The driving point of the film shifts when Hodiak learns of a murder committed before the war. Two men were seen walking along the docks, carrying a suitcase that supposedly contained $2 million. A third man was present, who either witnessed the murder or committed the murder. It is even more unclear who took possession of the suitcase. The protagonist begins to wonder if he was the murderer or if he was the witness. He desperately needs to find Larry Cravat to tell him who he is and to clear him of impending murder charges.

The high point of *Somewhere in the Night* is the waterfront scene, where Taylor and his newly acquired girlfriend stumble upon a suitcase that supposedly belongs to Larry Cravat. Until now, all we know is that Larry Cravat was the cad who left Taylor's girlfriend's best friend standing at the altar and then had the gall to send a postcard to the girlfriend. Other men wanted to kill this Larry Cravat. Even women despised him for what he had done. Where was Cravat?

In true film noir style, Taylor and his girlfriend are nearly lost in the fog and mist as they crawl up creaky, rotted steps near the waterfront. Then they find Cravat's suitcase, which contains not just money, but also another jacket that belongs to "Larry Cravat." The jacket has the same look and the same label that was seen in Taylor's civilian jacket that was recouped at the hospital where he underwent reconstructive surgery at the start of the film. The jacket label reveals Taylor's true identity: the label says "W. George, Tailor." The camera zooms in on the label, putting it in full view of the viewer, making the mistaken identity of "George Taylor" intuitively obvious, to both George Taylor and to the audience. Thus concludes the movie's MacGuffin. George Taylor realizes that *he* is Larry Cravat, as we and "Taylor" realize that the hospital clerk misspelled the label "George, Tailor" as "George Taylor."

To add intrigue, *cravat* is French for necktie. The necktie belongs with the jacket, in more ways than one. Taylor's assumed name was misread off a label that literally referred to a tailor. As they say, "clothes make the man." In this case, the tie and the jacket together make the man, and inform us of his identity. These clothes give him a civilian identity, just as his military uniform loaned him a wartime identity. Without these external accoutrements—the tie and jacket, or the Marine uniform and Purple Heart—this man without a memory has no identity.

The movie ends, but we still wonder who this man (or who any man) is. Is he the same man that he was before he entered the war? Is he still the serviceman with the assigned identity? If so, how can he have an identity if he is no longer in the service? Forties and fifties films pondered these psychological and sociological questions, and Vietnam vets fought about related issues in court, as they struggled to gain recognition for PTSD and to implicitly retain their wartime identities indefinitely as they get treatment through VA facilities.

Amnesia films became popular around this time, solidifying the significance of the psyche in cinema and fortifying Freudian, or psychoanalytic, concepts of the ego, or the I, or the [German] ich of identity. Unearthing memories about past lives or forgotten deeds did more than make good psychological sense; this was a perfect plot-driving device that was perfectly suited to the psychological thrillers that evolved around this time. Another thriller, Hitchcock's *Spellbound* (1945), was made a year before *Somewhere in the Night*. That film also revolves an amnesiac's quest to recover his memory and learn who he is so that he can clear himself of murder changes.

When *Manchurian Candidate* depicted psychological stresses among Korean War soldiers so directly in 1962, we realize how far film had come since 1946, and how much credibility the concept of psychological trauma had gained since World War II.

The next two decades brought a few important films about Vietnam. Sylvester Stallone's *First Blood* (1982) started his remarkably popular *Rambo* series. Those action-adventures were long on action, but short on psychology, and mid-range with respect to social commentary.

The Deer Hunter (1978), with Robert De Niro and Christopher Walken, was a different story. This thought-provoking and heart-rending "buddy film" told of the physical and psychological toll that Vietnam took on working-class youths who did not have college draft deferments. In the *Deer Hunter*, buddies who enlisted together witness the self-destruction (and war-induced destruction) of Nick's (Walken's) opiate addiction. They see his suicide, which finally frees him of his vice.

Poppy (opiate) addiction was fairly common in Vietnam, but repeated studies by addictionologists showed that most soldiers shook their habits before leaving for home.[2] Instead, Nick remains in Saigon, where he plays Russian roulette with a loaded pistol each evening. He collects cash to subsidize his habit and sends some of it home to his buddy, who lives out his life at a VA hospital, confined to a wheelchair because his legs were blown off. Considered to be one of the finest films of all times, *The Deer Hunter* is more than a war movie or a buddy film. It is also a tale about the dangers of drugs.

Jacob's Ladder (1989) is a film about war displacement, hallucinogenic drugs, and cross-cultural concepts of the afterlife. This bizarre film borrows ghastly artistic imagery from painter Francis Bacon. It goes far beyond PTSD or war trauma. It describes the Tibetan Buddhist bardos that the soul journeys through as it leaves earthly life and continues on to endless reincarnation. It compares the bardos to the proverbial stairway to heaven that the biblical patriarch Jacob ascends in Genesis (hence the title).

Until the movie ends, the viewer is uncertain if the battle and surgery scenes occurred on the battlefield, in an American hospital, or during a dream. Or maybe everything that Jacob experienced, as he lay dying in Vietnam, was part of an acid trip or an opium trance. Or perhaps the action really did occur in the bardos, or in heaven, or somewhere in the supernatural. For *Jacob's Ladder* began a trend of end-of-the-millennium films that caused even more mental confusion than paranoia or PTSD.

CHAPTER 10

DRUGS AND OTHER DEMONS

Drug and drink have appeared in film since film's inception. Sometimes these substances were the stars. Sometimes they were part of the setting. Sometimes they were in the foreground, other times in the background. Occasionally they were props. In the most memorable films about drink and drug—and there have been many—drug or drink take center stage.

Although we reflexively associate drug themes with the drug culture of the sixties and seventies, the fact of the matter is that drug and drink have very ancient origins, both in general history and in film history. These themes surfaced in silent films, such as Edison's *A Chinese Opium Den* (1894), which was made before Méliès transformed movies into magic.

Silent cinema captured drunken states, delirium tremens, drug withdrawals, and opium dreams just as well as "trippy" films from the heyday of the drug culture. Many film fans feel that early film's earnest and enthusiastic but simple special effects compete with and complement more sophisticated computer-generated imagery (CGI) found in films of the 1980s and 1990s.

In those decades "memoir movies" about the drug culture took advantage of CGI's abilities to manufacture drug-induced visions. By the twenty-first century, puppet animationists such as George Higham revisited Méliès's turn-of-the-century techniques, fusing arcane stop-motion animation with computerized editing. Higham's *Annabel Lee* (2002) conveys the uncanniness of Poe's laudanum-induced delirium through puppetry and voiceover narration.

SHORTS AND SILENTS

Just as contemporary society gloated over computer technology when it first appeared, early filmmakers similarly delighted in their cameras' newfound capabilities. They searched for every opportunity to show off their new skills. They needed themes that complemented this new moving medium. In America, train-robbery films were perfect for this purpose. In Europe, and in America as well, opium dreams were particularly popular, for several reasons.

For one thing, opium dreams were already well-enshrined themes in literature as well as in ballet (which is also a moving medium). Romantic era writers and choreographers created a taste for exotic opium dreams through such ballets as *La Bayadere*—a story about unrequited love, a venomous snakebite, a spectacular Indian palace, and delirious opium-induced visions.

Note that Edison produced the silent short, *Chinese Opium Den* (1894), at the start of cinema, when moving pictures were used for education or scientific documentation rather than entertainment or diversion. In 1908 Méliès used his special-effects skills to create a magical and mystical imagery for *Dreams of an Opium Fiend* (1908), which was as otherworldly as his *Trip to the Moon*. He merged the French intrigue with dissociated states with the sensual world of the Orient. Other filmmakers followed suit, and opium dreams appeared repeatedly on the silent screen.

The passage of the Opium Exclusion Act in the United States in 1909 opened the door for films about opium dens, drug dealing, and exotic overseas exploits, all of which offer inviting cinematic settings. As opium smuggling made headlines and attracted Americans' attention, opium also opened opportunities for "social problem" films, which mixed social messages, media skills, and money-making potential for moviemakers. These films exploited sensational themes to attract audiences, at the same time warning of the dangers of drugs and drink. It is interesting to look back in time, while we hear diatribes condemning our own contemporary sensationalist drug themes and exploitative films. For it is clear that current debates about appropriate film themes began in the early twentieth century, and have been rehashed over time.

CONRAD VEIDT

Drug and drink themes were not restricted to second-rate B movies. Conrad Veidt, an actor of great stature (and great historical significance), starred in a cautionary tale about opium in 1919, the same year that he appeared in the Expressionistic classic *Cabinet of Doctor Caligari* (1919). Robert Reinert's *Opium* (1919) is a less-respected example of German Expressionism, but it is an example of Expressionism nonetheless. The action of this German-subtitled, Austrian-directed film occurs in the "exotic Orient" of China and India, and not in the claustrophobic confines of *Caligari*.

Another important opium-related film appeared across the ocean in 1919. *Broken Blossoms* (1919) starred silent-screen favorite Lillian Gish. Directed by D. W. Griffith and based on Thomas Burke's story ("The Chink and the Chinaman") from *Limehouse Nights*, the film contrasts the seediness, dark shadows, drunkards, and drug addicts of Britain's Limehouse streets with the beautiful, Oriental-inspired abode of a Buddhist missionary. The missionary Cheng takes in Lucy, a "broken blossom" who has escaped her abusive alcoholic father and seeks Buddhist compassion. This film's dark and dismal visual style and subject matter inspired the German Expressionist giants Pabst, Stiller, and von Sternberg, as well as later European émigré directors who started American film noir style.

Burke's story portrays Cheng as a sordid Shanghai drifter who frequents opium dens and whorehouses after being conscripted into the navy. In the film, the drifter becomes a missionary who spreads Buddha's word to bring world peace—but he still frequents opium dens when depressed. Even at his lowest point, Cheng stops his gambling companions from fighting (and implicitly references World War I, which ended the year before the film's release).

This sentimental tale of abused children, damaged souls, reclaimed love, drug addiction, and depression starts in the "exotic Orient" but plays itself out on drug-infested British streets. Like other films of its era, it taps into the anti-Chinese sentiment that soared as Chinese immigration increased in America (the so-called yellow peril). Unlike most anti-Asian films, this film adds a drunken (rather than drug-addicted) Chinese father to the proverbial Oriental opium den scenes. However, Griffith hoped to promote tolerance, rather than intolerance, through film. As shown by his acclaimed but controversial *Birth of a Nation* (1915) and *Intolerance* (1916), Griffith readily tackled race-related themes, be it through panoramic staging or intimate drama.

Many decades later, Charlie Chan films linked opium and Orientalism in more offensive fashion. In fact, the connection between opium and Orientalism never fully fades away. The concept is stronger in some eras than others, but it often drifts in the background of all eras, like opium smoke itself. This exploitation of the "other," and the imputation of antisocial acts to this "other," peaks in blaxploitation films, where black pimps, prostitutes, drug dealers, and drug users supplant Oriental opium smokers.

CHARLIE CHAPLIN

In film's early years, Charlie Chaplin turned personal alcohol-related tragedies into slapstick comedy. Like his character in *The Tramp* (1915), Chaplin's father was alcoholic. Audiences laughed, and Chaplin laughed, but we wonder who "laughed through their tears" as tragedy turned into comedy. It is ironic that Adolf Hitler admired Chaplin's tragicomic character enough to adopt Chaplin's mustache. (Chaplin, however, did not reciprocate the admiration and made a film that mocked Hitler and led to a Nazi ban of all Chaplin films.)

Another Chaplin film about alcoholism is considered to be his funniest. *The Cure* (1917) tells the history of medical, psychiatric, and substance-use treatments at the same time that it shows slapstick comedy at its best. *The Cure* is set in a health resort that is devoted to the once-popular practice of "taking the waters" at mineral springs (such as Sharon Springs, Saratoga Springs, Cold Springs, Hot Springs, and Eureka Springs). When the movie was made, it was fashionable to spend a week at these expensive and exclusive spas. It was believed that mineral water cured whatever health problems plagued visitors, be it rheumatism, gout, polio, or alcoholism. Someone who went to a spa to get clean and sober was said to be taking the cure.

When Charlie's character arrives, he is pushed in a wheeled deckchair by a uniformed attendant but is obviously still intoxicated. Despite the familiar Chaplin mustache and his drunken slurred speech, he looks different from his lovable Little

Tramp. This Charlie remains disheveled, but his dapper ensemble, with light jacket, straw boater, and spotted tie, tells us that he is now a respectable citizen of far higher social status than the Little Tramp.

Like others spa-goers, he is (supposedly) there to dry out, probably at the insistence of friends or family. But Charlie has no intention of avoiding alcohol, for he filled his wardrobe trunk with bottles of booze (like Ray Milland in *Lost Weekend* [1945]). After an attendant offers him mineral water, he rushes to his room to wash out the taste of water with liquor. When his liquor stash is discovered by the resort's manager, the bottles are accidentally dumped into the spa's spring. Soon, everyone becomes as drunk and disorderly as Chaplin. This scene from the silent screen is strikingly similar to real-life scenes in twentieth-century rehabs.

Another classic about drugs that appeared on screen in the teens was *Dr. Jekyll and Mr. Hyde* (1912). Inspired by Robert Louis Stevenson's 1885 story about a doctor who transforms into a libidinous monster after ingesting a chemical potion that he concocted, this story would be told and retold on stage and screen many times over. When *Dr. Jekyll* made its way to Broadway in the 1990s, the story inspired devoted fan clubs, thereby attesting to the timeless appeal of this tale of transformation while "under the influence."

Rouben Mamoulian made the definitive version of *Dr. Jekyll & Mr. Hyde* in 1931, in a decade that produced some of the most successful horror films of all time, and in a decade that ushered in the worst horrors of the real world. (Hitler was elected chancellor in 1933 and the Holocaust began in 1938.) By the 1950s, times had changed. Comedians Bud Abbott and Lou Costello appeared in a version of Dr. Jekyll and Mr. Hyde. The campy counterculture *Dr. Jekyll and Sister Hyde* (1970) told the story of Jekyll's transvestite double. By 2007, imdb.com listed more than fifty remakes of *Dr. Jekyll and Mr. Hyde*!

The 1970s drug culture embraced Stevenson's story and delighted in remakes of this dated Scottish tale of drugs and sex. The sexual-freedom movement coincided with the 1970s drug culture and was fermented by the availability of oral contraceptives, legalized abortion, and feminism. These events found parallels in Hyde's story. Even though Stevenson's novella spoke of recent Darwinian discoveries about the "animalistic nature" of humankind, Stevenson's link between sex and drugs seemed tailor-made to this 1970s generation.

That era venerated other film remakes that were read as drug allegories. *Reefer Madness* (1936), originally intended as a docudrama about marijuana's dangers, was re-released in 1971 and became a favorite "midnight movie" from then on. The drug culture breathed new life into such old favorites as *The Wizard of Oz* (1939), *Alice in Wonderland*, and Disney's *Fantasia* (which was first made in 1940).

Frank Baum's turn-of-the-century stories about *The Wonderful Wizard* had turned into two different film versions—and several stage plays—even before Judy Garland starred as Dorothy Gale. Over the years, Baum's fantastic stories provoked many political interpretations. It is generally accepted that the Kansas farm girl's travails reminded 1939 American movie audiences of the farm failures of the thirties (even though Baum wrote it in 1900). *The Wizard of Oz* is considered to be the classic American myth of self-discovery and self-reliance, so it is fitting that it always airs on

the classic American holiday, Thanksgiving. Americans realize that their own inge-
nuity surpasses the abilities of the sham wizard who rules an illusory world.

The drug culture saw more than American myth or populist politics in *Wizard*.
The fact that Dorothy and friends romped through poppy fields, and saw scary hallucinations of flying monkeys along with breathtaking visions of glowing green,
proved that Frank Baum told hidden truths about hallucinogens. Curiously, a wild
grass known as *Lolium temultenum* is often infested by the same ergot-producing
fungus that is used to make LSD, and *Lolium* grass produces green vision without
the special glasses required by Emerald City.

The Wiz (1978) was based on a Broadway musical about an adult, African American
Dorothy (Diana Ross) who sings African American–inspired songs. Characters sing
and dance and prance around in seventies-style psychedelic garb. The mid-eighties
brought Disney's more sinister and less popular *Return to Oz* (1985), where
Dorothy's Aunt Em sends her for shock treatments to cure her of her dreams and
delusions about Emerald City. In the end, Dorothy escapes.

Disney's *Fantasia* was also deified by the drug culture, because it dramatized the
confusion between music and image that occurs during hallucinogen-induced synes-
thesia. Its fantastic creatures and high-key colors recollect psychedelic color changes
and hallucinosis. Adult mushroom users apparently appreciated Disney's *Fantasia*
(and the "mushroom dancers") more than its target children's audience. The fact that
the Greek god of dreams, Morpheus—the namesake of morphine—appears in the
first *Fantasia* made the fantastic film even more relevant to the drug culture.

Drug use was prominent in several late 1960s and early 1970s films. *Klute* (1971)
stars Jane Fonda as a reefer-smoking call girl, aspiring actress, and "liberated [white]
woman" who answers to her African American, drug-using pimp. She finds a new
life through a straight-shooting but open-minded cop (Donald Sutherland), who
investigates her "john's" murder. Another classic of that era, *Midnight Cowboy*
(1969), with Dustin Hoffmann and John Voight, morphed into *Drugstore Cowboy*
(1989). *Midnight Cowboy* shows a bleak vision of 1960s antiheroes who do drugs,
sell sex, and die young. Similarly, *Easy Rider* (1969) supposedly spoke for its generation as it showcased hapless youth, in this case Peter Fonda, starring as "Captain
America." The Depression-era comic book hero Captain America had become an
American flag–clad motorcyclist who rides cross-country, stopping only to light a
toke, until his meaningless life ends with an equally meaningless death.

The Seven Percent Solution (1976) spoofs the drug culture, Sigmund Freud, and
Sherlock Holmes together. It shows Freud as a cocaine user who deleted publications
about his personal cocaine use from his canonized "Collected Works." We see Freud
as another Timothy Leary: the High Priest of the Psychoanalytic Sect is little different from the professor-proselytizer for LSD. As one who authored a book about the
psychological significance of humor, Freud would agree that "many a truth is said in
jest." This 1970s parody predicted Freud's fall from grace in the 1990s, when protesters objected to the Smithsonian's federally funded show about Freud.

The film that best captured the essence of the drug culture—in spirit, image, and
word—is *The Trip* (1967). Directed by Roger Corman and starring the youthful
Peter Fonda, Jack Nicholson, and Dennis Hopper, this period piece flashes kaleidoscopic

colors on overexposed skin. Words like "groovy" occur too often, hinting at the conversational limitations induced by hallucinogen use. The film substituted for illicit LSD for the cautious but curious crowd.

THE DOWNSIDE OF DRUGS

The nihilism of early drug-culture films came to full flower (or should I say full wilt?) in Michael Cimino's *The Deer Hunter* (1978). The multi–award-winning *Deer Hunter* was both an antiwar and an anti-drug film, but its powerful presentation prevented it from becoming a polemic. The Vietnam War had finally ended, having dragged on far longer than student protesters ever expected. The mid-1970s recession collided with the social activism and overarching optimism of the 1960s. The national mood was now sober and somber.

The Deer Hunter is a buddy film that chronicles the interconnected lives of working-class, high-school chums who enlist together, with plans to fight together in Nam. Robert De Niro, Christopher Walken, and Meryl Streep play characters who are worlds away, both literally and physically, from the college kids who protested the war and robbed returning soldiers of the dignity enjoyed by World War II vets. *The Deer Hunter* shows the toll that drugs take on Christopher Walken's character. His buddy has lost his legs to a grenade and sits around idly in a VA hospital, collecting socks sent by friends. Walken remains able-bodied. He can walk and talk, but he lost more than legs in the war. His heroin addiction has turned him into a shell of his former self.

Unlike most vets, who kicked their heroin habits before returning to America, Christopher Walken continues his addiction and remains in Saigon, where he has a ready drug supply. To subsidize his habit, he plays high-stakes Russian roulette each night. He aims a loaded pistol at his head as frenzied crowds throw money at him and bet on his life. This act parallels the metaphorical "Russian roulette" that he plays each day in private, as he injects dope into his arm. He finally finds the peace he seeks through heroin when he is buried back home.

In contrast, most films that romanticized drugs and glorified the antisocial acts that often accompany drug use do not stand the test of time. Films meant to be viewed "under the influence," such as Stanley Kubrick's *2001* (1968), seem dull and dated when viewed through the sober eye of reason. Later generations are rarely as impressed by such cult classics as baby boomers were. Even boomers who view those films a second time around wonder what they liked in them.

The Beatles' *Yellow Submarine* (1968) epitomizes this genre. With its interesting animation, melting colors, morphing forms, and spinning flowers, *Submarine* was meant to be viewed after dropping an acid tab. Its animated flowers start to whirl when LSD kicks in, making the LSD experience more intense. The Beatles' lyrics recollect the group's own LSD experiments and implicitly condone spectators' drug use. Viewed without LSD, and without awareness of its cultural significance, this film is just another cartoon.

Psychedelic-era lyrics resurfaced in films about boomers' mid-life struggles. For instance, the Academy Award–winning *American Beauty* (1999) plays 1970s-style youth-culture songs to emphasize the futility of Kevin Spacey's quest for fulfillment in later life. *American Beauty* evokes the days when drug-induced reality promised more than "real" reality. In those days, the human potential movement eclipsed psychoanalysis, and advising followers to be "all that you can be" and forgetting about Freudian-style fatalism and psychological determinism.

In *American Beauty*, we watch the life—and death—of Kevin Spacey unfold before our eyes. He is a cuckolded husband and suburban father who lusts after his teenage daughter's cheerleader chum. He smokes weed, as he did as a teen. He wallows in memories of lost youth and anguishes over unrequited love. When the opportunity to consummate his passions for the teen-aged cheerleader arrives, an unexpected surge of morality overtakes him and he stops.

His daughter is disgusted by him, his wife is bedding another man, and his ex-soldier neighbor tries to kiss him. His advances rejected, the neighbor flies into a rage and shoots Spacey. Spacey lies dying on his suburban kitchen floor, surrounded by a flowing pool of blood that parallels the red petals of an American Beauty rose. The blood that flows from Spacey's dead head moves more than he did during his drug-induced reverie. So much for drug dreams.

Ironically, the film that best captured the LSD experiments of the sixties did not arrive until the eighties. Released in 1980, directed by Ken Russell and based on Paddy Chayefsky's novel, *Altered States* combines Darwinian evolution, Jungian archetypes, and Leary's chemical revolution in one. A young William Hurt stars as a Harvard professor who uses mind-altering drugs to research different states of consciousness. While using LSD inside an isolation chamber, he experiences physical as well as mental changes. His body journeys back in time as his mind regresses. He ends up as an ape.

A prolific filmmaker, the British-born Russell was known for his edgy themes and psychedelic art direction long before he made this film. He incorporated drug subtexts and hallucinogenic visions into other films, such as *The Devils* (1971), *Gothic* (1986), and *Lair of the White Worm* (1988). In spite of Russell's admiration for drug experimentation, *Altered States* is also an admonition against drugs.

Although the drug culture's cult films faded to gray, the drug culture's fascination with drugs made a permanent imprint on film history. Partly because of the importance accorded to visual hallucinations during the psychedelic sixties, film as a medium was elevated in importance. The long-standing struggle to acknowledge the "seventh art" was won. Film was the greatest hallucinogenic of all and was now a subject of serious academic study in America. Film studies blossomed in the early seventies.

During this time, independent filmmakers gained steam with the college crowd, who spurned mainstream in favor of alternative anything. Many indies glorified drug or alcohol use or produced slow-moving "moving pictures" (pictures that moved) rather than narrative films. The names of earlier filmmakers such as Stan Brakhage, Maya Deren, and Kenneth Anger appeared in university students' vocabularies.

Anger's *Inauguration of the Pleasure Dome* (1954) was based on Samuel Coleridge's drug-induced opium visions, described in his poem "Kubla Khan." Anger's films predated the drug culture and were ready and waiting when the drug generation was ready. Anger later became Jean Cocteau's lover and joined him in

Paris. Cocteau's *Beauty and the Beast* (1946) used simplified special effects to simulate opium-induced visions. His human-headed candelabras, with their moving
eyes and their waving arms, were venerated by the drug culture, even though
Cocteau's book about *Opium* described his two attempts to rid himself of his
opium habit and reminds readers that he produced his best work after he stopped
his opium excursions.

The drug culture was not just pro-drug. It was also anti-alcohol (or hard alcohol).
To justify their drug use, the youth culture/drug culture often alluded to the older
generation's overindulgence in drink. The drug culture bolstered its anti-alcohol
(and implicitly pro-drug) arguments by pointing to 1950s films about the downside
of drink (and prescription pills).

Some of the finest films ever made focus on the downward spiral caused by drug
or drink, although detractors claim that *any* film about drug or drink encourages
younger viewers to imitate the actions of the actors. *Valley of the Dolls* (1967)
appeared at a turning point, just after LSD was outlawed and just as the counterculture spread beyond the fringes. Based on Jacqueline Susann's best-selling novel, *Dolls*
stars Barbara Perkins, Sharon Tate, and Patty Duke as three recent college grads who
move to Manhattan, aspiring to act or sing. Their dreams turn into nightmares, as
prescription pills ("dolls") sabotage promising careers.

In real life, two of the three stars spiraled downward themselves. Patty Duke plays
the rags-to-riches singer who succumbs to sleeping pills and attempts rehab. Duke
herself developed a manic-depressive disorder that interrupted her acting career and
turned her into an advocate for lithium treatment. Sharon Tate was pregnant with
Roman Polanski's baby when murdered by the Manson clan. Eerily, Tate plays an
aspiring actress who marries a handsome entertainer who develops Huntington's
dementia. She pays his medical bills by appearing in X-rated films and then develops
breast cancer herself. She commits suicide with the "dolls" the day before she
is scheduled for a mastectomy. Only Barbara Parkins "survives," to star in the *Peyton
Place* TV series.

Decades before *Valley of the Dolls*, such films as *Lost Weekend* (1945), *The Man
with the Golden Arm* (1955), *Days of Wine and Roses* (1962), and *Night of the Iguana*
(1964) capitalized on the human drama intertwined with drug and drink. Some
films self-consciously tout the benefits of rehab or Alcoholics Anonymous (AA), but
Iguana minimizes alcoholism's contribution to Richard Burton's downfall as a
preacher and a person. Instead, the film focuses on Freudian-style repressed memories, sexual tensions, family conflicts, and human fulfillment, as would be expected
of the Freudian-influenced Tennessee Williams, whose story inspired the film.

Even *Lost Weekend* (1945), *the* classic film about the dangers of drink, shows a
romanticized and unrealistic view of the recovery process. Ray Milland plays a handsome and charming but unpublished and unrealistic writer whose fingers wrap
around the bottle rather than the typewriter. His old Underwood sits on his desk,
holding one partly written page. Milland's creativity is stifled, but he is endlessly
inventive at hiding his bottles from his older brother. He zips bottles into the vac-
uum cleaner bag. He wraps a rope around another bottle and suspends it outside his
window when he is scheduled to check into the sanitarium.

Early on, Milland meets an attractive and intelligent woman at the opera. She is charmed by his good looks and social status. Like any enabler, she skirts the fact that he spends more time in bars than with books. In the end, he suddenly decides to stop drinking, and supposedly succeeds, effortlessly. Even though the film shows heartbreaking scenes of self-destruction, the last scene shows none of the anguish of alcohol abstinence portrayed by *Days of Wine and Roses* (1962) or *Come Back, Little Sheba* (1952).

Lost Weekend is a movie with a message. It tells us that even the high and mighty and well-heeled can drop to the depths because of booze. In one especially memorable scene, we watch Ray Milland traipsing through a hard-scrabble neighborhood, futilely searching for an open liquor store after his local bar refuses to serve him anymore. It turns out that the day he runs out of drink is Yom Kippur, the Jewish Day of Atonement. The Jewish-owned liquor stores are all closed.

Milland breaks the store window to retrieve a bottle and soon after finds himself in a stark detox ward that is worlds away from the spa-like sanitarium that his brother offered him. Milland sees spiders as he lies on a cot in a crowded public hospital. Patients of all colors scream from drug withdrawal. The spartan ward is staffed by a sneering and cynical male nurse, whose over-the-top, stereotypical performance is as striking today as it presumably was in the 1940s.

While *Lost Weekend* tells of the world of the wealthy and well-bred alcoholic, *The Man with the Golden Arm* depicts a very different slice of life and social class. Frank Sinatra's Frankie Machine shows us what life might have been like for Jimmy Cagney's character, had he lived long enough to be paroled from prison and returned to the low-life world inhabited by Frankie and his card-playing cronies.

Otto Preminger's tale of a not-quite-working-class white man who struggles to pull himself out of the mean streets and gambling halls of the city slums, in order to avoid the harsher hold of heroin, is heartbreaking. Elmer Bernstein's jazz-inspired music adds pure pathos. The film salutes the drug rehab doctors who treat Frankie at the drug ward in Lexington Federal Prison. The film ends when Frankie's wheelchair-bound wife rises from her chair and jumps to her death, after it becomes apparent that she—and not Frankie—murdered a man. Until then, Frankie does whatever he can to comfort her, even though she cajoles him into card dealing so he can pay for her costly medical care. Frankie's wife is a different kind of enabler, an evil, ill-willed enabler who is polar opposite of Milland's unassuming but loving girlfriend.

Frank Sinatra's slum-dweller is particularly poignant because he desperately tries to "go straight" after his release from prison. He struggles to find a "real job" as a jazz musician so that he can avoid the company of drug-using cronies. Yet he is conscripted back into the con game and card game. He becomes a card dealer rather than a drug dealer. In one last attempt to make a big win, and get out of the game, he cheats at cards and gets caught. He tries to leave, but unwittingly loses the game for his backer, who is the same man who subsidizes his drug habit.

When the drug dealer who lures Frankie back into "the life" is accidentally shoved off a staircase by none other than Frankie's wife, spectators silently applaud. Then Frankie is framed for the dealer's death, while his wife escapes suspicion.

When Frankie's wife jumps to her death, she once again leaves Frankie feeling responsible, this time forever. The man "with the golden arm" seems doomed to suffer for his sins eternally, in this riveting drama about drugs.

AIDS and Drugs

It was hard to top the drama of *The Man with The Golden Arm*, with the synergistic skills of Preminger, Bernstein, and Sinatra. It would take decades—and the AIDS epidemic—before drug-related films could compete with Preminger's masterpiece about the diabolical power of drugs.

AIDS reared its ugly head in the early 1980s, initially attacking gay men, but soon enough appearing in users of injectable drugs. Until then, it was a poorly kept secret that drug users subsidize their habits by trading sex for money, and that many male drug users earn money from pay-for-play same-sex sex (gay sex). In the 1990s *Trainspotting* (1996) and *Requiem for a Dream* (2000) picked up where *Golden Arm* had left off, presenting newer and uglier realities to younger generations of movie viewers. In those years, other films revisited the drug-culture decades and presented drink and drug-related themes in a different light. *Leaving Las Vegas* (1995) and *Fear and Loathing in Las Vegas* (1998) are examples of such film flashbacks. Each ends badly and sadly, promising none of the high-flying hopes that *Lost Weekend* promised in the mid-forties.

Trainspotting was unfairly derided for romanticizing drugs (as happens to almost any film about drugs). For some strange reason, some people thought that scenes of a Scottish youth, his skin covered with fungus, dying of AIDS in the home of his unsympathetic parents were pro-drug. Or that shots of an amorous young man flinging feces-covered underwear around his girlfriend's parents' breakfast table after he had lost bowel control during drug withdrawal were romantic. Or that the sight of a dead baby, starved to death by drugged-out parents, was romantic.

It is likely that the film's most ardent critics never watched the full film. For anyone who watches this black comedy about the true-to-life Edinburgh drug scene comes away edified more than entertained. It is hard to believe that this film inspires people to use drugs, even though the surviving protagonists are smiling as the film ends. They enjoy the Scottish hillside as they celebrate their recovery from drug addiction.

Unlike *Trainspotting*, which uses black humor to make a dark subject palatable, Darren Aronofsky's *Requiem for a Dream* (2000) has no such veneer. *Requiem for a Dream* is as dark as a film could be, and as realistic as a drug-related film has been (save for the fact that it does not show the imprisoned black actor being raped and contracting HIV, as medical statistics predict).

Instead, *Requiem* shows the simple-minded mother of the heroin-injecting lead actor gulping down diet pills so she can fit into a dress that she wants to wear when she appears on TV. Instead of making her lose weight, her prescription pills make her hear her refrigerator talk. Her hallucinations send her to a psych ward for shock treatment. Her son, in the meantime, perpetually pawns her television sets so that he can get drug money.

Like any enabler, the mother refuses to listen to the shopkeeper's warnings and believes her son instead. It is fitting that Ellen Burstyn plays the mother of this devilish son, for she was mother to the possessed child in *The Exorcist* (1973).

In the meantime, the son's girlfriend, an aspiring designer, also gets hooked. She funds her drugs through live sex show performances that are far worse than the X-rated films from *Valley of the Dolls*. Her boyfriend loses an arm to an injection-site infection. This film could not be bleaker—or more correct. Two hours' reel time feels like a fast-forward of the real lives described by patients in a big-city methadone clinic. But real drug patients die at a higher rate than they do in the film.

RECOVERIES AND REHABS

Films about drug and alcohol rehabs are relatively rare, although movies about madhouses are abundant. This disparity becomes more remarkable when we see that substance-use disorders are the most commonly diagnosed "Axis I" psychiatric disorder today. ("Axis I" includes only the most serious and probably biologically based forms of mental illness and excludes the so-called personality disorders that may have social as well as biological causes.) Apparently, rehabs are not as entertaining as madhouse movies (Charlie Chaplin's slapstick sanitarium cure notwithstanding). Also, madhouse movies are a subgenre of horror films, and the horror of drug and alcohol addiction occurs during the addiction and not during the cure. If anything, a single scene is devoted to detox, as seen in *Lost Weekend* or *Valley of the Dolls.*

Still, there is an interesting subgenre of rehab and recovery films that revolve around "helping" professionals who need help themselves. Films about alcoholic or addicted doctors, police, preachers, attorneys, or emergency medicine technicians (EMTs) typically attract the attention of the public and fellow members of their profession.

This is not a recent trend that owes it growth only to the recovery movement of the eighties. In fact, one of the most impressive films about an alcoholic doctor was made in the pre-Code days, when dark topics were not yet outlawed by the Hayes Code. Michael Curtiz's *Mandalay* (1934) takes place in the South Seas. Unlike many movies about the "exotic Orient," this film focuses on the flaws of the American protagonists who are adrift, both literally and figuratively, in Asia. The Budapest-born Curtiz is better known for another film about an exotic locale, *Casablanca.*

In *Mandalay*, a beautiful woman is abandoned at sea by her lover and is forced to become a "hostess" in a decadent nightclub. She loathes her life, even though she is toasted across continents. She meets a doctor who left a comfortable life in America. He plans to practice in Mandalay. He explains his motivation to the "hostess": he was drinking before operating, and his patient died. To atone for his actions, he is making his way to Mandalay's malaria country, with no hopes of return. She leaves her own decadent life to accompany him. Like *Casablanca*, this film promises secular redemption through personal responsibility, in spite of past sins.

Three decades later, there was another memorable film about an alcoholic preacher who never confronts his alcoholism and never finds redemption. That film is *Night of the Iguana*. Starring Richard Burton and Ava Gardner, and set in a steamy Mexico resort where iguanas roam free—unless they are tethered to a rope at a resort—this film includes stunning performances and character portrayals, but it skips AA's anti-alcohol approach.

Richard Burton portrays a preacher who tempers his manic tirades with alcohol and then gets more disinhibited from drink. After losing control during a sermon, and getting suspended from another church, he becomes a tour bus driver in Mexico. He chauffeurs stuffy church ladies through the sweltering desert and carries on affairs with conduct-disordered adolescents. One young lady is chaperoned by a spinster group leader, whom Burton identifies as a moral woman but a repressed lesbian who cannot accept her unacceptable sexual impulses and deflects attention to the teenager's libido instead. The rum bottle that he holds in his hand, as he swings from his Mexican hammock, allows Burton to express Freudian-style explanations without the caginess expected in pre–sexual revolution films.

Burton never acknowledges the role that alcohol plays in his downfall (in that pre-lithium era). His widowed female friend, played by Ava Gardner, ends the film by offering him a proper "role for a man" at her resort. The implication is that gender-appropriate sex roles will cure all ailments, including alcoholism. This sorry attitude prevailed during the heyday of Freudian psychoanalysis, before scientific research about alcoholism overrode Freudian superstitions. Still, the superb acting and the interpersonal drama make this film worth watching.

In *The Verdict* (1982) an aging Paul Newman plays an alcoholic attorney whose professional and personal life have been destroyed by drinking. In a desperate attempt to recover his dignity, his professional skills, and his pride, he accepts an impossible-to-win malpractice case against a respected Boston obstetrician who practices at an even more respected hospital. In the process, he almost succumbs to the unscrupulous tactics of the defendant's attorneys, who send an attractive female associate to seduce him and to help him, and to find out about his progress on the case.

When he takes his case to court, he finds himself with a second-rate medical witness who is neither an anesthesiologist nor an obstetrician. He is a small-town general practitioner who still delivers babies. But he also finds a young nurse who was put out to pasture, and is now working as preschool teacher, because she witnessed the respected ob-gyn changing the medical record after she pointed out that the patient risked suffocation if anesthesia was administered so soon after eating.

In the end, the seemingly paranoid suspicions of the deceased patient's surviving sister are proven true. The young nurse takes the stand and reclaims her career, and Paul Newman proves that he, too, can win his case. Newman's character never makes a self-conscious effort to overcome alcohol. Like Ray Milland in *Lost Weekend*, he simply stops. Then he wins, in more ways than one.

David Duchovny plays a drug-addicted doctor in *Playing God* (1997). Duchovny's character is more plausible than Newman's in *The Verdict* (and much more plausible than his completely implausible, supernaturally tinged *X-Files* character). Duchovny was already a TV star when he appeared as a wayward surgeon who cannot practice medicine because his patient died while he operated under the influence. Yet the surgeon cannot resist resuscitating a man who is shot at a bar he frequents. His skills are noted by a black marketeer, who coerces Duchovny into becoming his personal physician.

An FBI agent also notes Duchovny's activities and threatens him with further legal action unless he cooperates with the feds. Duchovny is eventually released by his criminal captors after a shootout between the feds and criminals. Charged with practicing medicine without a license, he gets clean, pleads his case, and convinces the medical board that he broke the law to help others. His adventures have none of the poignancy of *Mandalay*'s doctor, but the film is an enjoyable action-adventure cum cautionary tale nonetheless.

Other films allude to the alcoholic state of their stars. One film in particular, *Lethal Weapon*, adds black comedy to action-adventure, and pro–racial peace propaganda to boot. It shows Mel Gibson as a drunken, divorced, nearly suicidal cop who is rescued by the happily married African American cop, played by Danny Glover. Glover brings his self-pitying, hard-drinking partner home to his loving family and provides him with a second family while he stops drinking.

Other notable examples of superstar actors playing down-and-out alcoholics who shake their habits and save the day are Clint Eastwood's *The Gauntlet* (1977), Bruce Willis's *Die Hard* series, and Denzel Washington's *Soul on Fire* (2004). At the other end of the spectrum is Jack Nicholson's Jack Torrence from Stanley Kubrick's *The Shining* (1980). The alcoholic Torrence is haunted by ghosts or psychic phantoms or alcohol-related hallucinations. He descends into madness and attempts to ax-murder his family as he chases them through a maze.

RACE AND RELIGION, DRUGS AND DRINK

Racial and national factors grow increasingly important in a new breed of films about drink and drugs: the action-adventure. *Lethal Weapon* exemplifies this genre. Action-adventures became popular when advances in photography made it easier to show high-speed car chases and other such adventures. The action-adventures of the 1980s were updates on the police procedurals from the 1930s, when Prohibition-era crime was a significant social concern. These early social problem films eventually evolved into sociological sagas.

Films such as *Once upon a Time in America* (1984) reminisced about the days of speakeasies, bootleggers, flappers, and bowler-wearing black men. Like other films of its ilk, *Once upon a Time in America* was a sociological saga and an ethnographic study as much as it was a psychological portrait of a particular person. In this case, the small-time Jewish hood is played by Italian American actor Robert De Niro, who also evokes images of Italian American gangsters from other films. *Goodfellas* (1990), with Ray Liotta, plays on Italian American mobster stereotypes and points out that the half-Irish Liotta cannot be "made" because he is not all-Italian. Because cocaine does not discriminate as much as the mob, cocaine addiction completely claims Liotta and indirectly leads to his arrest.

When outrage about such films from the Italian American community increased, Russian drug smugglers were substituted for Italian American movie mobsters. In fact, many later films shower more attention on racial, religious, and national myths (or truths) regarding drug use and drug dealing, deflecting attention from the individual drug experience itself. In *Empire* (2002), John Leguizamo portrays a rags-to-riches and riches-to-rags Colombian-American drug dealer. The street-smart dealer is duped by a suave-talking, Armani-wearing Soho real estate broker. This superficial psychological portrait makes an important statement about social class, ethnic identity, and "making it" in America. And it reminds us of Gilbert and Sullivan's song about "milk [that] masquerades as cream," on all sides of the ethnic and racial divide.

Latin America is overrepresented in cocaine sagas, largely because Latin America supplied cocaine when cocaine became chic in the 1980s. Cocaine themes are well suited to action-adventure films, partly because cocaine itself increases action (whereas heroin or marijuana decrease action). Like *Empire*, the earlier *Scarface* (1983) focuses on drug dealing that starts in South America before moving to Miami. *Scarface* chronicles the rise and fall of a poverty-ridden Cuban refugee (Al Pacino) who competes with more sophisticated Miami crime lords. He strives to rise above his station, first by marrying his former boss's blue-eyed, Baltimore-born mistress, and then by building a pretentious look-alike mansion in Miami. In the last scene, the mansion is riddled with bullets and reduced to rubble. The Baltimore-born wife succumbs to cocaine before she, too, is shot. In a paranoid fit induced by cocaine, Pacino kills the new husband of his dewy-eyed, adoring sister before crumbling under enemies' bullets himself. Everything ends unhappily ever after.

Race and ethnicity (and prostitution and pimping) are so closely intertwined with one subgenre of drug and alcohol film that these films earned a special name: blaxploitation. Born in the seventies, at a time of peak racial tension but increased social liberalization, blaxploitation films exploited the grittiest African American ghetto life. Blaxploitation was reviled by anyone with a social conscience but was adored by the box office and by the black youths it was aimed toward. The *Superfly* series, *Shaft* remakes, and *Cotton Comes to Harlem* (1970) are some memorable titles.

Blaxploitation was nothing new. By revisiting themes of opium and orientalism in early films, we see the start of cinematic racial stereotypes about drug dealing and opium smoking. As tempting as it is to claim that blaxploitation films or the Miami Vice–style *Scarface* story defame specific races, religions, or national origins, it is also apparent that ethnic-specific films add interesting costumes and set locations. Opium beds with their plush silk pillows, overgrown tropical South American gardens, and rugged Afghanistan mountain passes all provide pleasing backdrops that are as important as abstract ideas or social statements.

Moreover, there is the unforgettable *The French Connection* (1971), which takes a different turn and traces drug-dealing to Marseilles. Famed for its car-chase scene, *The French Connection* tells the story of two tough-talking New York City narcotics cops (one of whom is a bigoted alcoholic) who nail a suave French heroin smuggler. By the eighties, films about South American cocaine cartels, such as *Scarface* (1983), take center stage.

Oddly enough, the best-known American drinking films are not associated with alcohol at all, but are associated with the scene and setting that the genre is named for. That genre is the Western. What would a Western be without hard-drinking outlaws who frequent saloons before, during, and after shootouts? When they are not riding high on the trail, they are setting up camp in the brush and drinking full bottles of booze. Yet we never think of Westerns as "alcohol stories" or "drunkalogues," partly because society was not trained to think about alcohol abuse when Westerns reigned supreme, and partly because spectators are too awed by Western settings, cowboy boots, and horse saddles to think about alcohol bottles. Yet it impossible to envision a Western without a saloon smack in the center of town.

It would be convenient if we could attribute changes in cinema's depiction of drug and drink to changes in social attitudes or shifts in professionals' perceptions of mind-altering substances. But it would be inaccurate. For government censorship, along with the Legion of Decency and other social pressures, played a strong role in permitting or prohibiting drug-related themes. There were times when studios strove to depict Americans respectfully, even without legal pressure. For instance, patriotism overrode commercial pursuits during World War II. Moviemakers agreed to avoid negative portrayals of Americans or their allies. Even in Rick's Café, where much of *Casablanca*'s action takes place, none of the American ex-pats get embarrassingly inebriated, although they spend their evenings drinking. We surmise that Bogie took to drink after Bergman abandoned him at the station, but that sort of revisionist reading has yet to be made. Luckily, there was so much to be said about *Casablanca* that few of us, apart from Woody Allen in *Play It Again, Sam* (1972), feel the need to speculate about alcohol here.

CHAPTER 11

DOUBLES AND DOPPELGÄNGERS

DOUBLES AT THE TURN OF THE CENTURY

The concept of doubles and doppelgängers stems from ancient times. Interest in such concepts soared in the late nineteenth century, shortly before film arrived. Conveniently, cinema shows doubles on screen, capturing action as well as image and making it easier than ever to dramatize this age-old theme. Filmic depictions of doppelgängers pushed further than photography, theater, stage magic could. Doppelgängers became favorites of German Expressionists of the 1920s. Expressionists, in turn, influenced film noir's dark themes decades later. Doppelgängers resurfaced with a vengeance as the twentieth century ended, when the computer era and web chat rooms renewed interest in doubled identities.

Beliefs in second selves and psychic phantoms date to biblical times, if not earlier. Jewish mystics spoke of a double Genesis story, and a double of Eve, named Lilith. This Lilith allegedly copulated with Adam, the primordial man, and produced unborn demon-like creatures that live in limbo. (This Lilith resurfaced in *Nightmare Alley*, where the succubus-like psychologist sports her name and sucks men dry, as her namesake did.) The Christian Gnostics of the first century also believed in double creation, as did the ancient Manichaeans.

According to these mystics, one double is good, the other evil. The psychoanalyst C. G. Jung was intrigued by myths of double identities and double worlds. He wrote about Gnostics and claimed that a shadow self, or a dark side, inhabits the best of human beings. Many Hindu deities possess dual natures. For instance, Shiva the Creator is also Shiva the Destroyer. Like Greek and Roman gods, Hindu gods physically morph into other forms and alternative identities.

The list of double-identitied deities, and shadow sides of humans, goes on and on. Such concepts figure prominently in prescientific cultures and in primitive or mystical religion. But these ideas seemed unbecoming to modern societies that strove to shed the shackles of superstition. So psychoanalysis, which appeared at the same time as cinema, appropriated these archaic beliefs and couched them in more acceptable terms. Concepts such as the unconscious and the shadow self became buzzwords for the burgeoning new psychological era.

One hundred years later, as the twentieth century ended and the second millennium concluded, people again became preoccupied with the crossroads between science and spirit, and with doubles and doppelgängers, albeit for very different reasons. For the late twentieth century witnessed the invention of the Internet. The World Wide Web connected unrelated people from different continents through "the ether." This "ether" that engulfed everyone increased interest in noncorporeal existence and in virtual worlds.

Moreover, Internet users adopted alternative identities, either for security or for sport. These Internet identities catalyzed interest in double identities and doppelgängers. Web surfers were left wondering who was who and who was where and what was what. Some people pretended to be someone other than who they really were. Some interacted in ways that they would not otherwise interact. Some concealed identities or falsified identities, once they realized that they were invisible (and untraceable) on the Internet. Cyberspace turned the world topsy turvy. Information was more accessible, but proof of identity was more inconclusive. It became common knowledge that Web handles and Internet identities could not be trusted. Scholars such as Sherry Turkle wrote about such phenomena in *Life on the Screen* (1995).

Filmmakers took note of these trends and capitalized on them. Computer gaming intensified the impact of cyberspace and was dramatized in David Cronenberg's *eXistenZ* (1999), which shows gamers connected to probes that attach to their lower spinal cords (near their anuses), like umbilical cords, or even like other X-rated mechanical devices. These probes transmit virtual ideas into bodies and brains, so that gaming experiences "circulate" through players, like lifeblood that circulates through arteries and veins. Cronenberg's boundary-breaking erotic imagery was less shocking than edgier imagery from his earlier films, *Crash* and *Videodrome*.

It is not until the film's end that characters (and spectators) learn that their doubled identities experienced only pseudo-experiences rather than real sensations. Had Cronenberg made this film a few decades earlier, during the psychedelic era, spectators would have surmised that his virtual reality and double identities were drug-induced hallucinations. Because 1990s audiences knew about psychedelic drugs as well as virtual reality, the movie's messages reverberated even more strongly.

After September 11, 2001, Americans were forced to face the prospect of death, to a degree they had not faced since World War II. This event, along with the turn of the millennium that preceded it, reinvigorated interest in life after death and in doubly lived lives. Intrigue with reincarnation progressed beyond the counterculture and the days when Hari Krishna chanting reverberated through airports and college campuses. The bardos (the transitional states described by Tibetan Buddhists and trumpeted by psychedelic prophet Timothy Leary) were ripe for reinterpretation and were ready to be mainstreamed. Several feature-length films about Tibet and Buddhism appearing in the late twentieth century educated American audiences about Eastern religions and nontraditional spirituality. With knowledge of such esoteric ideas no longer restricted to spiritual seekers, eccentrics who traveled to Tibet, and hippies who read Timothy Leary's rendition of the *Tibetan Book of the Dead*, turn-of-the-millennium movies could safely capture the continuum between the psychological and the supernatural. Films such as *Jacob's Ladder, The Sixth Sense, Donnie Darko*, and *The Jacket* became cult classics or box office hits.

Such films used twenty-first-century technology, but their themes unearthed an ancient and atavistic era when psyches and souls were interchangeable. Psychoanalytically informed pseudo-sophistication of the mid-century seemed out of synch with this spiritually striving era. Films about doubled identities from the 1950s, such as *Three Faces of Eve, Psycho*, and *Fear Strikes Out*, with their psychoanalytic subtexts, looked like relics from the distant past.

There was a reason why psychoanalytic films looked so out-of-date at the same time that spiritually-oriented films about psyche-as-soul took on a timeless quality. By 1990 psychoanalytic theories were challenged almost as often as creationist theories, even though they were widely accepted in the fifties, when *Three Faces of Eve* (1957) appeared. Psychoanalysis was upstaged by brain-science research. The 1990s were dubbed the decade of the brain.

Psychoanalytic theory was not in the same class as phrenology, that quaint practice of predicting personality quirks by palpating bumps on the head. But its credibility was waning, even though it once served cinema well, providing plausible explanations for the screen's most memorable double personalities. How could Hitchcock have created *Psycho* without Freudian ideas about mothers and sons and Oedipus complexes? Who would believe that Norman Bates dressed as his mother, were it not for Freudian psychosexual theories?

But filmmakers—like any fiction makers—must make their audiences suspend disbelief temporarily. They accomplish this feat by retaining enough factual and plausible material to make the unreal *seem* real, at least for an hour or two. Psychoanalytic theory was no longer real enough to make viewers believe in the fiction of a film. Another driving device was needed for more modern times. And so cutting-edge films regressed to the distant past. They excavated age-old themes that lurk in the subterranean regions of the mind. Or they turned to campier and crazier sci-fi.

Film returned to a time when spirits and specters roamed the earth, and when people believed in spiritual doubles and doppelgängers, and in demons and dybbuks. As the millennium neared, apocalyptic ideas multiplied; then 9/11 proved that these fears were not purely paranoid. Filmmakers looked into their own filmmaking past and unearthed myths about mirror images that had served early film so well in its infancy. People often seek solace from the past when they face an uncertain future. Primitive ideas carried with us from childhood can resurface during times of stress. And those times were stressful indeed. What a strange time it was, but what a good time it was to see strange cinema!

MYTHS, MOVIES, AND MEDICINE

The early Greeks and later Romans had much to say about physical and psychological doubles. The Janus myth of a two-headed deity who looks backward and forward is immortalized in our month of January. Janus is a literal rendition of the double.

Even more important to our study of the psyche is the handsome young man named Narcissus, who grew so enamored with his reflection in the spring water that he bent to kiss his image but fell into the water and drowned instead. Echo, the wood nymph who was infatuated with Narcissus, shriveled up and died after Narcissus drowned. From then on, Echo existed as only a voice, and thus we hear eerie echoes at times, or vocal doubles.

Freud revived the Narcissus myth and worked it into his nascent psychoanalytic ideas. By turning to theater and legend, Freud dramatized his abstract concepts and made them more accessible to the masses. Using classical myth also made his theories more respectable, because classicism was highly esteemed in his era.

Nearly a century before Freud formulated his ideas about psychoanalysis, psychic doubles, and psychological projections, another writer made equally important observations that were destined to influence Freud's theories (and ballet, opera, theater, and film). That poet and writer was E. T. A. Hoffmann (1776–1822). A drunkard and writer by night who worked a dull bureaucratic day job (and thus lived a double life himself), Hoffmann said that the double is a "phantom of our own Self, whose intimate relationship with and deep effect upon our spirit casts us into hell or transports us to heaven."[1]

Hoffmann's Romantic writings still resonated at the fin de siècle, when Freud and his followers were busy translating Hoffmann's poetic terminology into psychological lingo. Freud acknowledged Hoffmann in his essay on *The Uncanny* and in *The Interpretation of Dreams*, and he admitted that poets and writers achieve insights into human behavior long before psychologists and scientists. Today some remember Hoffmann's works because of Freud's references to Hoffmann's mechanical doll in his essay on *The Uncanny*, but more people know about *The Nutcracker Suite* ballet, which is based on a Hoffmann story about an ugly nutcracker who comes alive and turns into his princely double. Clara, the young girl who receives the nutcracker for Christmas, lives a double life in the dreamy Land of the Sugarplum Fairies.

Hoffman's fantastic tales about doubles and automatons inspired Jacques Offenbach to compose the opera *Tales of Hoffmann*. The work became Offenbach's lifetime obsession and was his only opera among his many operettas. It was still in progress when he died in 1880, a year before its 1881 premiere in Vienna, right around the time that Freud finished medical school in Vienna. A Technicolor film of *Tales of Hoffmann* appeared in 1951, just as Disney's lighter-hearted animated fairy tales were winning the hearts of children.

Other men of letters echoed Hoffmann's intrigue with doubles. Dostoevsky, the morose Russian writer who influenced philosophy and psychology as much as literature, wrote a novella called *The Double*. Edgar A. Poe (1809–49), the American author who died from the ill effects of excessive drink and tuberculosis, wrote about doubles and proto-detectives and diabolism in general. Poe's works translated into cinema more easily than Dostoevsky's ruminative prose. Poe's original ideas have been interpreted and reinterpreted so many times over that many readers and viewers are unaware of how much their favorite films owe to Poe. Even *Caligari* can be credited to Poe, to a degree.

Occultists claim that dreams provide proof that doubles exist somewhere. Mirrors, which show mirror images, also promulgate beliefs about doubles. Some cultures say that mirrors capture the soul, and they warn that breaking mirrors brings bad luck. Folklore says that vampires have no mirror image, possibly because they do not possess souls and therefore have no spiritual doubles. Vampires who appear human are easily identified by holding a mirror before their faces. If there is no image, the being is not human.

This simple diagnostic procedure made its way into movies. Silent films about vampires, such as *Nosferatu* (1922), said a thousand words without uttering a single word, simply by showing a black-cloaked man standing before a mirror. Such "smoke and mirrors" illusions of primitive film borrowed from nineteenth-century stage magic and competed admirably against the cutting-edge editing techniques used for *Fight Club* (1994) doubles.

By 1913 cinematographers had mastered double-exposure tricks for their movies and produced an enduring depiction of the mirror-image double in *The Student of Prague* (1913). Also known as *A Bargain with Satan*, this film was adapted from Poe's story. Some say that *Student of Prague* was the first *true* horror film. (Edison's *Frankenstein* is not considered to be a *real* horror film.) The first *Student of Prague* starred Paul Wegener as the impoverished student. Smitten by Prague, Wegener proceeded to direct an equally eerie film about *The Golem* (of Prague). In 1926 Henrik Galeen made the definitive *Student of Prague*, starring Conrad Veidt.

Student of Prague entered the halls of psychoanalytic history, as well as film history, because renegade psychoanalyst Otto Rank referenced the film in his book *Art and Artists* (1932). *The Student of Prague* was shown to students of psychiatry from then on. Sadly, Rank's career did not weather as well as the film. He was ousted from the psychoanalytic "chosen," even though he had once sat on Freud's secret "committee" and contributed two new chapters—on myth and legend—to the 1902 edition of Freud's *The Interpretation of Dreams*.

There is a familiar ring to *The Student of Prague*. A poor student named Balduin needs money and inadvertently sells his soul to a mysterious stranger he meets at a beer hall. Believing that he has nothing worthwhile to trade, the student gives the stranger his choice of anything in the room, in return for 600,000 florines. The stranger chooses Balduin's mirror image. Balduin's "second self" emerges from the mirror, in a splendid split screen, but Balduin is forever after haunted by this double, who follows him around. He is blamed for a death that the double caused while fighting a duel that the real Balduin swore never to partake in. Obsessed with fear, Balduin lures his double into a garret and fires a pistol at him. When he shoots into the mirror, he falls dead himself. The stranger appears to collect his due: the soul of Balduin. Balduin is buried beneath a tombstone that reads "Here lies Balduin, the man who fought the Devil and lost."

Student of Prague bridged the supernatural and the psychological and connected the soul to the psyche. In her esteemed *The Haunted Screen*, Lotte Eisner identifies *Student of Prague* as a nodal point between German Romanticism and German Expressionism. To students of psychology and sociology, *Student of Prague* carries even more meaning. Even though the story line deals with the student's struggles as he confronts his dual identity, the film is also a metaphor about the struggles of early twentieth-century society, and its attempts to reconcile ancestral spiritual ideas with the advances in science, technology, and psychology.

DR. JEKYLL AND DORIAN GRAY

Decades before *Student of Prague* screened, literature reflected this same fascination with the double. *The Strange Case of Dr. Jekyll and Mr. Hyde*, written by Robert Louis Stevenson in 1886, is arguably the most influential and long-lived literary tale of the double. *Dr. Jekyll and Mr. Hyde* was a stage success from the start and lived many more lives in cinematic form. When it reappeared on Broadway in the 1990s, the play spawned large fan clubs. Silent cinema adapted this tale as early as 1908. Several short versions of *Jekyll and Hyde* appeared before the 1931 *Dr. Jekyll* begot an Oscar for Frederick March.

Critics complained that the 1920 *Jekyll,* starring John Barrymore, added elements of Oscar Wilde's tale about Dorian Gray, instead of remaining true to Stevenson's tale of a dual-natured doctor. But enhancing a story for the sake of enthralling audiences is a filmmaker's prerogative, if not also an obligation. The following decade, Rouben Mamoulian turned the tale into a horror classic. Mamoulian's 1931 version premiered around the same time as other Universal horror classics, such as *Frankenstein* and *Dracula*.

Mr. Hyde was more than a psychological or neurochemical double of Dr. Jekyll. Stevenson's story paraphrased the philosophical conflicts that shook the late nineteenth century. Even before Freud formulated his theories, *Jekyll* suggests Freudian-Darwinian ideas about an untamed animalistic beast that lurks within the most civilized and sophisticated human. Even the best of men are no better than id-driven monsters. This animal nature is contained by the outward manifestations of civility but is waiting for the right opportunity to emerge and to pounce upon its prey. Protestant theologians who believed that the soul reigns over the body, distinguishing humans from beasts, found their views challenged by such innovative thinkers as Freud and Darwin.

Freud never forgot the lessons of Darwin, or of Stevenson (even if he did not credit them directly). In his later years, Freud devoted himself to philosophical writings that lacked the clinical case histories of earlier essays. One of these latter-day books, *Civilization and Its Discontents* (1930), came to press after John Barrymore's acclaimed appearance in the 1920 *Jekyll and Hyde*. Although Freud never saw this film, he did articulate the same sentiment expressed in the film. In *Civilization and Its Discontents*, Freud emphasized that civilization cannot advance unless individual members of a society repress instinct-driven urges. It is also worth noting that Freud wrote *Cocaine Papers* in 1884, two years before Stevenson conceived of his story about a good doctor whose personality changes after he drinks an elixir.

Many decades later, the drug culture celebrated the chemical powers of this magical elixir as well as the libidinal urges it unleashed. The intrigue with spiritual doubles diminished, and the appeal of releasing repressed urges soared. Not surprisingly, 1970s audiences appreciated newer versions of *Dr. Jekyll and Mr. Hyde* and apparently identified with its portrayal of the chemical transformation of personality. One wonders if the post-Prozac sentiment of the 1990s added to the appeal of the Broadway play of that decade, or if the strength of the recovery movement increased interest in age-old ideas about diabolical natures unleashed by demonic drugs.

Oscar Wilde's *Portrait of Dorian Gray* also lived several lives. Wilde's double rivaled Stevenson's, but *Dorian Gray* revolved around a portrait of a narcissistic young man whose portrait aged while his own skin remained unwrinkled. The story stimulated the imaginations of portrait artists and resulted in several cinematic versions. Wilde himself attained cult status because he challenged Victorian-era bans against same-sex sex. He went to trial around the same time that Freudian psychoanalysis and early cinema appeared and thus became a bellwether of the social and sexual changes fermenting in the twentieth century.

In short, by the time cinema arrived as the nineteenth century closed, the concept of the double was well entrenched in the world of art and ideas. The double was more than a mere holdover from the days of superstition and spiritualism; it morphed into a new form through turn-of-the-century depth psychology, and metamorphosed again during the drug decade. The double took on new meaning for the recovery movement that followed the drug culture. The literary double literally took on a life of its own in film, just as it did in photography.

PHOTOS AND FILM

To appreciate how much moving pictures advanced the concept of the double, it is worth looking back to the start of photography in the 1830s. Photographers delighted the public with renditions of the waking dream and paved the path for moving pictures. Photography gave material form to mirror images and made it easy to contemplate psychic doubles.

Unlike mirrors, photographs captured that "other self" for posterity and created a permanent record for the scientifically minded or the spiritually inclined. Photos proved that all persons possess an inverse image of their individual identity. Leonardo da Vinci had experimented with the camera obscura three centuries earlier, using this device to project mirror images onto canvas and sketchpad. But photography, and cellulose nitrate, permitted the average person to see what only the artistic eye could see in centuries past. One no longer had to rely on imagination alone to see the specters of photography and to appreciate altered images of the self.

By the time that moving pictures distinguished themselves from still photography, the Western world was eager to exploit any and all scientific inventions that validated those long-held spiritualist and supernaturalist claims about souls or doubles. Scientific inventions were fine for science, but they were even more fun when adapted to promote the purposes of spiritualists.

Spirit photography delighted the Victorians (Queen Victoria died in 1902, the same year the Freud-Rank revision of *Interpretation of Dreams* appeared). Double-exposed photos and poorly developed photographic plates, with streaks in the silver developing gel, were used to prove the existence of "spirits." Faked fairy photographs of little creatures won an equally admiring audience.

The public's willingness to accept these double-exposed spirit photos and fake fairy photos attests to the strength of spiritualism during that transitional time. The allure of the world beyond endured as science advanced. Earlier in the century, the Fox sisters' sham table rappings and seances proved popular. Society embraced anything that affirmed the existence of two worlds—one material and one spiritual.

Moving pictures, or movies, offered more than photography. Filmmakers who worked in the spirit of magic, as Méliès did, soon learned to use dissolves, double exposures, and split screens to simulate doubles, doppelgangers, and images of otherwordly worlds. If we consider Marshall McLuhan's contention that "the medium is the message," we come to appreciate why doubles and doppelgängers were so well suited to the cinematic screen. Ghosts, as well as skeletons, were also popular during film's first decade and could be created by splicing negatives into the film reel. X-rays appeared around the same time as cinema, turning skeletal imagery into a sort of scientific cutting edge as well as a supernatural symbol.

DYBBUKS AND DOUBLES

It wasn't long before another film about a different kind of double appeared. The *The Dybbuk* remake in 1937 was one of the last silent films produced before talkies supplanted subtitled films in the late 1920s. The dybbuk was an older version of the double and was solely supernatural. Yet it paralleled psychological constructs that would soon compete with this quaint folk belief. The story of the dybbuk appeared on stage before making its way to screen. The plot was based on the folkloric tale by the Russian-Jewish author, S. Ansky, and was already much beloved. *The Dybbuk* theater poster from the original HaBimah production is one of the more iconic images of its era. A reproduction of this poster hangs in the entryway to the bookstore of the YIVO Institute for Jewish Research in New York City, tacitly announcing that the *Dybbuk* doubles as the unofficial symbol of the preeminent research center for Eastern European Jewry.

Part of the dybbuk story's charm stems from the fact that it deals with the psychoanalytic theme of dissociation, or double identity, from a purely supernatural point of view, at the very same time that depth psychologists such as Pierre Janet and Sigmund Freud were tackling this topic from an entirely different angle. The 1937 film, like the original story, offers a simplistic explanation for a sudden personality change seen in a love-smitten young woman. A related theme of repressed libido and sudden personality shifts is dramatized very differently in the psychoanalytically inspired fifties' classic, *Three Faces of Eve* (1957).

In *The Dybbuk*, a young yeshiva student is infatuated with a young woman who is betrothed to a more eligible, older, and more affluent (but unappealing) man chosen by her father. Upon learning that his beloved is about to wed his rival—in spite of the secret vows made by the young lovers—the love-stricken student uses forbidden Jewish magic to change fate. It is well-known that these kabbalistic rites are off-limits because they can cause insanity or suicide in the uninitiated.

Not unexpectedly, the young man does not succeed in altering fate and in dissuading the father from marrying his beloved to another. Instead, he goes mad and commits suicide, as predicted. However, he does succeed in becoming a dybbuk, or a "clinging spirit," that possesses the body of this young woman, speaks through her, and makes her behave in strange ways. She acts as if she herself is insane. She talks in a deep, disturbed tone that is dramatically different from her ordinary voice. A rabbi is consulted (rather than a psychoanalyst, as might have happened in Western Europe). The rabbi makes the diagnosis and suggests a solution.

The rabbi recognizes that the young woman is possessed by a dybbuk and that her personality was replaced by this spiritual double and dislocated soul (rather than by the repressed part of her personality that psychoanalysts spoke of). The rabbi prescribes prayers and penance for the girl's father, who had sold her soul so that he could collect a dowry by wedding her to a rich man. An exorcism is needed.

Sadly, the young woman's body cannot endure the rigors of the exorcism, and she succumbs during the ceremony. We watch the cleaving spirit (or *dybbuk* or psychological double) as it is banished from her body. Her father is left grieving after she departs. She presumably reunites with her lost love in another spiritual world. The similarities to *Student of Prague* are striking, although Anksy's original story is from a far older source than Henrik Galeen's cinematic rendition, and uses material from a region far from Edgar Allan Poe's pre–Civil War United States.

One might expect modern audiences of the 1930s to scoff at this silly and superstitious story. But just the opposite was true. At the same time Freud was gaining followers in Austria and America, people were flocking to see new renditions of Ansky's supernatural story of psychosis, suicide, and dissociative states. The dybbuk story appeared in ballet, opera, and puppetry. In 1937 the film was remade in Poland and renamed *The Vow*. Two years later, the Nazis annexed Poland. *The Vow* became one of the last Yiddish films produced in Poland. Two more years later, the Nazis began extermination of one-third of Poland's Jews. Two million Jews died in Poland alone.

But this film lived on, and the idea of the double or the dybbuk or the cleaving spirit gained even more meaning. This later film and its silent predecessors also function as doubles for a people that was vanquished in body but not in spirit. The fact that the film remains intact to this day (even though its technology is eerily outdated) provides further proof of the one-time existence of a now nonexistent world. Even more eerily, Freud died in 1939. His "scientifically" based psychoanalysis pushed superstition aside, at least for a while—until his psychoanalytic "science" turned into its own superstition that was touted by true believers and denounced by nonbelievers. The fictional dybbuk films, however, have enduring appeal.

DOUBLES AND MELODRAMAS

World War II left far more legacies than *The Dybbuk* and *The Vow*. Americans also endured loss of life and loss of love, even though they were not affected as profoundly as Europeans. These losses found expression in American melodrama, a genre that was wildly popular in the 1940s before fading from fashion. Melodrama, and film noir in general, were influenced by the mostly Jewish émigré actors and directors who fled Hitler and brought their cinematographic talents as well as their personal pain to safer American shores. They also transported their German

Expressionist heritage, with its emphasis on doubles and dark themes. Their experiences inspired multiple mid-1940s melodramas about doubles and double lives.

Melodramas were also called women's films because they attracted female audiences when the men were away at war. When men returned, and women left factories and (sometimes begrudgingly) returned home, women had less "alone" time to view these sentimental stories, so movie melodramas faded to gray. Then television appeared in most American homes by the mid-1950s, and daytime TV soap operas substituted for movie melodramas.

Until then, female film-goers watched movie doubles that did double duty. Films such as *Portrait of Jennie* (1948), *Cobra Woman* (1944), *Dark Mirror* (1946), and *A Stolen Life* (1946) performed social functions above and beyond entertainment and diversion. Sentimental and subtly supernatural, *Portrait of Jennie* reassured grieving war widows that life and love persisted beyond the grave. Other films focused on portrait doubles or twin sister doubles.

Twin sister doubles that featured opposite personalities with the same face helped women transition between traditional female gender roles to the Rosie the Riveter work roles they adopted to aid the war effort. Such films suggested that women (and perhaps all humans) had both male and female personas, just as Jungian psychology said, and just as ancient myths about hermaphrodites implied. Twin sisters could be good and evil, male and female, kind or cruel. These movies basically retold the biblical stories about brothers, such as Cain and Abel or Isaac and Esau, but they starred sisters rather than brothers and thereby appealed to women more than men. And, during wartime, it was important to woo women, since there were fewer men to pay admission to films.

A decade later double personalities morphed into something much more. In 1957 *The Three Faces of Eve* made it to the movies. By then, psychoanalysis had penetrated American society, had shaped our concept of the psyche, and was an accepted explanation for bizarre behavior. Americans were studying psychology in college (courtesy of the GI bill) and were reading self-help columns by psychologists, instead of instinctively consulting their clergy.

These men (as well as women) needed new explanations for the personality changes that they observed in women after the war. The wives and girlfriends who waited for them were not necessarily the same women they left behind years before. Everything, and everyone, had changed, sometimes dramatically so. Postwar America had a new need for the nineteenth-century doppelgänger. They turned this double into something more tangible and more relevant. The double was now represented by a dissociative identity disorder, or a split personality, that could be cured by a caring psychiatrist. *Three Faces of Eve* was just such a film.

Lee J. Cobb starred as the psychoanalyst who "cured" Eve White (and Eve Black) of her double personality. Using the couch cure, the talking cure, and the hypnosis-induced trance (to make for a more interesting film with more twists and turns to the plot), Cobb's psychiatrist helps the troubled Woodward acknowledge the existence of her two personas. Then she merges these disparate identities into a single personality, named Jane, that is more middle of the road. Jane wants to live her own life, apart from either Eve. Jane initiates an amicable divorce from her understanding husband, and the film, in turn, started a trendy—and still controversial—diagnosis of multiple personality disorder (MPD).

Unlike Stevenson's *Jekyll and Hyde*, Eve's secret personalities do not derive from drug or drink. Rather, it is a psychological trauma and repressed memory that unleash a lascivious Eve Black to overtake the prim and proper Eve White. More importantly, Eve White did not start out in search of a psychiatrist. Rather, headaches and blackouts send her for medical care. But she finds relief through psychiatry, rather than through neurology, which turns her into a poster child for psychoanalysis's promises. The film reminds viewers that Freud was first a neurologist who treated headaches and hysteria before he discovered psychoanalytic truth. The artistry of the film, as well as the powerful acting by both Cobb and Woodward, convinces viewers of the veracity of the still-controversial psychiatric diagnosis of dissociative identity disorder.

The following decade, a different sort of double surfaced on the screen. Alfred Hitchcock's *Psycho* (1961) starred Anthony Perkins. *Psycho* proved to be one of the most unforgettable films ever made. The shower scene, in which Janet Leigh is murdered, is still taught in film classes, because it is an example of three points of view: the victim, the kill, and the spectator (who looks through the shower head itself). Hitchcock owes much of the film's suspense to this sequence. *Psycho* is also psychoanalytically oriented and plays upon the psychological sophistication that audiences acquired from films like *Three Faces of Eve*.

Psycho is the story of a seriously disturbed young man who takes the life of an attractive but unlikable young woman who was a liar and a thief in life (but not a murderess). This young man has a dual identity of the *Jekyll and Hyde* variety. By day, he is a meek and mild hotel clerk at his family motel (when he is not playing taxidermist). At other times, he is a knife-wielding woman who dresses in his dead mother's clothes. Even the murdered sister and the living sister, who pursues her and helps stop the killer, are doubles of sorts. The "bad" sister is dead, but the "good" sister tries to track down her missing sister, much as a classical Greek heroine might.

Psycho became the first slasher film when it showed the graphic and gripping shower scene that claimed Janet Leigh's life. But it was much more than a simple slasher. It also marked a turning point in the authority bequeathed to cinematic psychiatrists. In contrast to Hitchcock's *Spellbound*, which was the first film to use psychoanalysts in lieu of detectives, *Psycho* uses a psychiatrist to explain the plot, after the fact, rather than to push the plot.

Psycho's finale shows a forensic psychiatrist speaking matter-of-factly as he sits in a cell, having just interviewed Norman Bates. The audience is agitated, but the psychiatrist is calm as he explains why Norman Bates adopted a dual identity that led to murder and mayhem. We hear how Norma Bates, a momma's boy, became a transvestite, taxidermist, and thrill killer. We understand why we "saw" Bates's mother moving behind her window shade, even though she was long dead.

Although Hitchcock's purpose was to tell a good story, and to intrigue his audience, rather than to proselytize for psychiatrists, he nevertheless acts as a missionary for this modern science of mind. By showing how psychiatrists make sense out of nonsense, and how they have rational explanations for irrational events, Hitchcock did as much to mold the mid-century mindset, and to set the concept of the psyche, as any scientific study. Through *Psycho* he undid the damage done in *Spellbound*, which revolved around a murderous older analyst, a love-smitten female psychiatrist, and a male psychiatrist who lost his identity. After watching two hours of *Psycho*, 1960s viewers have seen the light about psychiatry as surely as Paul saw the light on the road to Damascus. Viewers come away converted to a newfound belief in psychoanalysis.

Psycho was remade in 1998, starring Vince Vaughn. The film remained true to the original, in homage to Hitchcock. It was technically impeccable, but its psychological sway was barely perceptible. The remake hardly attracted audiences. Few people were willing to pay to see a second *Psycho*. Many serious Hitchcock fans opposed a remake of the "sacred text." Nor did psychoanalysis enjoy the same cachet in the late 1990s that it did in the early 1960s. Cross-dressing, double-identitied murders were not nearly so shocking as they were in the pre–Richard Speck, pre–Jeffery Dahmer, and pre–Hannibal Lecter era. The moral of the story: even a great film must address the social concerns of its era if it is to be appreciated.

Maybe movie-goers were too jaded or sated by Brian De Palma's *Dressed to Kill* (1980). Some say that *Dressed to Kill* was a rip-off of *Psycho*. Others say it was an homage to Hitchcock. Either way, *Dressed to Kill* was remarkably similar to *Psycho*, even if it reversed some key elements: it retained other classic Hitchcock touches, such as fragile blondes who push the plot.

De Palma is the son of a surgeon, so it is no surprise that he focused on physicians in his more memorable films. *Dressed to Kill* tells the story of a seemingly ordinary Upper East Side psychiatrist. The psychiatrist is played by Michael Caine, who had once played a government agent who uncovered paranoid plots against scientists in *The Ipcress File*. In *Dressed to Kill*, the psychiatrist has more in common with Norman Bates than with the *Psycho* psychiatrist, who plays a secondary role and appears only in the final scene. Like Norman Bates, Dr. Elliot lives a secret life as a transvestite. He murders a patient, played by an aging Angie Dickinson, in a claustrophobic elevator reminiscent of *Psycho*'s shower scene.

By reversing the role of the psychiatrist in *Dressed to Kill*, De Palma implies that the psychiatrist is indistinguishable from the patients he treats in his well-tended office. Not only does the psychiatrist have a double (in the form of a woman), but the patients also have their doubles, in the form of a psychiatrist. Angie Dickinson's sexually charged character has another double in the film: a high-priced prostitute who works in Angie's building. The prostitute is many social steps away from the affluent Angie but is apparently also affluent because of her career as a call girl. Angie's behavior mirrors the prostitute's, for Angie engages in an extramarital affair with a stranger, after discussing her husband's sexual shortcoming with her psychiatrist.

Angie dies in the elevator, a victim of a blonde, knife-wielding "phallic woman," but the call girl lives, becoming the best witness to the murder, and the next intended victim of the murderer, after having been the first murder suspect herself. Curiously, the prostitute is played by De Palma's then-wife Nancy Allen, in another interesting twist. After watching *Dressed to Kill*, we have no doubt that the golden days of psychiatry have passed. But, because De Palma's doubles work double-duty, we come away convinced that "doubles" and doppelgängers will be with us forever, given that they endured the test of time.

Before gaining fame from *Dressed to Kill*, De Palma worked on another film about doubles and diabolical doctors who turn into stalkers. *Sisters* (1973) is the story of a Siamese twin—played by pre-*Superman* Margot Kidder—whose twin sister Dominique is seen committing murder, in *Rear Window* or *Dark Mirror* style.

Dead Ringers (1988) is another odd film about a doctor and his double. *Dead Ringers* was directed by the persistently perverse David Cronenberg, who made many unusual films, and many with doubles: the double reality of the virtual world of *eXistenZ*, the double consciousness of a hallucinating schizophrenic who lives in a halfway house (*Spider*), and the double reality of a brain tumor patient whose TV talks to him and for him (*Videodrome*). Compared to the extraordinary characters in those other Cronenberg films, the twin doctors depicted in *Dead Ringers* live ordinary lives, at least on the surface.

Unlike *Dressed to Kill*'s fictional physician, the *Dead Ringers* doctors are based on fact. The fraternal twins practiced obstetrics-gynecology on New York's Upper East Side, just as De Palma's doctor does in *Dressed to Kill*. The fraternal twins looked alike and acted alike and operated out of a prestigious hospital near the East River. Then they disappeared and died within a day of one another. What originally looked like a possible murder-suicide in the real-life twin doctors turned out to be a drug overdose in one and death from barbiturate withdrawal in the other.

Until their highly publicized deaths, and a very sensationalized article in *New York* magazine, the obstetrician-gynecologists were supposedly well-respected physicians whose unusual behavior was not noted at their well-regarded hospital. They somehow succumbed to drugs and debauchery and then death. Conveniently, tragedy in life makes for high drama in film. Cronenberg makes a point of filming one twin doing a more-than-thorough medical history as he asks a pompous elderly lady if she ever has sex with dogs. The other twin engages in unusual sexual acts in private time. In this film, there is no good twin and no evil twin. Both are bad. Whether or not all the events are portrayed realistically is moot. What is indisputable is that the double—or twin brothers—appeals to audiences.

As the millennium was nearing its end, fiction continued to compete with fact, and the double resurfaced with more vigor than before. There was good reason why. Computers were commonplace by then. The Internet was everywhere. Web surfers discovered that they had two (or more) identities at their disposal, one real and one virtual. Extra alter egos were easily available.

"Early adapters"—as early Internet users are described by sociologists and financial analysts—assumed online "handles." The Web names disguised their true identities. They could have one, two, three, even four names for a single $20-a-month Internet account. Even their sites of origin were unspecified. Users could change names, ages, and genders at will. They could adopt different personas when they "spoke" online. One did not need a wig and a dress, as Norman Bates did in *Psycho* or as Dr. Elliot did in *Dressed to Kill*. One did not need a pill as Alice did in Wonderland. One simply needed an Internet account and a keyboard.

It was said that some people became confused about who they were as they pretended to be different people. Others gained self-confidence by speaking through the screen. The lucky ones were able to translate their polished online persona into real life, to improve social and professional contacts. Sociologist Sherry Turkel's *Life on the Screen* (1995) posited that identities were fluid, as well as false, in the Internet era. Later research, such as that published by me in *Racial Revelation in the Colorblind Cyberclass* (2002), found that more people prefer to be perceived as who they are, even when invisible on the Internet.

Whatever the upshot of such research, it was clear that double identities were back with a bang, both literally and figuratively. In *Fight Club*, Ed Norton's alter ego overtakes the otherwise boring thirty-something unnamed male who works at a dull insurance job in order to pay his condo fees and furnish his apartment in indistinguishable "Ikea contemporary" conformist style.

Fight Club was made into a film after the Oklahoma City bombing, and post–Columbine school shooting. In that climate, moviemakers had to push harder to make audiences sit up and squirm. That is what *Fight Club* did when it appeared in 1999, just before the second millennium closed, and two years before the World Trade Center collapsed.

Based on a novel by Chuck Palahniuk, *Fight Club* was directed by David Fincher. Fincher also directed *The Game* (1997), which deals with doubled lives and hints at hallucinogenic experiences through its theme song, *White Rabbit*. As good as *The Game* is in its own right, it is not nearly so unusual as *Fight Club*, largely because it recycles subject matter from the sixties and seventies and reminisces about Alice's abnormal adventures.

Fight Club stars Brad Pitt, Ed Norton, Helena Bonham Carter, and Meat Loaf. *Fight Club* gained a cult following, as well as opprobrium, more for its extreme violence than for its willingness to tackle forbidden "men's topics." Critics claimed that *Fight Club* was a commentary on men's vaporizing sense of self in the age of the metrosexual and in an era when women's rights and opportunities blurred the boundaries between the sexes and left men searching for old-fashioned male bonding. But *Fight Club* contains many layers of meaning, and its message is as much psychological as sociological, for it resurrects the double, or doppelgänger.

Ed Norton's character is intentionally nameless. He is a person without an identity or a sense of self. He is a distant relative of the student of Prague who sold his soul but lived to see his double step out of a mirror and live an independent life. Norton's character meets his secret self when he encounters a slippery soap salesman during a blackout on a plane. Astute spectators suspect that something is amiss when Ed Norton emphatically talks about "single servings" as he sits alone on the airplane.

Few viewers notice the blurred image lurking behind Ed Norton as he waits for his baggage to arrive at an airport terminal. It is not until the film nears its end that we realize that Brad Pitt stood behind Norton in several scenes, barely identifiable because of out-of-focus photography. By then, many fight clubs have been born, and the primal, primitive side of Norton has emerged and has proselytized to growing numbers of disenchanted young men. These men—some young, some old, some black, some white, some yellow—meet in basements to learn to fight and to bond.

They form secret "cells" that recollect the communist cells from the paranoid Cold War era.

One of those lost men is played by Meat Loaf. Meat Loaf's performance is as unforgettable as Norton's and Brad Pitt's. Norton meets Meat Loaf at a local cancer support group. Meat Loaf's character suffers from testicular cancer. He sports breasts (also known as bitch tits) that have resulted from hormone treatment (or possibly from steroid use that led to his testicular cancer). Meat Loaf's character is as close to a real-life hermaphroditic double as imaginable. His physical appearance is almost medically plausible, given what we know about the way that female hormones and androgenic supplements cause gynecomastia (breast engorgement) in men. Meat Loaf is a big, beefy, and breasty man who suffers psychologically and reminds us of ancient deities and alchemical symbols that were both male and female.

Meat Loaf's body double parallels Norton's psychological double, who is played by Brad Pitt. The dualistic theme of male-female/primitive-civilized runs through-out this film. Even though *Fight Club* is thoroughly postmodern and is set among late twentieth-century skyscrapers, its timeless story about doubles evokes Steven-son's *Dr. Jekyll and Mr. Hyde*. Both Dr. Jekyll/Mr. Hyde and Ed Norton/Brad Pitt undergo transformations that release instinct-driven doubles that take over the lives of otherwise ordinary men.

The film shows brutal fight scenes, some of which were outlawed in Europe, and for good reason. In *Fight Club*, we see buildings blown up, as men huddle together underground, living together in basements, in mock preparation for battle and a final Armageddon. *Fight Club*'s ambience is far removed from the Romantic-inspired silent films that Lotte Eisner wrote about in *The Haunted Screen*.

One of the few women in the film, Helena Bonham Carter, is also androgynous in her own way. She makes us wonder if Brad Pitt prefers women or men or both. Bonham Carter's Marla Singer is chronically suicidal, and she attends all support groups, including the testicular cancer group that Meat Loaf frequents. She claims to be even more entitled to attend the testicle-less group because she herself never had testicles. Marla forms a relationship with the relatively innocuous Norton but some-times finds herself in bed (literally) with the more primitive Pitt.

In the end, Bonham Carter tries to calm down the out-of-control Norton, who has holed himself up in a penthouse apartment and is about to destroy the city below. He holds the power over his supporters, but ultimately it is Marla the woman who holds the power over Norton/Pitt. It is she alone who can convince him to stop. By the time she arrives on the scene, Norton has already blown a whole in his own head. There is a gaping orifice in his jaw that recapitulates the film's hermaphrodite metaphor. Holding a gun in his hand, he turns to the audience, and shows off his battle scar. Bombs detonate in the background, and the film ends. The only way to destroy the double is to destroy everything altogether, at least according to Palah-niuk, Fincher, Norton, and Pitt.

Fight Club was an extreme statement, for sure. The brutality of *Fight Club*, and its hard-hitting message, was matched by the events that followed on 9/11. This eerie correspondence to future tragedies recollects *Manchurian Candidate*, which was pulled from theaters after Kennedy's assassination. Two years later, *Donnie Darko* would also have uncanny parallels to the events surrounding 9/11. *Donnie Darko* was also pulled from theaters and then re-released.

Donnie Darko was one of several "softer" stories about doubles, end-of-life, and life-after-death that made their way into film as the century ended. Donnie Darko is a young man who is infatuated with a young woman at the film's start. He lives in a building that is about to be hit by an airplane. His parents evacuate, but Donnie remains. But we do not know what happened until the film ends. Until then, we witness Donnie living out a fantasy with his fantasy girlfriend. Even after the curtain closes, so to speak, we are still uncertain if we were watching a near-death experience, an end-of-life reverie, or an afterlife where a double Donnie lives.

Several other films from the last decade of the twentieth century had similar themes, and were more supernatural than psychological. *Jacob's Ladder* (1990) was the first of this genre. *Jacob's Ladder* references the bible story about the patriarch Jacob, and his angelic double, who made his way to heaven by way of a ladder. This ladder is the proverbial stairway to heaven. *Jacob's Ladder* also draws upon Tibetan Buddhist belief in bardos that people pass through after death. Jacob himself endures a living hell, a hallucinogenic hell. Only later do we learn that Jacob Singer (Tim Robbins) never returned to New York because he died on the battlefield in Vietnam. The Jacob we watch during the film was a body double, a disembodied soul, or a hallucinogenic image that he experienced while smoking pot in Nam.

Less than a decade after *Jacob's Ladder* appeared and disappeared (known only to a small cadre of cult fans who appreciated the convoluted religious references), *The Sixth Sense* (1999) made its way to the movie theaters. *The Sixth Sense*'s story is more straightforward, and it requires no annotation to appreciate. When it was nominated for six Academy Awards, it became one of only four horror films in history to achieve such honors.

In *The Sixth Sense* a child psychologist (Bruce Willis) treats a seemingly psychotic young boy named Cole. Cole suffers from the same delusions and hallucinations endured by a previous patient, who suicided. The living boy believes, as the dead boy believed, that he can see dead people.

In the opening scene, Dr. Crowe (Willis) returns home with his wife, having just attended an event where he was honored for his professional efforts on behalf of children. The couple soon discover they are not alone in their home. A clearly disturbed, nearly naked man named Vincent (Donnie Wahlberg) appears in their doorway, holding a gun and saying, "I do not want to be afraid anymore."

Cole, the central character, utters the same words when speaking to Dr. Crowe sometime later. Before that happens, Vincent denounces Dr. Crowe because he is unable to help him. Vincent then shoots Dr. Crowe in the stomach, and then turns the gun on himself. Crowe's wife stands to the side, unfazed, like a bystander.

Months later, Dr. Crowe finds himself working with another frightened young nine-year-old who believes he can see the dead and speak with them. In a rather unprofessional gesture, Crowe asks Cole to demonstrate his clairvoyance by communicating with ghosts who need help with their unfinished business on earth. Cole is initially skeptical about Crowe's suggestion, but he soon identifies a young girl who was poisoned by her mother. Encouraged by this success, Crowe regains faith in himself and in his ability to treat Cole and free him from his hallucinations. He is also delighted that he has helped the boy put his uncanny abilities to humanitarian use.

Dr. Crowe now returns home and speaks to his wife as she sleeps, hoping that she will hear him. It is then that we learn Crowe has been dead since the start of the film, when he was shot by Vincent. We have been watching his psychic and spiritual double complete his own unfinished business on earth. Cole could see him, and respond to him, because Cole could see the dead. It is no accident that a psychologist is the protagonist of this Academy Award–nominated movie. For psychologists substituted the psyche for the soul, perhaps even more than psychiatrists, who are medical doctors who also believe in the *biological* construct of the brain.

Perhaps the leitmotif of this 1999 movie is that the soul lives forever, even as the psyche and other psychological constructs fade away. For we now know that the metaphysical "mind" was pushed aside by the end of twentieth century, supplanted in importance by the biological "brain." In a later chapter, we will look more closely at the psyche's competitors: the brain and the body. We will see if biological explanations of behavior will make for movies that are as compelling.

Before that happens, we can turn to *Next* (2007), a cinematic rendition of Philip K. Dick's story "The Golden Man." As always, Dick saw far into the future, even further into the future than his showman-seer main character (Nicholas Cage) does in his cheap magic acts in Las Vegas. Cris (Cage) is cursed with the gift of knowing what will happen in the next two minutes.

Unscrupulous FBI agents realize that Cris is the only man who can find stolen radioactive materials and thereby avert a nuclear bomb explosion. To accomplish this feat, Cris splits into doubles (and quadruples and more) and walks into the future to find the safest path to take. The amphetamine-addicted but prophetic Philip K. Dick apparently experienced the splitting of consciousness that gave way to these ever-appealing ideas about doubles. Fortunately, director Lee Tamahori also saw far enough into the future to realize what a wonderful film this subject, and this story, would make for twenty-first century cinema.

CHAPTER 12

WOODY ALLEN'S WORRIES

Whatever happened to Woody Allen and his worries? He was once a shining star of cinema and a self-appointed spokesperson for psychoanalysis. His name was a household word. The mere mention of "Woody Allen" (born Allen Konigsberg in 1935) evoked laughter, amusement, and chuckles, even before the film began. For Woody portrayed the eternal analysand who pokes fun at his own psychological shortcomings. A self-described agoraphobic, Woody Allen was always suffering, yet always joking, in true Jewish (and Kierkegaardian) style.

Woody Allen is the schlemiel, the goofy-looking guy who nevertheless gets the girl, even if she is a goofy-looking girl, like the floppy-fedora-wearing Diane Keaton in *Annie Hall* (1977). Woody was everyman, who suffered alone and in public, in the pre-Jerry Springer days, before America paraded personal peccadilloes and outrageous sexual behavior on daytime TV. Allen was a Jewish Christ figure, crucified on the couch and humiliated on the screen for his psychological sins. But he was also that Jewish achiever who became a star in spite of his insecurities and gave viewers hope that they, too, could find fame and fortune in spite of their faults.

Then that event happened with his semi-stepdaughter Soon-Yi. He left Mia Farrow, his wife and collaborator, and married the twenty-two-year-old Korean orphan whom Mia had adopted and whom Allen had helped rear. His name made more headlines than ever before, and not just because Soon-Yi was thirty-five years younger. The relationship was almost incestuous, or so said Mia. Farrow had starred in Allen's *Zelig* (1983), playing his psychoanalyst to boot. The good doctor tried to treat the multiple-personalitied Allen, who morphed into any form that was needed to gain acceptance in society. Allen played a soulless man in the movie, and now he proved to be soulless in life.

Audiences reacted badly to Allen's transgression. His affair with Soon-Yi was worse than cheating on one's wife, which, in and of itself, was not unusual in show biz. In spite of the critical acclaim accorded to many Allen movies, his name became such a bad box-office draw that his producers dropped his name from billboards when advertising his film *Match Point* (2005). In cavorting with, and then marrying Soon-Yi, Allen went several steps beyond Roman Polanski, the Polish-born, half-Jewish director who was married to Sharon Tate when she was murdered by the Manson Family. After Polanski was caught with a thirteen-year-old girl, he fled the country and became a fugitive to avoid facing child-molesting charges. Banned from reentering the United States, he became a stateless European exile, which is what he was when he first fled from Hitler decades before.

Polanski remains a shadowy figure to this day. His directorial talent surfaced in such creepy but acclaimed psychological thrillers as *Repulsion* (1965), *The Tenant* (1976), and *Rosemary's Baby* (1968), which starred Mia Farrow before she married and divorced Allen. One wonders how much Polanski's tangled life influenced the seedy and sordid psychological underground seen in his films. Then Allen went one better (or one worse) than Polanski. Allen coveted a much younger women who was older than Polanski's thirteen-year-old but was his semi-stepdaughter. (Allen says that he is not her stepfather because he never officially adopted Soon-Yi, even though he reared her as a father-figure.)

While there are cultures that condone child marriage, and there are cultures that permit polygamy, there are no cultures currently in existence that permit incest. (That practice died off with the ancient Egyptians.) Allen broke the universal taboo when he married Soon-Yi. Even though she was not his biological offspring, and even though her Korean features made it clear that she was not born of his own seed, and even though it was Farrow—rather than Allen—who legally adopted Soon-Yi, Woody Allen nevertheless committed an unpardonable "sin." This act was shocking for anyone, but it was especially shocking for someone who made a career of pre-tending to be a man who lusted only on his analyst's couch, and in his own head, but not in his own bed, and who talked and thought but never acted.

Clearly, this transgression put his career on the skids. It is unlikely that Allen's decline derived from a decline in his filmmaking skills, or even his own aging process, which made him a less-than-ideal male lead for his films. For he was never the ideal romantic lead. He was always that nerdy, nebbishy, unkempt, skinny, bespectacled boy from Brooklyn at a time when blond-haired, blue-eyed Robert Redford was the preferred romantic lead. It is also unlikely that lack of money—as Allen contended—made his movies less popular. For he always made low-budget movies that appealed to a certain audience.

It *is* likely that Woody's fall from grace helped hammer yet another nail into the coffin of the already moribund pseudoscience of psychoanalysis. For psychoanalysis figured so prominently in Woody Allen films and in his private life (which was made public). Woody Allen was psychoanalysis's latest and greatest PR agent, until he announced that he no longer needed analysis after he found his forbidden fruit. When Allen, the most public proponent of the couch cure, lost his credibility, he dealt the death blow to the couch cure and stopped resistance to encroaching neuropsychiatry, which was emerging as the new gold standard of psychiatry.

Until his marriage to Soon-Yi, it was assumed that the neurotic Allen never acted out his forbidden fantasies. Even though he directed the ground-breaking *Everything You Always Wanted to Know about Sex (but Were Afraid to Ask)* (1972), and even though he himself starred in a vignette about "Guess My Perversion," there was always comic relief in thinking that an average-appearing man who wore unfashionable glasses and had half-combed hair could harbor baser desires in his heart of hearts. But many a truth is said in jest.

Apart from Alfred Hitchcock, whose mystery-suspense movies and psychological thrillers were worlds away from Woody Allen's one-liners and Jewish humor, Woody Allen did more to familiarize the Western world with the couch cure than any other single filmmaker. Born in 1935, he was too old to be a baby boomer but too young to be a parent to the baby boomers. Yet his idiosyncratic blend of autobiography and philosophy spoke to the 1960s and 1970s generations, both literally and figuratively. He was a near-contemporary of Mel Brooks, another humorist whose *High Anxiety* (1977) spoofed the seriousness of Hitchcock's psychoanalytic stories *Spellbound, The Birds, Marnie, Frenzy, Vertigo,* and *Rear Window.*

Allen fused Freud with Nietzsche, Kierkegaard, and McLuhan, and then some. In one of his latter-day films, *The Curse of the Jade Scorpion* (2001), he referenced early silent films about exotic Oriental curses and the evils of hypnosis as well as the Chandu the Magician radio and film series of the 1930s. In mid-career he wrote *Play It Again, Sam* (1972), in which he plays a mild-mannered man who turns to the hard-boiled Humphrey Bogart for romantic advice after he is dumped by his wife. In the process, Allen helped turn *Casablanca* into the most-quoted movie ever.

His nerdy, nebbishy, couch-addicted Alvy Singer in *Annie Hall* convinced the world that all New Yorkers are neurotic enough to spend years in analysis, without accomplishing anything. Along with novelist Philip Roth, who also chronicled Jewish neurotics in such books as *Portnoy's Complaint,* Woody Allen implied that all Jews are neurotic and that most neurotics are Jews, and that psychoanalysts are Jewish, too (which was true for a time). Allen's ethnification of analysts and analysands helped make the phobic Italian American mobster in *Analyze This* and *Analyze That* so funny.

If we can forget Allen's personal shortcomings and focus on his achievements instead (and it is unclear if we can, considering that his films are so autobiographical, not just because he appears in his films but also because his themes foreshadow events of his own life), we can see how he once wielded so much power in promoting analysis to American audiences.

Let us look at the dialogue in *Annie Hall* (1977), one of Allen's most financially and critically successful films. In this telling scene, Alvy (Woody) first meets Annie (Diane):

WOODY ALLEN: I got time. I've got nothing 'til my analyst appointment.

DIANE KEATON: Oh? You see an analyst?

WOODY ALLEN: Just for 15 years.

DIANE KEATON: Fifteen years!

WOODY ALLEN: I'm going to give him one more year and then I'm going to Lourdes.

This film set the standard for romantic comedy. It also won Allen four Academy Awards, one of which was for Best Picture. *Annie Hall* also started a minor fashion trend when Diane Keaton, the female lead and Allen's then-lover, wore offbeat men's apparel, such as poorly tied neckties and rumpled men's fedoras. It made it even more fashionable to inject psychoanalytic jokes into dialogue. Allen tells, while Hitchcock showed. Allen dispenses with subtleties.

In the prologue, Alvy (Allen) alludes to psychoanalysis as he tells an old joke. He describes a man who is so worried about his brother that he goes to a psychiatrist for help. The man tells the psychiatrist that his brother thinks he is a chicken.

Shocked at the story, the doctor says, "Well, why don't you turn him in?", implying that the family should commit the brother to an institution. The guy says, "I would, but I need the eggs." Alvy goes on to explain that "that's pretty much now how I feel about relationships; y'know, they're totally irrational, and crazy, and absurd, and . . . but, uh, I guess we keep goin' through it because, uh, most of us . . . need the eggs."

Allen blurs the boundaries between reality and fantasy, first in his films and finally in his own life. After having advocated analysis for thirty-odd years, he left the couch when he got the chutzpah to mate with the most forbidden female.

Other Woody Allen films advocated analysis. *Zelig* (1983) stars a demure, sweater-wearing Mia Farrow, who is made to look much older than her true age. Mia, who at the time was still married to Allen in real life, is Zelig's (Allen's) analyst in the film. Allen says that he is a Siamese twin with a split personality, all of whom are in treatment with his therapist.

Old newsreel footage is spliced into the film, to help *Zelig* tell of a man who is so bereft of individual identify that his facial features morph whenever he keeps company with people with more definitive identities. When standing near Chinese, he looks like a Chinaman. When walking with soldiers of the Reich, he turns into a Nazi. Through black humor, Woody Allen tells us the story of our own times, a story described by sociologist-turned-psychoanalyst Christopher Lasch in *The Culture of Narcissism* (1979). Lasch commented on changing trends in psychiatric diagnosis, and on the reasons why "narcissicistic personality disorder" became so prevalent among members of the self-absorbed "me generation," which turns to such health and beauty magazines as *Self* to learn about their sense of "self."

Other Allen movies won critical acclaim. *Time* included *The Purple Rose of Cairo* (1985) in its list of 100 best movies of all times. In this film, Mia's character sits in the audience of an abandoned movie theater, ogling the actor in the screen, emoting with him, and secretly sharing his kisses. When the actor steps out of the screen and into the theater, sweeping Farrow off her feet, we see not just the action of the film, and a commentary on the fine line between fantasy and reality, but we also witness an enactment of state-of-the-art film theory about "spectatorship" and the interaction between the audience and the actor. Here Allen is one part Plato, another part Lacan, but still all Allen.

A year later, Allen cast Mia in *Hannah and Her Sisters* (1986) and dramatizes delicate intra-familial conflicts, as well as the hold that cocaine has over Hannah's older sister before she goes to rehab and gets clean. Like his earlier films, this story is timeless, and a throwback to Bergman's sensitivities, but it also incorporates commentary about the current cocaine subculture.

Allen continues to show the underside of upscale people in *Crimes and Misdemeanors* (1989) and foreshadows his own "shadow self" that will soon appear. Here, a prominent ophthalmologist finds himself blackmailed by his distraught mistress (Anjelica Huston), who threatens to reveal his financial misdeeds. To end the entanglement that endangers his career and his reputation, he contacts his shady brother, who uses his underworld connections to stage a convenient "accident." As a sideline, an earnest but ailing young rabbi seeks treatment from the eye doctor and offers him spiritual solace instead. The good rabbi goes blind in the end, but the bad doctor gets off free, proving that there is no justice in the world, just as Job said.

In 1992, the year of the Soon-Yi escapade, Allen turned to German Expressionism as inspiration. He put aside his standard imitations of Fellini and Bergman (whose *Persona* epitomizes blurring of the psychological boundary between a psychiatric nurse and her psychotic patient). Allen's *Shadows and Fog* (1992) includes a haunting Kurt Weill melody that recollects Weill's roots in the German Expressionist era. Like German Expressionism itself, which rose and fell within a decade, but left a larger-than-life legacy, Woody Allen's career rose and fell in a quarter of a century, but is still not forgotten.

It is curious that German Expressionism was denounced as "decadent" when the Nazis took power in the 1930s—even though this genre is much-appreciated today. For Woody Allen films that foreshadow his affair with Soon-Yi, and his eventual abandonment of analysis, have also been denounced as decadent. Imagine, the man whose name once guaranteed long lines around movie theaters now had to be marketed in a "plain brown wrapper," his name erased from the marquee. In order to draw crowds that DreamWorks demanded, *Match Point* could not be promoted as a Woody Allen movie—even though the film later won critical acclaim.

In spite of his manifold talents, his lust and libido were his undoing. In an increasingly conservative America, Woody's willingness to abandon his wife and claim a younger woman as his bride was unforgivable. For someone who once softened the advance of America's sexual revolution with a laugh-producing parody of *Everything You Always Wanted to Know about Sex (but Were Afraid to Ask)*, Allen was now worse than his film characters. When he cast Gene Wilder as the pompous physician who falls in love with his patient's sheep (after initially expressing disgust when told that his patient slept with the sheep), Allen made audiences laugh. He showed us that strange sexual behavior was a suitable subject for the (non-X-rated) screen, but his comedic treatments assured us that such strange behavior would not seep into real life.

When the self-deprecating filmmaker and clarinet player finally acted out his own fantasies, and abdicated the analyst's couch for the semi-incestuous marriage bed, he proved that the conservatives were right about Freud all along. They blamed Freudian psychoanalysis for the sexual permissiveness of contemporary society, and for bringing AIDS, fatherless children, and almost every other social ill into being. In the end, Allen also proved Freud right; for he showed that civilization (or at least Allen's cinema) will fall, unless baser urges are sublimated into something better.

Allen was able to sublimate when he spoke through cinema. When he abandoned this approach, his advocacy for analysis went by the wayside. Bereft of its chief cinematic promoter, psychoanalysis had few defenders left. The decade of the brain in the 1990s marched into the arena, unchecked, and not just because of neuropsychiatry's successes. Allen's personal couch cure was no longer funny. Now it was sad. Other parodies about psychoanalysis became popular after Allen's fall: *Analyze This* and *Analyze That* starred Billy Crystal as an analyst who is abducted and forced to treat a moping mobster who suffers from bad dreams and an unresolved Oedipus complex. The fact that we could laugh at—rather than with—this unlikely event confirmed that Allen-style analysis was fading into gray.

The lack of success of Allen's psychoanalytic treatment was one more reason why the mind finally morphed into physical form, and why the world was ready to accept that neurotransmitters and tangled brain connections were better equipped to cure mental distress than the couch cure that Allen had advocated. We are left wondering who will have the last laugh.

CHAPTER 13

THE PSYCHE ASSUMES PHYSICAL FORM

In the preceding pages, we traced the development of cinema as a media form and showed shifts in cinema's portrayal of the psyche. This is a relatively straightforward endeavor, for cinema and psychology (and especially psychoanalysis) go hand in hand. They are cousins who basked in the same birth water of fin-de-siècle society and grew up together in the twentieth century. In this book, we covered just over a century's worth of cinema, for cinema did not exist before 1895.

Because cinema started at the same time that psychoanalysis was invented, much (but not all) of our movie history mirrors the rise and fall of psychoanalysis. Chapter 12 tells how Woody Allen's abdication of his own analysis in 1992 coincided with the clinical decline of psychoanalysis as a treatment technique and with the meteoric rise of the post-Prozac era. We saw how hypnosis and behavioral conditioning, as well as drugs, drink, demons, doubles, and *doppelgängers*, played into the portrayal of the psyche and shaped the public's perception of the modern mind.

It stands to reason that psychoanalysis—and the psyche—were overrepresented in movies, not just because both were products of the turn-of-the-twentieth century, but also because psychoanalysis pushes the plot, fleshes out characters, and adds dramatic dream scenes. It also stands to reason that most mind-control movies turn out to be horror films (since most of us fear mind control). Curiously, asylum thrillers (a subgenre of horror) always include physical treatments for psychological conditions, such as shock therapy, straitjackets, or restraints. Those old asylum thrillers alerted us to the biological aspects of behavior, long before psychopharmacology supplanted psychoanalysis.

What has happened to cinema since psychoanalysis fell from grace? Modern science tells us that genetic endowments, neurotransmitter changes, and brain morphology influence our actions and attitudes as much as (or more than) repressed memories, family dramas, or interpersonal conflicts—even though family dramas are such fodder for film. Does this mean that neuropsychiatry will push psychoanalysis aside in cinema, as it did in psychiatric practice? Will movies mirror the most modern theories of mind and forget about past plot devices?

I doubt that such a complete break will take place, although a shift away from talk therapy has occurred in recent years. Comedies have taken up the slack in psychoanalytic subject matter instead. Psychoanalysis may be too outdated to mine for movies, but the last decade shows that a shift to the supernatural, in lieu of the psychological, is taking place as science shifts gears and deliberates the psyche's fate. Whenever people or cultures are in transition, religion resurfaces, offering a safe haven and a retreat from reality. We know that spiritual and supernatural beliefs persist, in spite of the preponderance of scientific evidence against them. Luckily, supernatural forces make for interesting films that never seem dated because they are already so outdated. Psychoanalysis, on the other hand, may soon be as outmoded as phrenology.

Furthermore, if we step back in time, we find that it took a while before psycho-analysis seeped into cinema. Psychoanalytic talk therapy penetrated movies after talkies replaced silent cinema. Until then, Méliès's silent film about hydrotherapy was more interesting than the immobile couch cure. After all, what good was talk therapy before we could hear dialogue, and discern inflections, as analysands told their stories? Inter-titles go only so far.

Dream themes, on the other hand, were fine for film from the start, because dreams showcase special effects superbly and are well suited for silent cinema. Fortunately, hypnosis existed as a treatment technique before talkies were born. Somnam-bulists did not need sound to tell the stories about psyches. Their closed eyes and distant gazes tell us all we need to know.

Given that psychopharmacology and neuroscience advanced with unprecedented speed near the end of the twentieth century, it may seem appropriate that the psyche assumed physical form from that point on. If movies mirrored actual medical prac-tice, then the material brain should have suddenly substituted for the metaphysical mind at the end of the millennium. But what should be is not necessarily what is. A look into film history shows us a very different trajectory.

In film's first decade, we find short silents about brain exchanges between humans and apes. These brain exchanges reflected Darwinian influences that prevailed when cinema started. Darwinism also inspired Freud. This new science of evolution, and the hubris that inspired Darwin to allege that humans descend from apes (rather than from angels), provoked fear as well as anger. Movies mined these emotions and turned them into plots throughout the century.

Decades after Freud coined psychoanalytic concepts, Darwinists and creationists did combat in Tennessee courtrooms, inadvertently inspiring plays and films that immortalized these cultural clashes. *Inherit the Wind* (1960) (and the 1955 play it was based on) owe their origins to debates about Darwinism. *Inherit the Wind* was based on events surrounding the arrest and trial of a high-school science teacher in Tennessee: in 1925 John Scopes was arrested for illegally teaching the theory of evolution.

The Tennessee teacher was defended by Clarence Darrow. His trial became known as the Scopes Monkey Trial. Scopes's story was co-opted by the play's author, who turned it into an allegory about the dangers of McCarthyism, which peaked in the mid-1950s and which made it dangerous to criticize political policy too directly.

H. G. Wells's turn-of-the-century novel *The Island of Dr. Moreau* (1896) was also inspired by Darwinism. The novel turned into three different film adaptations, one in 1933 with Bela Lugosi and Charles Laughton (*The Island of Lost Souls*). Two later versions also had all-star casts. The 1977 film starred Burt Lancaster and Michael York, and the 1996 version featured Marlon Brando and Val Kilmer. Wells was a brilliant sci-fi writer and storyteller, but he was more concerned with general medical controversies than with theoretical constructs of the mind. Vivisection and the distinction between humans and beasts were more important to Wells than the biology of behavior. Still, movie scenes showing humanized animals regressing to animal form, and losing command of vocabulary, recollects Freud's early career as a neurologist, when he studied aphasia, laboring to distinguish between the loss of words (aphasia) that follows psychological trauma and the loss of words produced by physical brain injury.

Well before the *Moreau* story was made into movies, Edison took a different turn and made the first Frankenstein film in 1910. The idea that scientists could construct humans from body parts was in the air, but even Mary Shelley's *Frankenstein* novel (1818) had supernatural source material. *Frankenstein* was rooted in the Jewish Golem legend, in which Rabbi Loew of Prague made a humanoid from clay, wrote holy words on a paper that he stuffed into the monster's mouth, and then commanded the Golem to obey his (holy) commands. But the Golem had no psyche and no soul. He was a purely supernatural creature who responded to divine will.

Frankenstein, on the other hand, was conceived in the scientific era and conveyed society's fear of science and the control of electricity. *Frankenstein*'s monster had a brain, and he also had feelings. By implication, he had a psyche (even if he had no soul because he was created by a human). The scientist's monster is rejected from the start. His feelings hurt and his pride offended, he seeks revenge, like a mortal. If that is not evidence of a psyche that stems from a physical form, then what is? Charles Ogle, who plays Edison's monster, is so horrified when he sees his appearance (which is made of raw meat thrown over skeleton bones) that he dissolves into nothingness.

When Universal Studios produced the first "real" *Frankenstein* film in 1931, and cast Boris Karloff as the monster, audiences got a glimpse of the future, plus flashbacks into the past. Dr. Frankenstein's monster was a pastiche of body parts. Because he accidentally received a criminal's brain, he commits criminal acts, to the chagrin of his "father," Dr. Frankenstein. This touch echoes recent psychiatric studies about genetic transmission of sociopathy.

Each successive *Frankenstein* film plays on the previous one. *The Bride of Frankenstein* is considered the best *Frankenstein* film. There, the monster suffers from loneliness and begs his "father" to make him a mate. He promises to disappear with this bride and abandon civilization altogether. Dr. Frankenstein reluctantly agrees, but the bride rejects the monster. Bereft of any remaining hope, the monster embraces a course of never-ending revenge (and never-ending sequels). He threatens to kill his "parents" but then shows compassion for them and attempts suicide instead. Not bad for a soulless being made only of brain!

Frankenstein films are composed of such cliches that Mel Brooks made a comedy called *Young Frankenstein* (1974), with Gene Wilder and Marty Feldman. Igor

(Feldman) is sent in search of a brain for the doctor. He writes the name of the chosen brain donor on his hand, but accidentally drops the intelligent brain and replaces it with a brain on the shelf that is labeled "ab-normal." When the monster goes berserk, the doctor (Wilder) insists that such bad behavior could not result from the esteemed brain he requested. He demands the name of the brain donor. Igor stammers, "Ab, Abbie Something or Other."

The mid-fifties ushered in the race to space of the Sputnik era, along with films about disembodied brains that overpowered human will and invasions by brains (and aliens) from outer space. *Donovan's Brain* (1953), *The Brain from Planet Arous* (1957), and *Fiend without a Face* (1958) deal with alien intelligence that takes control of earthlings' consciousness, and other variations on this theme. Intense inter-country competition goaded scientists to send men to the moon and stimulated production of low-budget sci-fi films—and the magician turned movie maker foresaw these events in 1902 when he made *A Trip to the Moon*. Horror and sci-fi films of the 1950s were also reactions to the horrors of Hiroshima, and they often expressed fears of another bomb.

Still, psychoanalysis was alive and well in the fifties, and enjoyed its golden years in cinema—paradoxically, it seems, in retrospect. A schism between the psychological psyche and the scientific psyche was about to take place, but the fantasy aspects of sci-fi made it easier to accept such a radical shift, which was still decades away. The next decade's drug culture would provide a transition between the purely metaphysical mind and biologically based behavior.

George Romero's *Night of the Living Dead* (1968) was a zombie movie that was pure sixties. Romero ensured us that biological brains control zombies, even the cannibalistic zombies in this film. The proof? Zombies must be shot in the brain to be stopped. *Invasion of the Body Snatchers* (1956) and its remake (1978) arrived a decade before and after *Living Dead*. Initially intended as an allegory for McCarthyism and the Cold War, *Body Snatchers* revolves around pod people who replace real people, usurping their memories but not their emotions. These pods were planted in small-town basements by enterprising aliens who intend to overtake earth.

Both the original and the remake of *Body Snatchers* could allude to zombifying effects of Thorazine, the anti-psychotic tranquilizer introduced to America in 1954. Thorazine and related meds freed schizophrenics from frightening hallucinations but turned them into zombies who walked with a stiff "Thorazine shuffle" and had mask-like, emotionless facial expressions.

As we saw above, most movies about brains—rather than minds—were usually sci-fi, fantasy, or horror films. Movies based on Philip K. Dick's novels are paradigmatic of this genre. Dick was remarkably prolific, and remarkably paranoid—courtesy of his amphetamine habit, which produces paranoia and increases productivity. For a while, Dick himself feared that he had descended into the no-return realm of paranoid schizophrenia.

Before succumbing to stimulants, Dick produced a vast body of work that is remarkable for its breadth, quality, and uncanny insight. Dick's novels and short stories are as relevant today as they were when *Blade Runner* (1982) became the first film based on a Dick story. Dick's stories are still mined for movie plots, even though he left this earth long ago. It is not surprising that a man who used chemical brain fuel was so attuned to the physical counterpart of the so-called psyche. *Blade Runner* is the story of an artificially manufactured android who attains near-human status when she realizes that she can dream. This automaton has no soul to speak of, yet her physical form and her self-regulating brain morph into feelings and dreams.

Total Recall (1990) and *Minority Report* (2002) are other excellent examples of Dick's insight into body-brain connections. *Total Recall* has futuristic scenes of trips to Mars and "memory boluses," which are pushed into the brain through the nose to instill false memories of imagined vacations and destroy real memories of actual events. This "memory bolus" pushes the plot and mirrors medical fact. For surgery on the pituitary gland that lies at the base of the skull is carried out through the same intranasal technique that Quaid (Arnold Schwarzenegger) undergoes in this film. Of course, one might say that snorting cocaine through the nose could also have inspired this technique, given Dick's fascination with drugs. Either way, Dick's fanciful story was temporarily believable because details are accurate enough.

Minority Report (2002), a different sort of adaptation of a Dick short story, was directed by Steven Spielberg and stars Tom Cruise. *Minority Report* deals with Dick's favorite themes—free will and the nature of reality—as it traces the movements of a futuristic "Pre-crime Squad" that arrests criminals before they commit their crimes. Fetus-like creatures who were born of crack-addicted mothers bask in embryonic fluid and predict the future. They try to come to a consensus to solve crimes before they occur. It is not until Tom Cruise is accused of a future crime that he begins to doubt the credibility of the Pre-crime Squad. Curiously, all of Dick's stories were based on "real" psychotic experiences that he himself experienced during his drug days and beyond.

If films made from Philip K. Dick stories deserve special mention because of their ability to capture the physical form of the psyche, then films made by Canadian-born filmmaker David Cronenberg also deserve attention. In one of Cronenberg's three distinct phases, he consistently gives visual expression to biologically based psychotic states better than any other single filmmaker. Cronenberg directed *The Brood* (1979), *Videodrome* (1983), and *The Dead Zone* (1983). Later, he directed *eXistenZ* (1999), a movie about probes that plug into computer game players' spinal cords to produce a virtual reality that is indistinguishable from ordinary reality.

His later film *Spider* (2002) chronicles the tragic course of a chronic schizophrenic man who endures hallucinations produced by his brain, along with humiliations inflicted by the compassionless lady who runs his "adult residence." *Spider* is as bleak and reality-based as a movie about mental illness can be. *eXistenZ* is the exact opposite in its confusion between body and brain and physical aspects of the psyche and the conflation of chemically induced hallucinations and computer-transmitted delusions.

If we examine Cronenberg's earlier film *Videodrome* (1983), we see a continuum between *Videodrome* and *eXistenZ*. In *Videodrome,* a lowlife cable TV operator discovers a sadomasochistic "snuff TV" broadcast called "Videodrome." Then he discovers that "Videodrome" is more than a TV show. It is an experiment conducted by a drug-addicted psychology professor. It uses TV transmissions to permanently alter the viewer's perceptions by producing brain damage. The TV screen turns out to be the "retina of the mind's eye." The screen is part of the brain itself, and part Video-drome transmission as well. The concept is completely confusing, but such confusion is permissible in sci-fi. In the end, we learn that Videodrome creates brain tumors in the viewer. The creator of Videodrome claims that the hallucinations cause the tumors, even though it is accepted wisdom in the medical world that strategically situated brain tumors can cause hallucinations.

Compared to *Videodrome, Scanners* and *The Brood* are easy to view. In *The Brood*, disturbing thoughts and obsessions take on physical form and become embryonic, translucent twins, triplets, and quintuplets of the person who imagines them. Thoughts are no longer mere thoughts but bodies that personify the thoughts. This film is a far cry from the psychoanalytically inspired films about multiple personality disorder (MPD) that stop with the psyche. Similarly, *Scanners* gives physical form to schizophrenia. People who are hypersensitive to environmental stimuli (as schizophrenics are) develop large heads with engorged veins that burst wide open. To protect these "scanners" from harm, they are separated from society, not in a mental hospital, but in a secluded and nurturing environment (as hospitals should be).

There is a distinctly different subgenre of lobotomy films that affirm that the mind is controlled by the brain. There is no dearth of cheesy, low-budget, direct-to-video films of this ilk, but there are also some highlights. *Planet of the Apes* (1969) deals with both Darwinian evolution and American race relations. By default, it also deals with physical aspects of existence and experience. It is only fitting that Charlton Heston, who brought the law to the Israelites in Cecil B. DeMille's *The Ten Commandments* (1956), tries to right society's wrongs when he discovers that his pal was lobotomized by enemy apes and made less than human.

Decades later, Hannibal Lecter demonstrates the meaning of a good lobotomy—and a gourmet meal. In a startling scene in a well-tended kitchen, Dr. Lecter makes a nearly bloodless incision into Ray Liotta's brain. He dissects out the frontal lobes (which control volition and motivation). He then sautés his guest's brains and serves them for dinner. Liotta sits at the table politely, showing no signs of pain or perception. This scene is remarkably true to fact, for brain operations are nearly bloodless, and neurosurgical patients remain awake during surgery, since the brain has no pain receptors.

Other films, such as *Flatliners* (1990), are horror-supernatural films that use electroencephalograms (EEGs) and near-death experiences as driving devices for supernatural action adventure and moralistic movies. In *Flatliners*, medical students experiment with near-death experiences to achieve transcendent states that the drug generation sought through hallucinogens. They shock classmates until their EKGs and EEGs "flatline," and losing their characteristic curves. And then they resuscitate the subject—but the time comes when resuscitation fails and the "flatliner" goes through heaven and hell, and back again. Like any good moral tale, some subjects die, some go insane, and all subjects come away knowing that humans should not usurp responsibility for life-and-death decisions without good guidance.

Oddly enough, the film that best exemplifies the crossover between the psychological and the supernatural also doubles as one of the best examples of the netherworld between mind and brain, and the transition between psychiatry and neurology. That film is *The Exorcist* (1973), with Linda Blair as the possessed child and Ellen Burstyn as the child's mother. When Linda first shows signs of odd behavior—which includes urinating in public as she sleepwalks in a dream state—she is sent for an epilepsy evaluation. Her physician recognizes that temporal lobe seizures cause dreamy states, and that epileptics lose bladder control during seizures. So we see state-of-the-art EEG machinery in *The Exorcist*—along with the atavistic religious rituals of exorcism. This attention to medical detail, and to the distinctions between the psychoanalytic construct of the psyche and the medical model of the brain, is one of the many true-to-life touches that made *The Exorcist* so suspenseful, and so successful at making us suspend disbelief.

In 2004 the *Manchurian Candidate* remake introduces audiences to neurosurgery and lobotomies. This time, the impact is underwhelming, partly because the original *Manchurian Candidate* was so overwhelming. The original's use of Pavlovian conditioning (read Russian/communist conditioning) carried political implications that were critical to the meaning of the movie. When a neurosurgery scene is added to the remake, it updates the medical aspect of the movie but it makes the movie meaningless. The omission of the brainwashing scene endured by American soldiers during their captivity in North Korea strips the film of its most important implications. Newer political issues about race relations substitute for preoccupations with communist plans and actual Korean brainwashing of American sailors. The remake fails. Spectators are not impressed when they see a world class film turned into a *Total Recall* rip-off.

Eternal Sunshine of a Spotless Mind (2004) is a very different type of film, a film that could not have been imagined in the psychoanalytic era, before the psyche officially assumed physical form. It is fitting that this film followed such movies as *The Cell* (2000), *Memento* (2000), and even *Pi* (1998). For *Memento* focuses on a biologically based brain defect that interferes with memory construction and that robs victims of their sense of selfhood and personal fulfillment. Both the insurance agent in *Memento* and his hapless client incur physical injuries that obstruct their abilities to remember. The thrust of this film is diametrically different from the rash of repressed-memory movies of the fifties, sixties, and even seventies, such as *Three Faces of Eve* and *Sybil*. In *The Cell*, Jennifer Lopez plays a social worker turned psychotherapist who uses high-tech equipment that literally "tries to get into the head" of her patients, and into the head of a comatose serial killer, whose consciousness is clearly physical rather than metaphysical.

In *Eternal Sunshine*, a lonely loser is contemplating suicide. Then he meets "the girl" who gives him a reason to live, at least for a while. This "girl" wears an orange sweater, sports crimson hair, and is named Clementine. Then something stranger happens. He realizes that he remembers aspects of Clementine, and their past meeting. It turns out that the movie mostly takes place in Joel's mind, as he struggles to recover memories of his lost love. For he (and his ex-girlfriend) visited a psychiatrist who performed a procedure that erases painful memories, including memories of lost love.

However, Joel learns that erasing unpleasant memories also erases good memories, and most other memories. He realizes, in retrospect, that much of his memory, and the very fabric of his experience, is intertwined with memories of Clementine. The movie ends, not as a love story gone wrong, but as a commentary on the value of memory in an era of biomedical advances. For the day may soon arrive when patients indeed ask psychiatrists to ablate memories, just as patients ask dermatologists to erase wrinkles. In fact, studies on treating post-traumatic stress disorder (PTSD) in such a way are reportedly underway.

As I conclude this book, we are facing a new frontier in neuropsychiatry. Vagal nerve stimulation, brain implants and pacemakers, and gene transplants have moved from the Michael Crichton novel and film *The Terminal Man* (1974), to experimental stages, to the clinical arena. It remains to be seen which of these "invasive" neuropsychiatric treatments will be successful and push ahead, and which will take us two steps back instead. For scientists cannot predict the future the way that such luminaries as Philip K. Dick, Méliès, and even Edison could. It is unclear if these new treatment techniques will turn into horror films, or if they will become better dramas as they impact the human condition and intensify interpersonal interactions. This determination is left for the future. In the meantime, filmmakers will tell us where these new medical treatments will take us. For filmmakers need not be correct; they just need to be entertaining.

Unlike physicians and scientists and psychiatrists, who must abide by ethical restraints on human experimentation, filmmakers and other inventors of fiction are free to produce plots that extrapolate on these experiments. Interestingly, some of the finest researchers I know tell me that they themselves turn to science fiction when they wonder what the future will bring. Likewise, we, too, are free to enjoy fictional films, and to see what happens when the psyche fully and finally morphs into physical form (if indeed it does). Such ambiguity is frustrating for the physician, but it provides fodder for filmmakers' imaginations. *Have a lovely film future!*

CHAPTER 14

CONCLUSION

It is now necessary to conclude this book, knowing that it will always be incomplete. For the subject of the psyche and the cinema never ends. Filmmakers will always find inspiration from psychological themes, and students of psychology and practitioners of psychiatry will inevitably muse about depictions of the mind, and of mental health practitioners, in movies.

The good news is that this is an endlessly fertile subject that will (I hope) continue to stimulate as much thought after the cover of this book is closed. The bad news is that an open-ended topic like this one is bound to cause as much frustration as fascination. For there will always be films and filmmakers that deserve so much more attention than there is time or space available for in a single volume.

Hopefully, there will be a never-ending supply of movies about the mind in the future. I invite each of you to add your own selections to the films mentioned above, and to speculate about past and future films, and the portraits that they paint of the psyche or mind, and to think about how those films affect you and reflect you in particular.

FILMOGRAPHY

American Beauty (1999): Sam Mendes.
Analyze That (2002): Harold Ramis.
Analyze This (1999): Harold Ramis.
Anatomy of a Murder (1959): Otto
    Preminger.
Angels with Dirty Faces (1939): Michael
    Curtiz.
Annabel Lee (2001): George Higham.
Annie Hall (1977): Woody Allen.
Annie Oakley (1935): George Stevens.
The Arrival of a Train at the Station (1895):
    Lumière brothers.
The Artist's Dream (1898): Georges Méliès.
The Astronomer's Dream (*The Man in the
    Moon*) (1898): Georges Méliès.
The Avenging Conscience (1914):
    D. W. Griffith.

Batman Begins (2005): Christopher Nolan.
Beauty and the Beast (1946): Jean Cocteau.
Bedlam (1946): Mark Robson.
Beetlejuice (1988): Tim Burton.
The Beggar's Dream (1898): Georges
    Méliès.
The Birds (1963): Alfred Hitchcock.
The Birth of a Nation (1915): D. W.
    Griffith.
Blade Runner (1982): Ridley Scott.
The Brain from Planet Arous (1957):
    Nathan Juran.
The Bride of Frankenstein (1935): James
    Whale.

Brokeback Mountain (2005): Ang Lee.
Broken Blossoms (1919): D. W. Griffith.
The Brood (1979): David Cronenberg.

The Cabinet of Dr. Caligari (1919):
    Robert Weine.
Cape Fear (1962): J. Lee Thompson.
Cape Fear [remake] (1991): Martin
    Scorsese.
Carmen Jones (1954): Otto Preminger.
Casablanca (1942): Michael Curtiz.
Cat People (1942): Jacques Tourneur.
Cat People [remake] (1982): Paul Schrader.
The Cavalier's Dream (1898): Edwin S.
    Porter.
The Cell (2000): Tarsem Singh.
Cendrillon [*Cinderella*] (1899): Georges
    Méliès.
Chandu the Magician (1932): William
    Cameron Menzies, Marcel Varnel.
Charlie and the Chocolate Factory (2005):
    Tim Burton.
Un Chien Andalou (1929): Luis Bunuel.
A Chinese Opium Den (1894): Thomas
    Edison (producer).
The Christmas Dream (1900): Georges
    Méliès.
Citizen Kane (1941): Orson Welles.
The Clockmaker's Dream (1904): Georges
    Méliès.
A Clockwork Orange (1971): Stanley
    Kubrick.

er</sup>

FILMOGRAPHY

Close Encounters of the Third Kind (1977): Steven Spielberg.
Cobra Woman (1944): Robert Siodmak.
Come Back, Little Sheba (1952): Daniel Mann.
Convicted by Hypnotism (1912): Eclair (production company).
Cotton Comes to Harlem (1970): Ossie Davis.
Crimes and Misdemeanors (1989): Woody Allen.
The Criminal Hypnotist (1909): D. W. Griffith.
The Cure (1917): Charles Chaplin.
The Curse of the Cat People (1944): Gunther von Fritsch, Robert Wise.
Curse of the Crimson Idol (1914): Phoebus (production company).
Curse of the Hindoo Pearl (1912): American Standard (production company).
Curse of the Jade Scorpion (2001): Woody Allen.
Curse of the Scarabee Ruby (1914): Gaumont/Eclipse/Urban (production company).

Days of Wine and Roses (1962): Blake Edwards.
The Dangers of Hypnosis (1923): Hugo Werner-Kahle.
Dark Mirror (1946): Robert Siodmak.
David and Lisa (1962): Frank Perry.
The Dead Zone (1983): David Cronenberg.
The Deer Hunter (1978): Michael Cimino.
The Defiant Ones (1958): Stanley Kramer.
The Devils (1971): Ken Russell.
Dial M for Murder (1954): Alfred Hitchcock.
Die Hard (1988): John McTiernan.
Die Hard 2: Die Harder (1990): Renny Harlin.
Die Hard with a Vengeance (1995): John McTiernan.
Dr. Dippy's Sanitarium (1906): American Mutascope (production company).
Dr. Jekyll and Mr. Hyde (1912): Lucius Henderson.

Dr. Jekyll & Mr. Hyde (1920): John S. Robertson.
Dr. Jekyll and Mr. Hyde (1931): Rouben Mamoulian.
Dr. Jekyll and Sister Hyde (1970): Roy Ward Baker.
Dr. Mabuse, der Spieler [*Dr. Mabuse, the Gambler*] (1922): Fritz Lang.
Dr. Strangelove (1964): Stanley Kubrick.
The Doctor's Secret [*Hydrotherapie Fantastique*] (1910): Georges Méliès.
Donovan's Brain (1953): Felix E. Feist.
Dracula (1931): Tod Browning.
Dream of the Ballet Master (1903): Georges Méliès.
Dream of a Hindu Beggar (1902): Georges Méliès.
Dream of an Opium Fiend (1908): Georges Méliès.
The Dream of the Poor Fisherman (1904): Georges Méliès.
Dream of a Rarebit Fiend (1906): Edwin S. Porter, Wallace McCutcheon.
Dream Street (1921): D. W. Griffith.
Dressed to Kill (1980): Brian De Palma.
Drugstore Cowboy (1989): Gus Van Sant.
The Drunkard's Dream (1897): Georges Méliès.
The Dybbuk (1937): Michal Waszynski.

Easy Rider (1969): Dennis Hopper.
Empire (2002): Franc. Reyes.
The Eternal Jew (1940): Fritz Hippler.
Eternal Sunshine of a Spotless Mind (2004): Michel Gondry.
Everything You Always Wanted to Know about Sex (but were afraid to ask) (1972): Woody Allen.
eXistenZ (1996): David Cronenberg.
Exodus (1960): Otto Preminger.
The Exorcist (1973): William Friedkin.
The Exorcist II: The Heretic (1977): John Boorman.

Fail-Safe (1964): Sidney Lumet.
Fantasia (1940): James Algar, Samuel Armstrong.
Fear and Loathing in Las Vegas (1998): Terry Gilliam.

Fear Strikes Out (1957): Robert Mulligan.

Fiddler on the Roof (1971): Norman Jewison.

Fiend without a Face (1958): Arthur Crabtree.

Fight Club (1999): David Fincher.

The 5,000 Fingers of Dr. T (1953): Roy Rowland.

Flatliners (1990): Joel Schumacher.

Frankenstein (1931): James Whale.

Fred Ott's Sneeze (1894): William K. L. Dickson.

The French Connection (1971): William Friedkin.

Frenzy (1972): Alfred Hitchcock.

Freud (1962): John Huston.

The Game (1997): David Fincher.

Gaslight (1944): George Cukor.

The Gauntlet (1977): Clint Eastwood.

Girl, Interrupted (1999): James Mangold.

The Golem (1920): Paul Wegener, Carl Boese.

Good Will Hunting (1997): Gus Van Sant.

Goodfellas (1990): Martin Scorsese.

Gothic (1986): Ken Russell.

The Great Train Robbery (1903): Edwin S. Porter.

Greed (1924): Erich von Stroheim.

Guess Who's Coming to Dinner (1967): Stanley Kramer.

Gun Crazy (1950): Joseph H. Lewis.

Hannah and Her Sisters (1986): Woody Allen.

Hannibal (2001): Ridley Scott.

High Anxiety (1977): Mel Brooks.

Horrors of the Black Museum (1959): Arthur Crabtree.

House on Haunted Hill (1959): William Castle.

House on Haunted Hill [remake] (1999): William Malone.

The Hypnotic Eye (1960): George Blair.

The Hypnotic Violinist (1914): Warner Brothers (production company).

The Hypnotic Wife (1909): Pathe (production company).

Hypnotism (1910): Lux (production company).

The Hypnotist at Work [*Le Magnetiseur*] (1897): Georges Méliès.

I Confess (1953): Alfred Hitchcock.

I Never Promised You a Rose Garden (1977): Anthony Page.

In Like Flint (1967): Gordon Douglas.

Inauguration of the Pleasure Dome (1954): Kenneth Anger.

Intolerance (1916): D. W. Griffith.

Invasion of the Body Snatchers (1956): Don Siegel.

The Ipcress File (1965): Sidney J. Furie.

The Island of Dr. Moreau (1977): Don Taylor.

The Island of Dr. Moreau (1996): John Frankenheimer.

The Island of Lost Souls (1933): Erle C. Kenton.

The Jacket (2005): John Maybury.

Jacob's Ladder (1990): Adrian Lyne.

Jaws (1975): Steven Spielberg.

Johnny Guitar (1954): Nicholas Ray.

Judgment at Nuremberg (1961): Stanley Kramer.

King of Hearts (1966): Philippe de Broca.

Klute (1971): Alan J. Pakula.

Kustom Kar Kommando (1965): Kenneth Anger.

Lair of the White Worm (1988): Ken Russell.

Leaving Las Vegas (1995): Mike Figgis.

Let There Be Light (1946): John Huston.

The Life of an American Fireman (1903): Edwin S. Porter.

Lilith (1964): Robert Rossen.

The Lost Soul, or The Dangers of Hypnosis (1923): Hugo Werner-Kahle.

The Lost Weekend (1945): Billy Wilder.

M (1931): Fritz Lang.

The Maltese Falcon (1941): John Huston.

Man on Fire (2004): Tony Scott.

The Man with the Golden Arm (1955): Otto Preminger.

The Manchurian Candidate (1962): John Frankenheimer.

The Manchurian Candidate [remake] (2004): Jonathan Demme.

Mandalay (1934): Michael Curtiz.

Manhunter (1986): Michael Mann.

Marnie (1964): Alfred Hitchcock.

Match Point (2005): Woody Allen.

The Matrix (1999): Andy Wachowski, Larry Wachowski.

The Mayor of Hell (1933): Archie Mayo.

Memento (2000): Christopher Nolan.

Metropolis (1927): Fritz Lang.

Midnight Cowboy (1969): John Schlesinger.

Minority Report (2002): Steven Spielberg.

The Mummy (1932): Karl Freund.

Next (2007): Lee Tamahori.

The Night of the Hunter (1955): Charles Laughton.

Night of the Iguana (1962): John Huston.

Night of the Living Dead (1968): George Romero.

Nightmare Alley (1947): Edmund Goulding.

A Nightmare on Elm Street (1984): Wes Craven.

Nosferatu (1922): F. W. Murnau.

Now, Voyager (1942): Irving Rapper.

On a Clear Day You Can See Forever (1970): Vincente Minnelli.

Once upon a Time in America (1984): Sergio Leone.

One Flew over the Cuckoo's Nest (1975): Milos Forman.

Opium (1919): Robert Reinert.

Our Man Flint (1966): Daniel Mann.

Pandora's Box (1929): George Wilhelm Pabst.

Une Partie de Cartes (1896): Georges Méliès.

Peeping Tom (1960): Michael Powell.

Pi (1998): Darren Aronofsky.

Pick-Up on South Street (1953): Samuel Fuller.

Pinky (1949): Elia Kazan.

The Plainsman (1936): Cecil B. DeMille.

Planet of the Apes (1968): Franklin J. Schaffner.

Play It Again, Sam (1972): Herbert Ross.

Playing God (1997): Andy Wilson.

Porgy and Bess (1959): Otto Preminger.

Portrait of Jennie (1948): William Dieterle.

Possessed (1947): Curtis Bernhardt.

Pressure Point (1962): Hubert Cornfield.

Prime (2005): Ben Younger.

Psycho (1960): Alfred Hitchcock.

Psycho (1998): Gus Van Sant.

Purple Rose of Cairo (1985): Woody Allen.

Quills (2000): Philip Kaufman.

Rainman (1988): Barry Levinson.

The Rajah's Dream (1900): Georges Méliès.

The Razor's Edge (1946): Edmund Goulding.

Rear Window (1954): Alfred Hitchcock.

Red River (1948): Howard Hawks.

Reefer Madness (1936): Louis J. Gasnier.

Repulsion (1965): Roman Polanski.

Requiem for a Dream (2000): Darren Aronofsky.

The Return of Chandu (1934): Ray Taylor.

Return to Oz (1985): Walter Murch.

Rope (1948): Alfred Hitchcock.

Rosemary's Baby (1968): Roman Polanski.

Scarface (1993): Brian De Palma.

The Search for Bridey Murphy (1956): Noel Langley.

The Seashell and the Clergyman (1929): Germaine Dulac.

Secrets of the Soul (1926): George Wilhelm Pabst.

The Seven Percent Solution (1976): Herbert Ross.

Shadow of a Doubt (1943): Alfred Hitchcock.

Shadows and Fog (1992): Woody Allen.

Shaft (1971): Gordon Parks.

Shaft [remake] (2001): John Singleton.

Shaft in Africa (1973): John Guillermin.

Shock (1946): Alfred L. Werker.

Shock Corridor (1963): Samuel Fuller.
The Silence of the Lambs (1991): Jonathan Demme.
Silent Hill (2006): Christophe Gans.
Sisters (1973): Brian De Palma.
The Sixth Sense (1999): M. Night Shyamalan.
The Snake Pit (1948): Anatole Litvak.
Somewhere in the Night (1946): Joseph L. Mankiewicz.
Song of Russia (1944): Gregory Ratoff.
Spellbound (1945): Alfred Hitchcock.
Spider (2002): David Cronenberg.
Stalag 17 (1953): Billy Wilder.
Star Wars (1977): George Lucas.
The Stepford Wives (1975): Bryan Forbes.
A Stolen Life (1946): Curtis Bernhardt.
Stranger on the Third Floor (1940): Boris Ingster.
Strangers on a Train (1951): Alfred Hitchcock.
The Student of Prague (1913): Paul Wegener, Stellan Rye.
The Student of Prague (1926): Henrik Galeen.
Superfly (1972): Gordon Parks Jr.
Superfly T.N.T. (1973): Ron O'Neal.
Suspicion (1941): Alfred Hitchcock.
Sybil (1976): Daniel Petrie.
The System of Dr. Tarr and Professor Fether (1912): Maurice Tourneur.

The Talented Mr. Ripley (1999): Anthony Minghella.
Tales of Hoffmann (1951): Michael Powell.
The Ten Commandments (1956): Cecil B. DeMille.
The Tenant (1976): Roman Polanski.
The Terminal Man (1974): Mike Hodges.
The Testament of Dr. Mabuse (1933): Fritz Lang.

The Texas Chainsaw Massacre (1974): Tobe Hooper.
This Gun for Hire (1942): Frank Tuttle.
The Three Faces of Eve (1957): Nunnally Johnson.
The Tingler (1959): William Castle.
Total Recall (1990): Paul Verhoeven.
Trainspotting (1996): Danny Boyle.
The Tramp (1915): Charles Chaplin.
The Trip (1967): Roger Corman.
A Trip to the Moon [*Le Voyage Dans La Lune*] (1902): Georges Méliès.
Triumph of the Will (1935): Leni Riefenstahl.
2001: A Space Odyssey (1968): Stanley Kubrick.

Valley of the Dolls (1967): Mark Robson.
The Verdict (1982): Sidney Lumet.
Vertigo (1958): Alfred Hitchcock.
Videodrome (1983): David Cronenberg.
A Vilna Legend (1924): Zygmund Turkow.
The Vow (1937): Henryk Szaro.

Whirlpool (1949): Otto Preminger.
Willy Wonka & the Chocolate Factory (1971): Mel Stuart.
Witchcraft through the Ages (1922): Benjamin Christensen.
The Wiz (1978): Sidney Lumet.
The Wizard of Oz (1939): Victor Fleming.
Woman in the Window (1944): Fritz Lang.

Yellow Submarine (1968): George Dunning.
Young Frankenstein (1974): Mel Brooks.

Zelig (1983): Woody Allen.

NOTES

CHAPTER 1

1. John W. Hesley, and Jan G. Hesley, *Rent Two Films and Let's Talk in the Morning: Using Popular Movies in Psychotherapy*. New York: John Wiley and Sons, 1998.

2. Parker Tyler, *The Hollywood Hallucination*. New York: Simon & Schuster, 1970.

CHAPTER 3

1. Hays Code (Production Code) of 1930: Specific restrictions, or "Particular Applications" included the following:

- Nudity and suggestive dances were prohibited.
- The ridicule of religion was forbidden, and ministers of religion were not to be represented as comic characters or villains.
- The depiction of illegal drug use was forbidden, as well as the use of liquor, "when not required by the plot or for proper characterization."
- Methods of crime (e.g., safe-cracking, arson, smuggling) were not to be explicitly presented.
- References to "sex perversion" (such as homosexuality) and venereal disease were forbidden, as were depictions of childbirth.
- The language section banned various words and phrases that were considered to be offensive.
- Murder scenes had to be filmed in a way that would discourage imitations in real life, and brutal killings could not be shown in detail.
- The sanctity of marriage and the home had to be upheld. "Pictures shall not infer that low forms of sex relationship are the accepted or common thing." Adultery and illicit sex, although recognized as sometimes necessary to the plot, could not be explicit or justified and were not supposed to be presented as an attractive option.
- Portrayals of miscegenation were forbidden.
- "Scenes of Passion" were not to be introduced when not essential to the plot. "Excessive and lustful kissing" was to be avoided, along with any other treatment that might "stimulate the lower and baser element."

- The flag of the United States was to be treated respectfully, and the people and history of other nations were to be presented "fairly."
- "Vulgarity," defined as "low, disgusting, unpleasant, though not necessarily evil, subjects" must be treated within the "subject to the dictates of good taste." Capital punishment, "third-degree methods," cruelty to children and animals, prostitution and surgical operations were to be handled with similar sensitivity.

2. Harvey Roy Greenberg, *Screen Memories: Hollywood Cinema on the Psychoanalytic Couch*. New York: Columbia University Press, 1993.

3. Louis Gianetti and Scott Eyman, *Flashback*, 3rd edn. Englewood Cliffs, NJ: Prentice Hall, 1996.

Chapter 4

1. Hortense Powdermaker, *Hollywood, the Dream Factory*. New York: Little, Brown, 1950.

2. John M. MacGregor, *Discovery of the Art of the Insane*. Princeton, NJ: Princeton University Press, 1992.

3. Tony Pellegrino, film instructor and editor, School of Visual Arts and New School University.

4. Eli Zaretsky, *Secrets of the Soul*. New York: Knopf, 2005.

5. Henri Ellenberger, *The Discovery of the Unconscious*. New York: Basic Books, 1970.

6. See Sandy Flitterman-Lewis, "The Image and the Spark: Dulac and Artaud Reviewed" in *Dada and Surrealist Film* (ed. Rudolf E. Kuenzli). Cambridge, MA: MIT Press, 1996, and A. L. Rees, *A History of Experimental Film and Video*. London: BFI, 1999.

7. See P. Sitney Adams, *Visionary Cinema*, 2nd edn. Oxford: Oxford University Press, 1979; Parker Tyler, *The Underground Film*. New York: Da Capo, 1995; and James Peterson, *Dreams of Chaos, Visions of Order*. Detroit: Wayne State University Press, 1994.

Chapter 5

1. See S. S. Prawer, *Caligari's Children*. Oxford: Oxford University Press, 1980; and David Robinson, *Das Cabinet des Dr. Caligari*. London: BFI Publishing, 1997.

2. See David Soren, *The Rise and Fall of the Horror Film*. Baltimore: Midnight Marquee Press, 1997; and Lottie Eisner, *The Haunted Screen: Expressionism in German Cinema*. Berkeley: University of California Press, 1969.

3. Mark Salisbury, *Burton on Burton*. New York: Faber & Faber, 1995.

4. Castle tried to make movie-going more appealing in the television era; his gimmicks included flying paper skeletons over audiences in *House on Haunted Hill* (1958) and sending sham electric shocks through wired theater seats in *The Tingler* (1959).

Chapter 6

1. *A History of Psychiatry: From the Era of the Asylum to the Age of Prozac*. New York: Wiley, 1998.

Chapter 9

1. Sheri Chinen Bisen, *Blackout: World War II and the Origins of Film Noir*. Baltimore: Johns Hopkins University Press, 2005.

2. Joyce H. Lowinson, Pedro Ruiz, Robert B. Millman, and John G. Langrod, *Substance Abuse: A Comprehensive Textbook*, 4th edn. Philadelphia: Lippincott, Williams & Wilkins, 2005.

CHAPTER 11

1. Lucy Fischer, "Two-Faced Women: The 'Double' in Women's Melodrama of the 1940s," *Cinema Journal*, 23.1 (Autumn 1983), pp. 24–43.

BIBLIOGRAPHY

AoF: Atkinson on Film (www.Atkinsononfilm.com).

Arnheim, Rudolf. *Film as Art.* Berkeley: University of California Press, 1957.

Bartov, Omer. *The "Jew" in Cinema.* Bloomington: Indiana University Press, 2002.

Bazin, Andre. *The Cinema of Cruelty.* New York: Seaver Books, 1982.

Bergfelder, Tim, Erica Carter, and Deniz Gokturk. *The German Cinema Book.* London: BFI, 2002.

Bergstrom, Janet (ed.). *Endless Night.* Berkeley: University of California Press, 1999.

Bernstein, Matthew, and Gaylyn Studlar (eds.). *Visions of the East.* New Brunswick, NJ: Rutgers University Press, 1997.

Biesen, Sheri Chinen. *Blackout: World War II and the Origins of Film Noir.* Baltimore: Johns Hopkins University Press, 2005.

Bould, Mark. *Film Noir: From Berlin to Sin City.* London: Wallflower, 2005.

Bourde, Raymond, and Etienne Chaumeton (trans. Paul Hammond). *A Panorama of American Film Noir: 1941–1953.* San Francisco: City Lights, 2002.

Budd, Mike (ed.). *The Cabinet of Dr. Caligari.* New Brunswick, NJ: Rutgers University Press, 1990.

Ceram, C. W. *Archaeology of the Cinema.* New York: Harcourt, Brace & World, n.d.

Channan, Michael. *The Dream that Kicks*, 2nd edn. London: Routledge, 1980.

Charney, Leo, and V. R. Schwartz. *Cinema and the Invention of Modern Life.* Berkeley: University of California Press, 1995.

Conraad, Peter. *The Hitchcock Murders.* London: Faber & Faber, 2000.

Craddock, Jim (ed.). *Videohound's Golden Movie Retriever 2007.* Detroit: Thomson Gale, 2006.

Eberwein, Robert T. *Film & the Dream Screen.* Princeton: Princeton University Press, 1984.

Eisner, Lotte. *Fritz Lang.* New York: Da Capo, 1976.

———. *The Haunted Screen.* Berkeley: University of California Press, 1952.

Elon, Amos. *The Pity of It All.* New York: Picador. 2002.

Elsaesser, Thomas. *Fassbinder's Germany.* Amsterdam: Amsterdam University Press, 1981.

———. *Weimar Cinema and After.* London: Routledge, 2001.

Ezra, Elizabeth. *Georges Méliès.* Manchester: Manchester University Press, 2000.

Gabbard, Glen, and K. Gabbard. *Psychiatry and the Cinema*, 2nd edn. Washington, DC: American Psychiatric Press, 1999.

Gabler, Neal. *An Empire of Their Own.* New York: Anchor Books, 1988.

————. *Life: The Movie: How Entertainment Conquered Reality.* New York: Vintage, 2000.

Giannetti, Louis, and S. Eyman. *Flashback*, 4th edn. Upper Saddle River, NJ: Prentice Hall, 2001.

Gould, Michael. *Surrealism and the Cinema.* London: Tantivy Press, 1976.

Greenberg, Harvey Roy. *Screen Memories.* New York: Columbia University Press, 1993.

Gunning, Tom. *The Films of Fritz Lang.* London: BFI, 2000.

Halpern, Leslie. *Dreams on Film.* Jefferson, NC: McFarland & Company, 2003.

Hammond, Paul (ed. and trans.). *The Shadow and Its Shadow*, 3rd edn. San Francisco: City Lights, 2000.

Hayward, Susan. *Cinema Studies*, 2nd edn. London: Routledge, 2000.

Heard, Mervyn. *Phantasmagoria.* Hastings, UK: The Projection Box, 2006.

Heath, Stephen. "Cinema and Psychoanalysis," in *Endless Night*, ed. J. Bergstrom. Berkeley: University of California Press, 1999, pp. 25–56.

Hesley, J. W., and J. G. Hesley. *Rent Two Films and Let's Talk in the Morning: Using Popular Movies in Psychotherapy.* New York: Wiley, 1998.

Hill, Geoffrey: *Illuminating Shadows: The Mythic Power of Film.* Boston: Shambala, 1992.

Hoberman, J. *The Dream Life.* New York: The New Press, 2003.

Hoberman, J., and Jeffrey Shandler. *Entertaining America.* Princeton: The Jewish Museum with Princeton University Press, 2003.

Hyler, Steven H., Glen Gabbard, and Irving Schneider. "Homicidal Maniacs and Narcissistic Parasites: Stigmatization of Mentally Ill Persons in the Movies." *Hospital and Community Psychiatry* 42 (October 1991): 1044–1048.

The Internet Movie Database (www.imdb.com).

Jones, Gerard. *Men of Tomorrow.* New York: Basic Books, 2004.

Kalat, David. *The Strange Case of Dr. Mabuse.* Jefferson, NC: McFarland & Company, 2001.

Kaplan, E. Ann (ed.). *Psychoanalysis & Cinema.* New York: Routledge, 1990.

Kinnard, Roy. *Horror in Silent Films.* Jefferson, NC: McFarland & Company, 1995.

Kolker, Robert. *A Cinema of Loneliness*, 3rd edn. New York: Oxford University Press, 2000.

Kracauer, Siegfried. *From Caligari to Hitler.* Princeton: Princeton University Press, 1947.

————. *From Caligari to Hitler: A Psychological History of the German Film.* Princeton: Princeton University Press, 2004.

————. *Theory of Film.* Princeton: Princeton University Press, 1997.

Kuenzli, Rudolf E. (ed.). *Dada and Surrealist Film.* Cambridge, MA: MIT University Press, 1998.

Langdale, Allan (ed.). *Hugo Munsterberg on Film.* New York: Routledge, 2002.

Langford, Barry. *Film Genre: Hollywood and Beyond.* Edinburgh: Edinburgh University Press, 2005.

Lapsley, Robert, and M. Westlake. *Film Theory: An Introduction.* Manchester: Manchester University Press, 1988.

Lebeau, Vicky. *Lost Angels.* London: Routledge, 1995.

————. *Psychoanalysis and Cinema.* London: Wallflower, 2001.

Lichtenfeld, Eric. *Action Speaks Louder.* Westport, CT: Praeger, 2004.

Macfie, Alexander Lyon. *Orientalism: A Reader.* New York: New York University Press, 2000.

Mast, Gerald, and Marshall Cohen. *Film Theory and Criticism.* Oxford: Oxford University Press, 1985.

McCarthy, John. *Movie Psychos and Madmen.* New York: Citadel Press, 1993.

McGinn, Colin. *The Power of Movies.* New York: Pantheon, 2005.

McGowan, Todd, and S. Kunkle. *Lacan and Contemporary Film.* New York: Other Press, 2004.

Mijolla, Alain de. "Freud and the Psychoanalytic Situation on the Screen," in *Endless Night*, ed. J. Bergstrom. Berkeley: University of California Press, 1999, pp. 188–199.

Mitry, Jean (trans. Christopher King). *The Aesthetics and Psychology of the Cinema.* Bloomington: Indiana University Press, 1990.

Morris, Peter. *David Cronenberg: A Delicate Balance.* Toronto: ECW Press, 1999.

Naremore, James. *More Than Night: Film Noir in Its Contexts.* Berkeley: University of California Press, 1998.

Neugroschel, Joachim (ed. and trans.). *The Dybbuk and the Yiddish Imagination.* Syracuse, NY: Syracuse University Press, 2000.

O'Brien, Geoffrey. *The Phantom Empire.* New York: Norton, 1993.

Oliver, Kelly, and Benigno Trigo. *Noir Anxiety.* Minneapolis: University of Minnesota Press, 2002.

Osborne, Jennifer. *Monsters.* New York: Del Ray Books, 2006.

Packer, Sharon. "The Colorblind Cyberclass: Myth and Fact," in *Race in the College Classroom: Politics and Pedagogy*, ed. Bonnie TuSmith and Maureen Reddy. Piscataway, NJ: Rutgers University Press, 2002, pp. 264–276.

———. "Consciousness and the Novel: Connected Essays" (book review). *Psychiatry Services* 54 (November 2003): 1554.

———. *Dreams in Myth, Medicine, and Movies.* Westport, CT: Praeger, 2002.

Parkinson, David. *History of Film.* New York: Thames & Hudson, 1995.

Polan, Dana. *Power and Paranoia.* New York: Columbia University Press, 1986.

Prawer, S. S. *Caligari's Children.* Oxford: Oxford University Press, 1980.

Ramsaye, Terry. *A Million and One Nights.* New York: Simon & Schuster, 1954.

Rausch, Andrew J. *Turning Points in Film History.* New York: Citadel Press, 2004.

Rees, A. L. *A History of Experimental Film and Video.* London: BFI, 1999.

Robinson, David. *Das Cabinet des Dr. Caligari.* London: BFI, 1997.

Salisbury, Mark. *Burton on Burton.* London: Faber & Faber, 1995.

Schelde, Per. *Androids, Humanoids, and Other Science Fiction Monsters.* New York: New York University Press, 1993.

Sievers, W. David. *Freud on Broadway.* New York: Hermitage House, 1955.

Silver, Alain, and Paul Ursini. *Film Noir*, edited by Paul Duncan. Los Angeles: Taschen, 2004.

———. *Film Noir Reader 4.* New York: Limelight Editions, 2004.

Silver, Alain, and Elizabeth Ward. *Film Noir*, 3rd edn. Woodstock, NY: Overlook Press, 1992.

Sitney, P. Adams. *Visionary Film*, 2nd edn. (ed. Paul Duncan) Oxford: Oxford, 1979.

Slocum, J. David. *Violence and American Cinema.* New York: Routledge, 2001.

Soren, David. *The Rise and Fall of the Horror Film*, rev. edn. Baltimore: Midnight Marquee, 1997.

Stevenson, Jack. *Addicted: An Illustrated Guide to Drug Cinema.* Creation Books, 2000.

Stokes, Melvyn, and R. Maltby (eds.). *Hollywood Spectatorship.* London: BFI, 2001.

Thomson, David. *The New Biographical Dictionary of Film.* New York: Knopf, 2004.

Tredell, Nicholas. *Cinemas of the Mind.* Cambridge: Icon Books, 2002.

Turkle, Sherry. *Life on the Screen.* New York: Touchstone, 1995.

Tyler, Parker. *The Hollywood Hallucination.* New York: Creative Age Press, 1944.

———. *Underground Film.* New York: Da Capo Press, 1999.

Vernet, Marc. "The Fetish in the Theory and History of Cinema," in *Endless Night*, ed. J. Bergstrom. Berkeley: University of California Press, 1999, pp. 88–95.

Walker, Janet. *Couching Resistance.* Minneapolis: University of Minnesota Press, 1993.

Zizek, Slavoj (ed.). *Lacan: The Silent Partners.* London: Verso, 2006.

INDEX

About the Author

SHARON PACKER, M.D., is a psychiatrist in private practice in New York City and Woodstock. She has authored many academic articles and book chapters, including *Dreams in Myth, Medicine and Movies* (Praeger, 2002), which was *Choice*'s "best academic book of 2003."